THE DIGITALLY DISPOSED

Racial Capitalism and the Informatics of Value

SEB FRANKLIN

Electronic Mediations 61

University of Minnesota Press
Minneapolis
London

Every effort was made to obtain permission to reproduce material in this book. If any proper acknowledgment has not been included here, we encourage copyright holders to notify the publisher.

A different version of chapter 5 was published as "Racial Capitalism and the Informatics of Value: Forms of Disposal," *Social Text* 39, no. 2 (Summer 2021). A different version of chapter 12 was published as "Cleverness and Drive, or the Cybernetic Fantasy of Value: R. S. Hunt's 'Two Kinds of Work,'" *Grey Room,* no. 68 (Summer 2017): 32–59; doi:10.1162/GREYa00223.

Copyright 2021 by the Regents of the University of Minnesota

All rights reserved. No part of this publication may be reproduced, stored in a retrieval system, or transmitted, in any form or by any means, electronic, mechanical, photocopying, recording, or otherwise, without the prior written permission of the publisher.

Published by the University of Minnesota Press
111 Third Avenue South, Suite 290
Minneapolis, MN 55401-2520
http://www.upress.umn.edu

ISBN 978-1-5179-0714-3 (hc)
ISBN 978-1-5179-0715-0 (pb)
Library of Congress record available at https://lccn.loc.gov/2021058756.

The University of Minnesota is an equal-opportunity educator and employer.

THE DIGITALLY DISPOSED

Electronic Mediations

Series Editors: N. Katherine Hayles, Peter Krapp, Rita Raley, and Samuel Weber

Founding Editor: Mark Poster

61 *The Digitally Disposed: Racial Capitalism and the Informatics of Value*
    Seb Franklin

60 *Radical Secrecy: The Ends of Transparency in Datafied America*
    Clare Birchall

59 *Perpetual Motion: Dance, Digital Cultures, and the Common*
    Harmony Bench

58 *Playing Nature: The Ecology of Video Games*
    Alenda Y. Chang

57 *Sensations of History: Animation and New Media Art*
    James J. Hodge

56 *Internet Daemons: Digital Communications Possessed*
    Fenwick McKelvey

55 *What Is Information?*
    Peter Janich, Eric Hayot, and Lea Pao

54 *Deconstruction Machines: Writing in the Age of Cyberwar*
    Justin Joque

53 *Metagaming: Playing, Competing, Spectating, Cheating, Trading, Making, and Breaking Videogames*
    Stephanie Boluk and Patrick LeMieux

52 *The Perversity of Things: Hugo Gernsback on Media, Tinkering, and Scientifiction*
    Hugo Gernsback
    Edited by Grant Wythoff

51 *The Participatory Condition in the Digital Age*
    Darin Barney, Gabriella Coleman, Christine Ross, Jonathan Sterne, and Tamar Tembeck, Editors

50 *Mixed Realism: Videogames and the Violence of Fiction*
    Timothy J. Welsh

(continued on page 255)

CONTENTS

Introduction: Forms of Disposal   1

PART I. THE INFORMATICS OF VALUE

1 Things Communicated: Messages, Persons, Goods   31

2 Reliable Circuits, Unreliable Components: How Capital Connects   38

3 The Informatics of Dispossession   59

4 Differentiation as Regulation   69

5 Two Models: Samuel R. Delany's *Neveryóna*   78

PART II. MEDIA HISTORIES OF DISPOSAL

6 Human Use, or The Digital-Liberal Person   97

7 Elemental Space: Coloniality and Flexibility   104

8 Deplorable Alternatives: "Mechanical Slaves" and Upgradable Labor   112

9 The Digital Atlantic: Sondra Perry's *Typhoon coming on*   120

10 Redundant Life: Intellectual Workers and Street Nuisances   126

11 Anatomizing "Freedom": Carceral Digitality   138

12 The Cybernetics of Capacity: R. S. Hunt's "Two Kinds of Work"   158

Coda: *The Human Surge* 175

Acknowledgments 187

Notes 189

Index 241

INTRODUCTION

Forms of Disposal

A GLOBAL MARKETING CAMPAIGN launched by HSBC in July 2018 comprises a triptych of images under the heading "Trade. Building a future on bytes and boxes."[1] The first of these images shows fiber-optic cables running underneath the concrete of a freeway interchange. In the second, a circuit diagram appears below grids of shipping containers. In the third, rows of 1s and 0s are superimposed onto a handwritten table of numbers on paper. In each of these images, the technologies of electronic digital computing—the cables, the circuit diagram, and the 1s and 0s—appear in the shape of the bank's "iconic" hexagon logo. In the words of the campaign, this logo "becomes a lens through which to look at the world, showing how the influence of the bank can help individuals, businesses and communities to grow and flourish." And what HSBC is able to "see" is a series of connections between the complex of infrastructures and abstractions that subtends commodity circulation and the technologies of digital communication. It is the bank's intimate knowledge of these connections, the campaign suggests, that will allow its customers to thrive.

Almost exactly a year later, in late June 2019, Google announced a new private subsea cable to run from Portugal to South Africa, with the first of several branching units expected to land in Nigeria. Following a company tradition of naming cables for "historical luminaries"—after Curie (Los Angeles to Valparaíso) and Dunant (Virginia Beach to the west coast of France)—this cable bears the name *Equiano*.[2] Here, as in the HSBC campaign, the transmission of data is equated with commodity circulation. But making explicit the fact that for centuries the circulation of commodities between Europe, West Africa, and the Americas centered on the purchase, sale, and forced labor of enslaved Africans does not appear to

· 1

Trade. Building a future on bytes and boxes.

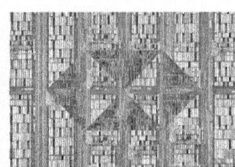

Figure 1. Bytes and boxes. HSBC. 2018.

be the intention behind this choice of name. The sentence in Google's announcement that explains the use of Equiano's name emphasizes abolitionism and writing over enslavement before shifting to a celebration of the cable's technological sophistication.

> Named for Olaudah Equiano, a Nigerian-born writer and abolitionist who was enslaved as a boy, the Equiano cable is state-of-the-art infrastructure based on space-division multiplexing (SDM) technology, with approximately 20 times more network capacity than the last cable built to serve this region.[3]

This extraordinary sentence registers an equation between freedom, self-expression, and data transmission capacity. Enslavement provides the counterweight necessary to elevate those values and that capacity. In other words, Equiano's name is used to signify the attainment of liberal personhood and to imply that high-speed internet access will confer the prospects with which that form of personhood is associated. From another perspective, the sentence makes it clear that the promises of digital culture remain relationally bound to Atlantic slavery and its afterlives.

The associations disclosed in the HSBC and Google campaigns—between digital technologies, prosperity, freedom, and the capacity for self-expression—exemplify a conjuncture in which the language and organizational logics of digitality are central to the operations of global capitalism. By "digitality" I do not mean discrete representation in general but rather the complex of technologies, concepts, imaginaries, metaphors, and fantasies that today bear on social life from the Googleplex to the

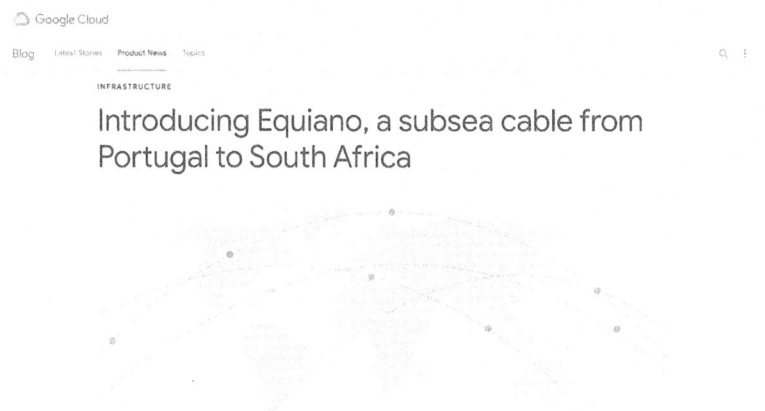

Figure 2. Introducing Equiano. Google. 2019.

app-mediated service economy, from national and local governments to hospitals, prisons, schools, and universities, and from extraction sites to the factories in which electronic devices are assembled. The latter definition constitutes what might be called the cultural logic of contemporary capitalism, while the former has a much longer and more diffuse history that certainly feeds into but is not exhausted in that logic.[4] Digitality as a cultural logic both produces and is produced by users who experience their devices as media of frictionless connection. In the present, that experience both requires and invisibilizes a massive carbon footprint, vast amounts of waste, and myriad forms of disposable labor. As Sean Cubitt puts it, there is a "myth of immaterial media" that requires the projection of "consumer goods that have no history: no mines, no manufacture, no freighting, and no waste."[5] The terms in which this myth appears across the HSBC and Google campaigns invite questions about the longer histories of dispossession and disposal that ground it. Why does the conflation of commodities and data appear to be the key to individual and collective flourishing? What are the causes and effects of this way of thinking? If digitality makes it both possible and desirable to name an internet cable for an enslaved person in order to amplify its promises of extended freedom and expressive possibility, what other kinds of violence do its logics and historical conditions effect and obscure?

These questions are at the heart of this book. Answering them requires a historical scope that goes beyond the emergence and wide distribution of electronic digital computers. Indeed, some of the details required to respond to them in a rigorous manner can be found in Equiano's *Interesting Narrative*. Consider the following passages, the first recalling the pestilential conditions aboard the slave ship and the second the "usual manner" of the slave auction:

> The stench of the hold while we were on the coast was so intolerably loathesome, that it was dangerous to remain there for any time, and some of us had been permitted to stay on the deck for the fresh air; but now that the whole ship's cargo were confined together . . . the air soon became unfit for respiration . . . and brought on a sickness among the slaves, of which many died, thus falling victims to the improvident avarice, as I may call it, of their purchasers.[6]

> We were not many days in the merchant's custody before we were sold after their usual manner, which is this:—On a signal given . . . the buyers rush at once into the yard where the slaves are confined, and make choice of that parcel they like best. The noise and clamor with which this is attended, and the eagerness visible in the countenances of the buyers, serve not a little to increase the apprehension of the terrified Africans, who may well be supposed to consider them as ministers of that destruction to which they think themselves devoted.[7]

In these passages, Equiano precisely illustrates a network of relations between abstraction, acquisitive personhood, and material violence that centers on the figure of the enslaved person rendered as "cargo." In the first he identifies "improvident avarice" as the root cause of the lethal conditions in the ship's hold. It is what Marx calls the "voracious appetite of the capitalists for surplus labour," the structurally determined drive to purchase, to accumulate economic-legal abstractions—value and property—that leads to the hold becoming "so crowded that each had scarcely room to turn himself," and thus to the deadly proliferation of diseases.[8] In the second passage, the buyers' apprehension of slaves as exchangeable abstractions—*parcels*—evokes visceral reactions. The hunger for accumulation that is written on the faces of the purchasers and sounded in the clamor they create amplifies the enslaved Africans' terror, indexing the relationship between the abstract form of the commodity and the destruction of individual and collective life to which the entire trade is perdurably bound.

The "eagerness" to acquire a "parcel" exemplifies the link between pleasure and possession that, as Saidiya Hartman has shown, "can be explained in part by the fungibility of the slave—that is, the joy made possible by the replaceability and interchangeability endemic to the commodity."[9] The prospect of buying or selling a "parcel" leads to a kind of excessive performance of the very personhood that is denied to the enslaved. And the fungibility that makes purchase and sale possible, the exchangeability and replaceability that marks commodity exchange, is what will later allow boxes to be rendered as bytes. Note how closely *parcel* resonates with *packet,* as in packet switching, that system of disaggregation and grouping for the purpose of optimal circulation that lies at the heart of distributed electronic communication. One must only think of the "fatal morning" on which Equiano's sister was "torn from [him] forever" to see another way in which the spatial logics of digital communication— here the packet-switching system's method of separation for the purpose of efficiently "allocating channel capacity"—are foreshadowed by the separation and transmission of lives rendered as economic data and technologies of accumulation.[10]

This book is about the logics, practices, fantasies, and imaginaries that connect the conditions documented by Equiano to the visions exemplified in HSBC's campaign and Google's cable. It is also about the processes of dispossession, abjection, and differential valuation through which capital and digitality effect social organization. In order to focus attention on these linked dynamics, I argue that capital accumulation reproduces a specific kind of relation—the *form of disposal*—that determines the meaning and effects of a range of social forms, exemplarily the "free" human subject. In so doing, this relation positions certain bodies and things within, outside, or across the threshold of form in order to maximize the functionality and reach of the system it constitutes.[11] As HSBC, Google, and Equiano all suggest, albeit in very different ways, the logic through which this mechanism operates is centered on *value.*

In "Can the Subaltern Speak?" Gayatri Chakravorty Spivak writes that "under capitalism, *value,* as produced in necessary and surplus labor, is *computed* as the representation/sign of objectified labor (which is rigorously distinguished from human activity)."[12] This formulation appears especially striking when read alongside those found in standard English translations of Marx, where one is more likely to find values described as "*congealed quantities* of homogeneous labour" than as *computed signs* of such labor.[13] The use of *computed* where one might otherwise find *congealed* dramatizes the historical dynamics I want to examine over the course of this book.

Although they are often said to have converged in the techniques and technologies of logistics that are so central to capital accumulation today, value and digitality appear, on the surface at least, to result from distinct historical and logical processes. But Spivak's use of *computed* in place of *congealed* hints at a more fundamental relationship between capitalist and digital modes of abstraction. If value represents a "phantom-like objectivity," an empty abstraction that is borne by but somehow remains separate from and determines the concrete relationships between persons and things, then *computed* may capture some essential dynamics that are obscured by the direct, material process implied by *congealed* (as well as by the depiction of commodities as "crystals" of "social substance").[14] If value constitutes the social forms in which disparate things, including quanta of social activity, become commensurable and thus interconnected—the forms that subtend the specifically capitalist mode of emergent social synthesis—then its basal operations appear closer to the logic of digital computation, and of networked computation in particular, than they do to the process of boiling down animal matter to produce a jelly.

Which isn't to say that the physical and psychic effects of exploitation and forms of violence not directly intelligible as exploitation aren't essential to capital's computations (or to computation under capital). Rather, it is to argue that the processes evoked by *congealed* may not fully capture either the structural logic of extraction and resource allocation or the dispensation of violence that is specific to capitalism. The production of a congealed quantity—or *Gallerte*, gelatin, in Marx's German—implies the direct extraction of matter and energy from an organic body.[15] And it implies that this extraction either destroys or severely depletes that body. *Computed* implies an entirely different kind of extraction process. It suggests that what is extracted is an abstraction, something that has no specific connection to the individual bearer. In this process, the return of the bearer to the site of computation is not impeded and in fact appears entirely facilitated by the value relation, which proceeds as if the entire operation takes nothing from and leaves no mark on the bearer. *Computed*, then, describes a mode of processing bodies that in the same stroke abstracts their social product and facilitates their reproduction, their capacity to return to the production process day after day. *Congealed* describes extraction that does not facilitate this apparently perpetual return, instead leading to the degradation and eventual destruction of the living bearer of labor power. As I will argue over the following pages, the conditions that make value relations intelligible as *computed,* and which make possible the commingling of capital and digitality, both require and obscure these conditions of material degradation. For now, I want to say that *computed* describes an idealized state of value-mediated social relations, a state that organizes all waged and unwaged labor but into which no concrete laborer has ever fully entered. In practice, capitalist social relations entail the computation of all activity that produces a commodity, and capital only recognizes as valid that which is computed. At the same time, all labor entails some degree of *congelation*. The distribution of conditions primarily intelligible as computation and those which tend toward congelation depends on and informs a multitude of historical factors, some of which we might understand in terms of race, gender, sex, and capacity.[16] Equiano's *Narrative* is but one record of the way in which the computation of certain bodies produces conditions that tend toward their degradation.

The structural implications and the modes of social distribution indexed by *computed* and *congealed* are sketched in an extraordinary passage from the 1955 seminar on "Freud, Hegel, and the Machine" in which Jacques Lacan states:

> People who had slaves didn't realise that one could establish equations for the price of their food and what they did in their *latifundia.* There are no examples of energy calculations in the use of slaves. There is not the hint of an equation as to their output. . . . It took machines for us to realise they had to be fed. And more—they had to be looked after. But why? Because [machines] tend to wear out. Slaves do as well, but one doesn't think about it, one thinks that it is natural for them to get old and croak. And later on, it dawned on people, something which was never thought of before, that living things look after themselves *all on their own,* in other words, they represent *homeostats.*[17]

I want to note four things about this passage. First, Lacan is here describing, in the most efficient terms possible, how "free" and enslaved social reproduction appear from the point of view of capital, which is to say, from the perspective in which social relations are valid only so far as they are computed. As Stephanie Smallwood puts it in an account of the "scientific enterprise" of turning captives into commodities, the processes Lacan glosses as feeding and looking after "reflected a calculation balancing the cost of the slaves' maintenance against their purchase price"—which is to say, against the projected value of the labor they embody.[18]

Unlike slaves and machines, "free" workers appear to reproduce themselves automatically, to reappear in the production process in what Marx called a never-ending circle (*fehlerhaften Kreislauf*).[19] Second, I say "appear" because (and this is no great surprise, as Marxist and black feminist analyses have shown) racialized and gendered differentiation are entirely absent from Lacan's account of "living things" that can be distinguished from both machinery and slaves on the basis of their self-reproducing character. The passing reference to enslaved people's *latifundia* acknowledges the incalculability of non-market-mediated production and reproduction, but not the possibility that such reproduction takes place across a vast range of abjected, oppositional, and/or indifferent ways of living and relating to land and other "living things"—a possibility Sylvia Wynter has located in the co-constitutive and antagonistic relationship between plot and plantation.[20]

Third, Lacan distinguishes "living things" from machines and slaves, which is to say, he locates the enslaved outside the zone of life. Nonlife is here a cipher for social death.[21] And fourth, Lacan uses the language of informatics to describe the distribution of enslaved and putatively self-reproducing "free" life. This language runs through the 1954–55 seminar, which includes references to William Grey Walter's robot tortoises of 1948 and an analogy between repetition compulsion and the operation of a binary switch "which proceeds by opening and not opening, the way an electronic lamp does, by yes or no."[22] But the informatic language in the passage on energy, "free" social reproduction, and slavery is not analogical. It uses the new vocabulary made available by cybernetics to describe the differentiating effects of historical processes that precede that vocabulary by several centuries.

In Lacan's account of reproduction, "living things" differ from slaves and machines because they are homeostats, self-regulating systems. Since machines and slaves are formally and practically equivalent in this account, the differentiating factor—the thing that makes "living things" homeostatic—must be voluntary participation in money-mediated exchange. This voluntary participation—as seller of labor power and buyer of commodities—positions "free," waged workers closer to the *computed* aspects of capitalist social relations; the impossibility of such participation places slaves closer to those aspects that cause life to wear down as it congeals in its products. The purchasers in the slave auction Equiano describes are performing computations; the lives of the slaves are to congeal. The implications of this distribution are extended when Lacan goes on to define the machine (and thus, by extension, the slave) in terms of desire that is strictly circumscribed by subsistence: "Machines which reproduce themselves," he claims, "have yet to be built, and have yet even to be conceived of—the schema of their symbolic has not even been established. The sole object of desire which we can presume of a machine is therefore its source of nourishment."[23] Recalling Lacan's earlier grouping of machines with slaves on the side of things that cannot (or do not appear to) reproduce themselves, one might reformulate this claim to observe the connection it makes between homeostatic and nonhomeostatic things and the distribution of *expectation.* Those whose ongoing reproduction is secured by a primarily computational relationship to value can desire beyond subsistence. Those whose reproduction is not secured in this way cannot.

Value, "as produced in necessary and surplus labor, is *computed* as the representation/sign of objectified labor (which is rigorously distinguished from human activity)." And in this computation, distinctions are produced between those whose reproduction appears homeostatic— and who can thus desire more than mere survival—and those who will be either cut off from or worked to death by the demands encoded in value's abstract operations. The two possibilities—abstract computation and material degradation—represent the two poles between which value-mediated social forms are materialized. So it is significant that Spivak's formulation of value as computation appears in the middle of an essay on the erasures that are sanctioned when even the most putatively radical accounts of struggle remain centered on a universalized figure of *the* worker. Theoretical appeals to "*the* workers' struggle," Spivak reminds her readers, obfuscate the technologies of accumulation that array individuals and groups across the continuum between abstract computation and material degradation: "the subject-production of worker and unemployed within nation-state ideologies in [the overdeveloped] Center; the increasing subtraction of the working class in the Periphery from the realization of surplus value and thus from 'humanistic' training in consumerism; and the large-scale presence of paracapitalist labor as well as the heterogeneous structural status of agriculture in the Periphery."[24] If the abstract social form designated by *the* worker is a figment of the social matrix in which value appears to be simply computed from labor, the technologies whose effects Spivak lists produce structural positions that appear somewhere between that form and the space in which bodies and social relations are either destroyed by direct violence or subject to the kinds of slow death that result from debilitating conditions of reproduction.[25] This system—of differential computation grounded in the concrete violence of dispossession—comprises what Cedric Robinson and many after him have named *racial capitalism*.[26]

What can formulating the value relation as differential computation reveal about the historical and practical relationships between digitality and racial capitalism? Value's abstract operations are too often posited as unconnected to or even incommensurable with material violence and social differentiation. Yet the commonalities between such disparate materials as HSBC's advertisements, Google's cable, and writing by Equiano, Lacan, and Spivak hint at a fundamental yet constantly shifting relationship between the "geometric whole" formed of value-mediated social relations and the ascriptive processes and forms of violence that, as a result of the modes of perception those relations reproduce, tend to be "tossed . . . into the imagined abyss signified by precapitalist, noncapitalist, and primitive accumulation."[27] Close examination of this relationship offers a way to understand the differential mechanisms that inform digital culture, but which precede the development of computing machinery, algorithms, and databases.[28]

Spivak offers a way to begin thinking through these questions of abstraction and differentiation toward the end of "Scattered Speculations on the Question of Value," an essay published three years before "Can the Subaltern Speak?" Here, after an exhaustive interrogation of value as it is deployed in Marxist, poststructuralist, and neoclassical economic writings, Spivak concludes that inquiries into its operations and outcomes must move through and beyond a singular focus on "abstract labor time." The "premises of *Capital I*," Spivak writes, are "dependent upon *a gesture of reduction that may be called a construction*" that makes such a singular focus unviable.[29] Spivak is here arguing that value—the expression of abstract labor, or that which is *computed* from human activity—both contains and determines much more than can be represented in quantitative terms. Her formulation recalls the tension between Marx's observation that "not an atom of matter enters into the objectivity of commodities as values," and his acknowledgment that those values form and are formed by concrete social processes through which "a definite quantity of human muscle, nerve, brain, etc. is expended" and thus has to be "replaced" (or reproduced) for production to resume.[30] At the same time, Spivak maps that tension onto the racial-capitalist dynamics of dispossession and differentiation that allow value to circulate within global networks as if it were an "automatic" and "dominant" subject.[31] This mapping shows how the parsing of abstract and concrete labor cleaves to the rigorous distinction between "objectified labor" and "human activity in general" that accompanies Spivak's account of the value relation as computation. Anything that takes the form of computed value is promulgated. All that does not is abjected. The constantly shifting boundary between the two produces supported and outlawed forms of those abstract yet materially consequential phenomena that can be analytically separated into race, sex, gender, and desire. Reduced in the construction of *the* worker, then, are the materiality of social reproduction, the ongoing forms of dispossession, and the histories of racialized and gendered differentiation that make possible the computation of labor as value. These processes of reduction allow capital accumulation to function under the sign of race- and gender-blind computation.[32]

I want to show how these value-mediated protocols of separation, integration, reduction, and construction—of the *computation* and the *wearing-down* of life—inform the modes of abstraction, representation, and organization that shape and are shaped by digitality: cybernetic concepts of information, communication, self-regulation, and distributed networking; and the images of capital accumulation that coalesce around them, which include post-Fordism, logistics, supply-chain dynamics, the information economy, and so-called immaterial labor. My thesis, already sketched in the above readings of Equiano and Spivak, is that the historical practices and conceptual structures exemplified in HSBC's bytes and boxes campaign and Google's cable are forged and bound together by the value abstraction centuries before the language of digitality takes shape around the electronic digital computer.

Consider, for example, the discussion that followed Ralph W. Gerard's talk "Some of the Problems concerning Digital Concepts in the Central Nervous System" at the seventh Macy conference, held in New York in March 1950. In the course of this discussion, a group of preeminent figures from the fields of computing, cybernetics, and information theory—including Gregory Bateson, Julian Bigelow, J. C. R. Licklider, Warren McCulloch, Walter Pitts, Claude Shannon, John von Neumann, and Norbert Wiener—attempt to specify the meanings and utility of the terms "analog" and "digital." In an attempt to circumscribe "some of the terms more precisely," von Neumann offers the following complication:

> An electrical computing machine is based on an electric current, which is an analogical concept. A detailed analysis of how a responding elementary unit of the machine (a vacuum tube or an electromechanical relay) stimulates

another such unit, which is directly connected to it, shows that this transition of stimuli is a continuous transition. Similarly, between the state of the nerve cell with no message in it and the state of the cell with a message in it, there is a transition, which we like to treat conceptually as a sudden snapping; but in reality there are many intermediate shadings of stages between these two states, which exist only transiently and for short times, but which nevertheless exist. Thus, both for the man-made artefact as well as for the natural organ, which are supposed to exercise discrete switching actions, these "discrete actions" are in reality simulated on the background of continuous processes.[33]

Discrete actions are "in reality *simulated* on the background of continuous processes." Von Neumann is here suggesting—at a historical moment in which the meaning of the term has yet to be standardized—that *digital* describes a mode of abstraction that relies not only on an illusory or imagined discreteness but also on the support and the disavowal of its material substrate. The digital is a simulation, but it is always simulated on a "background of continuous processes." Later in the same discussion, von Neumann is even clearer about the abstract-concrete character of the digital when he claims that "one must say that in almost all parts of physics the underlying reality is analogical, that is, the true physical variables are in almost all cases continuous, or equivalent to continuous descriptions," while the "digital procedure is usually a human artifact for the sake of description."[34]

The conceptual separation von Neumann sets out in the Gerard discussion recalls the fraught imbrication of abstract and concrete that Marx identifies in his comments on the immateriality of value and the necessity of material expenditure in the social processes that form and are formed by it. And, as his comments on "underlying reality" and the artifactual status of the digital procedure make clear, this separation reproduces the externalization of "Nature" from "Society" that Jason W. Moore posits as capitalism's "governing conceit."[35] The continuities between von Neumann's and Moore's formulations are amplified by the latter's terminology: the Nature/Society separation, Moore writes, leads to relations based on the principle that "Nature is external and may be *coded, quantified,* and *rationalized* to serve economic growth."[36] The computation of value is "simulated" against a background of real processes, and that "simulation" has real preconditions and real effects. And, as Marx, von Neumann, and Moore all insist, the discretely coded artifacts cannot be separated from their continuous preconditions. The phenomena von

Neumann associates with the continuous, nonsimulated space of "reality" are the energy basis (electricity) and life processes (nerve function) upon which the discrete abstractions are simulated.

I am not interested in valorizing the analog over the digital on the basis that the former is the site of some unmediated concrete reality and the latter merely a "simulated" abstraction. Such an approach would reproduce what Iyko Day, following Neil Levi, identifies as a romantic anticapitalist view that too hastily separates abstract from concrete, glorifying the latter while casting the former as "evil."[37] I do, however, want to examine the relationships of determination and subordination into which the two sets of terms—analog/concrete and digital/abstract—are cast in digital and capitalist imaginaries. The computation of value without any material cost to the bearer of labor power can only happen—or be imagined to happen—in a simulated reality of the type von Neumann defines as the realm of the digital. But since the computation of value is fundamental to capital accumulation, and since capital accumulation occurs through and dominates a world of people and things, concrete life processes are necessarily reduced in and constructed around that computation.

In 1995, Nicholas Negroponte, founder of the Architecture Machine Group and the Media Lab at MIT, wrote: "The change from atoms to bits is irrevocable and unstoppable."[38] Many studies of the so-called information age have addressed the subordination of concrete to abstract—the process of *reduction* that is fundamental to the digital imaginary.[39] Fewer have examined the *construction*, the synthesis toward which that reduction is oriented. It is, after all, the synthesis of complex systems from independent parts, rather than reduction as such, that informs the logics and historical practices whose most recent developments are depicted in the examples that open this book. Two years after the seventh Macy conference, in a lecture at the California Institute of Technology titled "Probabilistic Logics and the Synthesis of Reliable Organisms from Unreliable Components," von Neumann reiterated the conceptual separation at the heart of the Gerard discussion in order to theorize the effective synthesis of larger organisms, or automata, from components such as neurons and electronic valves. Following foundational work by Alan Turing and McCulloch and Pitts, von Neumann first shows that "logical propositions can be represented as electrical networks or (idealized) nervous systems" because "logical propositions are built up by combining certain primitive symbols," and networks are material systems "formed by connecting basic components, such as relays in electrical circuits and neurons in the nervous system."⁴⁰ Having established this relationship between abstract representation and concrete synthesis, von Neumann details the excess that characterizes the relationship of logic to its bearer.

> There is one important difference between ordinary logic and the automata which represent it. Time never occurs in logic, but every network or nervous system has a definite time lag between the input signal and the output response. A definite temporal sequence is always inherent in the operation of such a real system. This is not entirely a disadvantage. For example, it prevents the occurrence of various kinds of more or less overt vicious circles (related to "non-constructivity," "impredicativity," and the like) which represent a major class of dangers in modern logical systems. It should be emphasized again, however, that *the representative automaton contains more than the content of the logical proposition which it symbolizes*—to be precise, it *embodies a definite time lag.*⁴¹

"Logic," as Neumann here describes it, stands in the same relationship to "the operation of . . . a real system" as the digital does to the analog in the Gerard discussion. And, tellingly, it also stands in the same relationship to its substrates as does value to its concrete conditions of production and circulation. Indeed, von Neumann's use of time as the mark of the difference between logic and material substrate mirrors Marx's commentary on the contradiction between the abstractly determined fantasy of "continuity of production" and the delays introduced by the concreteness of production and circulation. Like the logic in which time never occurs and the laggy network or system required to materialize that logic, the "conditions of production arising out of the nature of capital itself contradict each other." Capital, Marx writes, "travels through the different phases of circulation not as it does in the mind, where one concept turns into the next at the speed of thought, in no time, but rather as situations that are separate in time. It must spend some time as a cocoon before it can take off as a butterfly."⁴² And in the case of capitalist production and circulation, those "situations that are separate in time" entail different temporalities, each indexed to techniques for imputing capacity to differently racialized and gendered bodies and for allocating and organizing labor accordingly. Value, which (1) appears to exist in an abstract register apart from concrete or underlying "reality," in order to (2) account for and determine the material conditions that avail capital accumulation, should be understood as analogous to the logic detailed by von Neumann. Fully homeostatic social reproduction is only thinkable from the perspective of a "simulated" social matrix, which is to say, one that only recognizes the movement of value. But, just as the desired "logical propositions" or idealized networks determine the shape of the assemblages of "basic components such as relays in electrical circuits," value determines the shape of the social reality that bears it.

In this respect, the relationship of logic to representative automaton is identical to that of capitalism to slavery sketched by Marx and more fully theorized by Walter Johnson.[43] In both cases, the latter is the former's pedestal, insofar as the pedestal is understood as a structural or spatial (rather than temporal) metaphor.[44] The concrete grounds the abstract, and the abstract disciplines the concrete. No amount of periodizing chatter about immaterial information or immaterial labor can turn the relationship into one of temporal succession. Of course, Johnson's analytic focus is significant here. Slavery isn't a placeholder for a more general set of material processes upon which capitalism depends. Nonetheless, it represents a particularly violent and particularly profitable outcome of the multithreaded harnessing, expropriation, and wearing down of material life through which capitalism operates, but which the matrix of value relations cannot admit. Identifying this commonality between von Neumann's formulation of the relationship between logic and its substrates and Johnson's reading of the capitalism-slavery relation helps to emphasize the fact that the consignment of populations to zones of compromised reproduction remains a structural foundation of the homeostatic social matrix that value relations appear to sustain.

Reading von Neumann with Marx, Spivak, and Johnson reveals striking similarities between value and digitality. But how can this be? How can the conceptual and discursive norms surrounding a species of technical operation—digitality—reproduce the abstract logic of a much older system of social organization? Or, how can this reproduction be understood without resorting to expressive causality?[45] Understanding value and digitality as linked modes of abstraction certainly affords useful insights into the ways that digital tools and their associated ways of seeing and knowing facilitate control of production and distribution across increasingly granular and distributed social formations. Technological and infrastructural developments such as computerization; distributed networks; so-called immaterial, cognitive, or communicative labor; supply-chain management; and the platform-enabled shift from employees to "partners" promise to "free" value from the spatiotemporal limitations embodied in living labor and finite material resources, bringing material conditions of production and circulation closer to value's spectral ontology. As such, the relationship between value and digitality might simply be taken as a relatively recent outcome of the process through which, in Alfred Sohn-Rethel's analysis, "the abstractness operating in exchange and reflected in value" finds "an identical expression" in "the abstract intellect, or the so-called 'pure understanding'—the cognitive source of scientific knowledge," so that "the valid foundations of the science of an epoch are those in keeping with the social synthesis of the epoch."[46] Throughout this book I will examine the ways in which digital notions of information, communication, and self-regulation cleave to conceptual frames that are grounded in the logic of value and its associated historical conditions. But I want to argue that this cleaving is not one of incidental resemblance or linear causality. Digitality is not an allegory of value. Rather, value is (or appears) informatic *avant la lettre,* and this is why it so precisely furnishes digital imaginaries with their form and conceptual efficacy.

Which isn't to say that value and digitality are identical. Value is a real abstraction. It emerges not from some realm of pure thought but from concrete actions of exchange, and it has concrete outcomes.[47] These real preconditions and operations are rendered opaque by the systemic conditions they generate; value-mediated social synthesis and its attendant processes of coordination and commensuration happen in secret— "behind the backs of the producers."[48] By contrast, digitality names a set of abstract operations that promise direct, unmediated control over an increasingly complex set of real relations—a promise that is exemplified in the commonplace notion that to click or to code is to immediately *do something.* Where value *hides its real effects,* digitality *flaunts its illusory realness.* This explains why the latter mode of abstraction becomes most overtly conjoined with the former during the economic downturn of the long 1970s, in that extended (and ongoing) period in which the challenges posed by waning growth necessitate increasingly granular control over globally dispersed labor.[49] In identifying the conceptual and imaginative continuities between value and digitality, I want to insist that both exist within a shared history—a history that is fundamentally organized around scientific, economic, and philosophical apparatuses for maximizing the extraction of surplus value against shifting structural requirements.[50] I want to argue that the rearticulation of value's structural logic in digitality is grounded in the synthesis of putatively self-regulating systems from idealized components—sometimes called *the* worker, at others the subject, the human, or the user; always made possible by dispossession, differential valuation, and disposal—that is assumed in and modulated by the organizational logics of digitality.

Because, as is implied in quite different ways by HSBC, Google, Equiano, Spivak, Lacan, and von Neumann, value-determined and digital processes of reduction and construction—or abstraction and synthesis—are reciprocally bound to gradated iterations of free personhood in more or less compromised conditions of reproduction. As I hope to show over the course of this book, the digital image of optimally homeostatic self-reproduction in a value-mediated social matrix grounds feelings and ideas of freedom, acquisitiveness, and self-possession that are not guarantees but rather promises extended to dispossessed persons in return for their repeated participation in networks of accumulation. These promises underwrite *the* worker and the capitalist alike. They are visible in Equiano's account of the "improvident avarice" of the purchasers and the clamor and noise of the auction. Elsewhere, they can be located in the often minimal possibilities of protection, survival, and futurity that aggregate around the waged relation, whether the latter is direct or, as is more and more often the case, platform-mediated. And the same promises underwrite the individuals and communities whose thriving is imagined to depend on HSBC's knowledge of bytes and boxes or Google's high-capacity cable.

In her landmark essay "Whiteness as Property," Cheryl I. Harris shows how Locke's pronouncement that "every man has a 'property' in his own 'person'" crystallized a modern legal and political-philosophical concept of personhood that is defined against enslaved and colonized populations. Where the former is grounded in the linked dynamics of self-ownership and the prospect of possessing external forms of property, the latter are positioned outside or only partially within those dynamics precisely in order to subtend them.[51] Central to Harris's argument is Margaret Radin's earlier theorization of personhood as partly constituted through the anticipation of future plans, the realization of which requires an ongoing sense of "control over objects."[52] By identifying its foundationally racialized character, Harris is able to show how this future-oriented, property-mediated form of personhood is grounded in an unevenly allocated "expectation" that is exemplified (but not exhausted) by whiteness, the "quintessential property for personhood."[53] Harris's theorization of self-possession, expectation, and personhood makes it possible to clarify the structural and historical significance of Lacan's claim that non-homeostatic life can desire nothing more than its "source of nourishment."[54] According to this value-mediated distribution of expectation, to be self-reproducing—to be "free" because waged—is to be granted access to a wide field of desire, albeit one that remains circumscribed by equally value-determined norms of propriety. If this homeostatic form of personhood requires mediation by an abstraction—value—that is comparable to that of von Neumann's "ordinary logic," it follows that everything which cannot access that level of abstraction falls into a space of nonhomeostasis, or limited self-possession. And since homeostatic life appears, as in Lacan's schema, to be a cipher for wage-mediated reproduction, that lower space must necessarily be a space of unmet needs, or compromised survival.[55]

All of this is to say: any analysis of the imbricated histories of capital and digitality must account for the ways that those histories produce, maintain, modulate, and instrumentalize what Wynter names the distinction between "selected" and "dysselected" life.[56] This distinction is implemented not only through separation, exclusion, and regulation but also, and more fundamentally, through protocols for instituting, disciplining, and synthesizing value-mediated forms of life and sociality. And describing those protocols tends to require the language of digitality: "Value and authority," Wynter writes, constitute "the governing code by which human 'forms of life' are instituted and their specific ensemble of behaviors regulated. And because this code is everywhere instituted about the representation of symbolic 'life' (projected as *culture*) and death (projected as *raw nature*), it both governs the processes by means of which each human mode of the subject is socialized as such a subject and defines the semantic closure principle that integrates each order as a living system."[57] In the context of waning growth, those codes furnish increasingly dynamic and granular methods for sorting, distributing, and extracting value from populations allocated more or less reliable conditions of reproduction. And these methods are embodied in and effected by the techniques and technologies that exemplify capital's post-Fordist convergence with digitality. This is why Lisa Nakamura insists at the start of an extraordinary essay on the brief history of electronics manufacturing on Navajo land in New Mexico that understanding "how digital labor is configured today" necessarily involves "seeing into it, into the histories of its platforms, both machinic and human."[58] Following Nakamura, I suggest that "seeing into" digitality requires seeing into value and its effects, both the "logical proposition[s]" that drive social synthesis and the differentiated bodies and unmet needs that constitute "more than the content of" those propositions.

Figuring value and digitality as linked forms of disposal can aid in this process of "seeing into" in a number of ways. First, thinking of value and digitality as forms of disposal emphasizes how both constitute feedback loops of abstractions and their material preconditions and effects. As I show in Part I, the foundational instance of such a loop is composed of value mediation, market dependence, dispossession, and differential valuation.[59] This is the loop of value-mediated self-reproduction that informs HSBC's byte-like boxes, Google's association between high-capacity cable and freedom, and Lacan's theorization of homeostatic personhood, all of which require as a foundation and a counterpoint forms of life whose structurally determined expectations—or permitted needs—appear on a spectrum whose lower end falls below the threshold of survival. This dialectical operation makes intelligible as *form* all that is subject to the process of mediation. And it always entails disposal: of anything that makes non-value-mediated life possible; and of everything that, cut off from that possibility, falls fully or partially outside value's circuits.[60]

Second, thinking of value and digitality as linked forms of disposal makes it possible to move beyond Sohn-Rethel's analysis of the "cognitive source of scientific knowledge" as an "identical expression" of the exchange abstraction in order to grasp how value is (or appears) informatic long before the emergence of the cybernetic sciences. Digitality becomes intelligible as having emerged through (rather than simply mirroring) capitalism's "perceptual economy."[61] And, as a result, it reproduces the latter's structural dynamics as well as its surface appearances. This perspective emphasizes the role of disposal in digital systems, introducing questions of how the latter stage and intensify the processes of social bifurcation and differential valuation that are indexed to survival prospects. Since digital imaginaries are grounded in forms of thought that are shaped by the value relation, they reproduce not only capitalism's abstract logics but also the mechanisms for sorting populations into spaces of homeostatic and nonhomeostatic, selected and dysselected, or human and nonhuman life that are driven by those logics.[62]

Third, viewing value and digitality as linked forms of disposal helps to demonstrate their common recursivity. This has major implications at two levels, the first concerning the historical relationship between capital and computation, and the second concerning the relationship between formalization and abjection that each institutes. Value-mediated social synthesis was informatic in character centuries before the language of cybernetics was formalized, but the ways of seeing and knowing crystallized in the cybernetic sciences have real effects via the development of new techniques for the distribution and management of persons and things. Value informs digitality, and digitality entails methods for the intensification and control of value-mediated social organization. Each provides the other with inputs, and each shapes the other's outputs. And in both cases, anything abjected through the process of formalization can be integrated at a later time and thus becomes raw material for the expansion or continuation of the system. The second of these recursive operations helps to explain both the structural centrality of abjection and the conceptual valorization of the offline in digital culture.

As these three perspectives suggest, the project of making legible the ways in which value and digitality shape social reality and modulate the distribution of prospects, personhood, and subjectivity requires analytic strategies capable of holding together phenomena that exist at different structural levels and in putatively distinct registers. The strategy I pursue here involves reading historical and theoretical material alongside aesthetic formulations—in fiction, visual art, and film—that depict explicit articulations of value and digitality as they shape and function within models of social reality. Over the course of this book I will present readings of Samuel R. Delany's novel *Neveryóna*, Sondra Perry's video installation *Typhoon coming on*, and Eduardo Williams's film *El auge del humano (The Human Surge)*. For now, by way of a preliminary study of the aesthetics of form and disposal, I want to consider the promises that tangibly shift from value to digitality in conditions of compromised possibility in Elena Ferrante's *Those Who Leave and Those Who Stay*.

After escaping her violent marriage to the merchant Stefano Carracci, Lila, one of the two protagonists of Ferrante's Neapolitan novels, moves into an apartment in the suburbs of Naples with her childhood friend, Enzo. While working at a sausage factory and raising her young child, Gennaro, she helps Enzo study for a correspondence course in computer programming that largely entails producing block diagrams on paper.[63] After Lila confronts her boss, Bruno, with a list of complaints about the debilitating work conditions and systematic sexual harassment in the factory, he gropes her. Everything about this assault "except the smell of the salamis" reminds her of her husband's violence, and "for several seconds she felt annihilated, she was afraid of being murdered" (*TWL* 111–12). Lila punches Bruno in the face and between the legs, threatens to castrate him, and leaves, but the need to obtain means of subsistence for herself and Gennaro compels her to continue working at the factory. As her supervisors torment her with constant role changes, excessive hours, and obscene remarks as punishment for her "contemptuous indifference" (113), her interest in computer programming intensifies.

Enzo is motivated to begin the correspondence course by a promise that computation began to embody in the years during which the novel is set—the late 1960s to the late 1970s—and which is ubiquitous in the present discourse of post-Fordist production, circulation, and reproduction. He is "convinced that the languages of computer programming held the future of the human race, and that the elite who first mastered them would have a resounding part in the history of the world" (*TWL* 108). But Lila locates in programming a different promise, one that goes beyond access to the emerging information economy. She finds in the logic of computation a promise of security in abstraction. This promise leads her beyond the exercises set out in the correspondence course and into the diagramming of "daily life," or social reproduction: "the door opening," "knotting the tie," "tying Gennaro's shoes," "making coffee in the *napolitana*."

> From the simplest actions to the most complicated, they racked their brains to diagram daily life . . . not because Enzo wanted to but because, as usual, Lila, who had begun diffidently, grew more and more excited each day, and now, in spite of the cold of night, she was frantic to reduce the entire wretched world they lived in to the truth of 1s and 0s. She seemed to aspire to an abstract linearity—the abstraction that bred all abstractions—hoping that it would assure her a restful tidiness.
> "Let's diagram the factory," she proposed one evening.
> "The whole process?" he asked, bewildered.
> "Yes."
> He looked at her, he said: "All right, let's start with your job."
> An irritated scowl crossed her face; she said good night and went to her room. (*TWL* 114)

Why does this shift of focus, from the factory as an aggregate of processes to her job within it, lead to irritation and then refusal? Lila's desire to diagram the factory, like the preceding diagrams of "daily life," is driven by the promise of an "abstract linearity" that can impose "restful tidiness" over a world whose wretchedness would otherwise be too proximate. Even when directed at sites of waged or unwaged labor, this diagramming process can maintain a spatial and conceptual distance, abstracting from the arrangement of bodies and objects a series of causal relationships. Starting from Lila's concrete position in the factory, however, makes this diagrammatic reduction of the "wretched world" impossible. It represents a shift from labor and reproduction imagined as nothing more than the tasks that comprise them, which can be diagrammed and thus controlled by individuals, to the material conditions that necessitate and constrain those tasks, over which most individuals cannot exercise control on the basis of diagrammatic knowledge.

Two chapters later, Lila tells a group of student activists something of the wretchedness that cannot be shown in or resolved through block diagrams. It encompasses "eight hours a day standing up to your waist in the mortadella cooking water," "fingers covered with cuts from slicing the meat off animal bones," and workers going "in and out of refrigerated rooms at twenty degrees below zero" for minimal cold compensation pay (*TWL* 121). It also encompasses "the women [who] have to let their asses be groped by supervisors and colleagues without saying a word" (122). Indeed, it encompasses the entire history of capitalist dispossession and its effects: methods of separating people from non-market-mediated access to their means of subsistence in order to necessitate their entry as sellers into the market for labor power; slavery, colonialism, imperialism, and the ongoing racial and national formations that operate in their footprints; and, as Silvia Federici has shown, a series of religious and philosophical principles directed toward "the development of a new sexual division of labor subjugating women's labor and women's reproductive function to the reproduction of the work-force" and "the mechanization of the proletarian body and its transformation, in the case of women, into a machine for the production of new workers."[64] Lila's structural position and the local events that bear on it—events that are depicted in forensic detail across Ferrante's Neapolitan novels—are shaped by those dispossessive forces, most directly Marshall Plan industrialization and the integration of southern Italians into the national (and thus, increasingly, world) economy as cheap, disposable labor, a process whose early development is closely connected to late nineteenth-century colonial expansion in Libya, Somalia, Eritrea, and Ethiopia.[65]

From the midst of this "wretched world," the prospect of mastering programming's "abstract linearity" feels like the possibility of existing apart from the requirement to meet basic needs through waged labor and the attendant exposure to debilitating labor conditions, fettered desire, and direct violence. And this is where the subjectivity-shaping effects that recur across value and digitality become most apparent. Where Enzo views programming as a technical skill that will reshape the capitalist economy, Lila imagines the "truth of 1s and 0s" as leading not to accumulation, to wealth as such, but to "restful tidiness." The idea of computation is here shown to connect abstraction to the possibility of homeostatic life—to life lived as if computed rather than congealed—without passing through the material conditions that make exposure to value's computations possible and necessary. In other words, programming appears to embody in a more perfect and more explicit form the promises of freedom, security, and self-possession through which value-mediated social relations constitute liberal personhood. And it makes explicit a perfected form of this promise at the precise historical moment at which shrinking growth mandates intensified dispossession and the integration of the newly dispossessed into a capitalist economy whose capacity to meet even the basic needs of those it exploits has started to (perhaps irreparably) wane.

This transfer of the promise of security from waged reproduction to digitality is underscored later in the novel when Lila tells Lenù Greco, the novel's other protagonist, of her desire to "*reduce myself to diagrams,*" to "*become a perforated tape*" so that "*you won't find me anymore*" (*TWL* 345). The "abstraction that bred all abstractions," here imagined in inverted form, as digitality rather than computation by value, promises an amplified capacity for self-determination that, at its most extreme edge, allows the subject to become untethered from matter. In this respect, Lila's fantasy of digital restfulness is shown to emerge through the processes Grace Kyungwon Hong identifies in her analysis of the shared capacity of abstract labor (exemplified by Taylorist management) and digitality (exemplified by the Hollerith-machine-tabulated 1903 census of the Philippines) to produce a subject that is "disembodied, rendered objective and omniscient, and presented as devoid of materiality." This subject, Hong observes, is animated by a promise of "ostensibly protected and comfortable domesticity" that, in specific combination with abstract labor, "produces the particular formation that is the white working class."[66]

But diagrams and perforated tape are material substrates. They are bearers of abstractions. And Lila cannot begin to render the "wretched world" abstract if she starts from her own material position, which is to say, not from *the* worker but from a specific feminized worker *and* a specific kind of nonworker in a determinate proximity to impoverishment and direct violence. If the promises that inhabit Lila's desire for abstract linearity mark the continuity between digital and capitalist abstractions, her refusal constitutes a visceral recognition of the fact that much of what determines her structural position cannot be computed either as program or as value. She already knew this, of course, when she attacked her boss. The wretchedness of disposal is determined by an abstraction: value. But it can't be resolved through abstractions, whether command over the methods of machine computation or a closer proximity to the ideal of liberal personhood that informs the figure of *the* worker—a figure whose implied security Lila later describes as "hot air to sweeten the pill of . . . a terrible condition" that must be "eliminated," not "improved" (*TWL* 163). This impossibility is mapped onto the imbricated dynamics of production and reproduction when Lila describes the computer hardware and the working conditions in the underwear factory outside Naples in which she and Enzo have secured roles as computer operators:

> The central unit of the machine is as big as a wardrobe with three doors and it has a memory of 8 kilobytes. You can't imagine how hot it is, Lenù: *the computer is worse than a stove*. Maximum abstraction along with sweat and a terrible stink. (*TWL* 262; emphasis added)

Here, 148 pages after her furious recognition that the debilitating effects of concrete labor, the devaluation of her productive and putatively unproductive activities, and the gratuitous gendered violence that is linked to both cannot be abstracted away through programming, Lila evokes the materiality of computation through a direct analogy to the labor of social reproduction. The connections in this passage—of "maximum abstraction with sweat and a terrible stink," of the unmarked figures of *the* worker and the digital with the discomfort arising from their substrates, and of the computer with the stove that metonymically evokes devalued forms of waged service labor and unwaged domestic labor—represent one way of diagramming the investments of the present book. Mastering the techniques necessary for machine computation will not allow Lila to undo the history of divisions that produce the wretched world and position her in it. But they promise to. And, as Hartman has revealed, such promises, with their emphasis on "will, mastery, autonomy, and volition," require the racialized and gendered imposition of "submission, docility, fear and trembling."[67]

This co-constitutive relationship between autonomy and fear exemplifies the distribution of expectations and material conditions across those constituted as homeostatic "living things" and those posited as having to be maintained or left to die. Lila's fraught pursuit of programming as a substitute for the unrealizable promises that cohere around "free" labor shows how the linked abstractions of value, digitality, and personhood become legible at the threshold between value-mediated reproduction and social abjection. Throughout this book I aim to show how the ascriptive, exclusionary, and differentiating processes which operate at that threshold shape and become legible within digital optics, the kinds of disinterested viewing positions from which questions of life and death appear either absolutely irrelevant (as in the engineering problems of communication theory) or so abstract as to become entirely detached from material life (as in predictive models). To give a sense of how these ways of seeing inform and are reproduced through the archives of digitality, I want to consider an exchange between the British cybernetician W. Ross Ashby and the neurophysiologist John A. V. Bates concerning biology, hardware, and the nature of information.

In May 1952, Ashby published an article titled "Can a Mechanical Chess-Player Outplay Its Designer?" in the *British Journal for the Philosophy of Science*. Several major cyberneticians had already addressed the subject of chess playing machines. But where earlier pieces by Wiener and Shannon focus more or less exclusively on technical questions of design and programming, Ashby is more concerned with the question of what it means for a machine to *outplay* (rather than simply play against) its designer. To this end, he includes a section on "Evolution and Design" that engages questions of complexity in biological and mechanical systems through the language and conceptual framework of information theory.[68] In that section, Ashby formulates biological evolution as an information system with two sources of input: genetic inheritance and "mutations" determined by the external environment. "The law that information cannot be created is not violated by evolution," Ashby writes, "for the evolving system receives an endless stream of information in the form of mutations. Whatever their origin, whether in cosmic rays or thermal noise, the fact that each gene may, during each second, change unpredictably to some other form makes each gene a typical information source."[69] Consequently, Ashby argues, any mechanical system built to "evolve" beyond its designed parameters (such as a chess machine able to outplay its designer) should operate according to the same principle.[70]

In a letter dated May 6, 1953, Bates praises Ashby's "ingenious approach to the mechanical chess player problem" but is "bothered" by the section on evolution and design. "I . . . do not like your development in the second paragraph on page 51," Bates writes. "If you regard a gene mutation as a source of information," he continues, "you should it seems also regard, for example, the variation in the behaviour of a component in an electronic machine as a source of information. This again is using information in a sense which is so wide that it confuses the concept, to my mind."[71] Ashby's concept of information troubles Bates because it is insufficiently disembodied and insufficiently yoked to intent and, thus, to will and volition; it introduces the possibility that information can name more than what occurs in "particular situations where the prior probabilities are known and finite."[72] These objections are grounded in Bates's understanding of information as an abstraction that emerges from certain "pure" forms, carries particular intent, and flows through without being touched or added to by the substrates—the concrete organisms, the concrete components—that bear it. On the basis of this understanding, his response takes the form of an ontological justification for the placement of entities inside or outside a closed circuit of communication and the allocation of value on the basis of that placement. In these ways, Bates's discomfort with Ashby's formulation of genetic mutation as a source of information—and his assertion of equivalence between such a mutation and the variations arising from the concreteness of an electronic component, which is to say, the unreliability of that component—rests on an articulation of abstract and concrete that reproduces in explicitly informatic terms the processes through which racialized and gendered forms are posited, under capitalism, as the outside of value-mediated social relations. In this way, Bates's letter models how the social processes that extend from value to allocate or withhold "free" personhood inform ostensibly nonsocial abstractions such as information.

If Bates's complaint positions the unforeseeable output of genes and electrical components outside the realm of information through a logic of exclusion, Ashby's response is equally revealing for the way it models the integration of that which is marked as aberrant. After noting that the majority of criticisms directed at his article rest on "what is primarily a question of vocabulary—was the word 'information' used accurately?"— Ashby appeals to Shannon's insistence that there is "no intrinsic difference between information and noise" in order to propose an illustrative case, which he has "put to several pundits":

> Experimenter A is studying electronic emission from a hot cathode, wanting to know particularly its variance of fluctuation; he shows it on a C.R.O. [cathode-ray oscilloscope], and then finds that interference is bringing some telephone conversation on to his wires.[73]

"In this case," Ashby observes, "the evidence of thermal agitation is his 'information' and the conversation his 'noise.'" This theoretical experiment, he continues, resolves the objection. "All of the pundits, after being momentarily shaken by this reversal of their established habits, have agreed that this is so." Where the anxieties crystallized in Bates's letter arise from a fixed, ontological distinction between a universalized abstraction and a concrete particularity that is always already aberrant, Ashby's example suggests that inclusion is not circumscribed by preexisting ontological distinctions but is afforded by connection to a system whose coherence is entirely derived from the movement of the governing abstraction—in this case, "information." As long as it is parsed by this mechanism, any phenomenon, even one arising from putatively faulty or abnormal components, can be accounted for, modeled in, and thus determined by the system's organizing logic. Like Bates's objection, this definition of information rests on a conceptual articulation of abstract and concrete. But unlike that objection, it affords integration as well as exclusion.

Following his account of the electronic emission/telephone conversation experiment, Ashby goes on to state that he has found it difficult to find the right word to describe the abstraction that can encompass signal and noise. He writes that he "wanted some word to express 'change or fluctuation' in contrast to 'no change'—to distinguish between the loudspeaker that is emitting some sound from one that is silent, while not distinguishing whether the sound is of interest to anybody." Having considered "information" and "entropy," he wonders whether "all objections would be removed if I spoke of 'variety' or 'variation.'"[74] This tentative observation leads Ashby to define the *law of requisite variety*, which holds that "the restriction of the outcomes to the subset that is valued as Good demands a certain variety in R [the regulator or control mechanism]."[75] In other words, Ashby's concept of variety undergirds the principle that homeostasis or self-regulation at a systemic level can only be effected by a mechanism able to accommodate that which it might otherwise abject. If Bates's discomfort with admitting genetic mutations or component noise as sources of information is analogous to (or informed by) essentialism, Ashby's variety is analogous to (or informed by) liberal-capitalist protocols of difference: protocols that repurpose essentialism by subjecting differentiated bodies to increasingly granular and precarious relations of integration in order to ward off the destabilizing effects of volatile conditions.[76]

Ashby's concept of variety and Bates's discomfort with its nascent expression in the informatic conceptualization of biological and electronic errors show how cybernetic ontologies reproduce the logical operations of ascription and differentiation, those mechanisms which, under capitalism, produce a multitude of social forms. Across their exchange, the processes of marking and differential valorization that produce noise, materiality, and information are obfuscated by the abstraction "information" just as surely as the allocation of personhood and the centrality of dispossession, unwaged reproduction, and slavery to capital accumulation are obfuscated by the putatively self-determining operations of the abstraction "value."

Lila's encounter with digitality as a cluster of promises and Ashby and Bates's disagreement about the possible sources of information offer a glimpse at the range of mediations that exist between the commodification and abjection narrated by Equiano and the digital-economic fantasies disclosed in HSBC's "bytes and boxes" and Google's cable. Where Ferrante shows value and digitality as linked abstractions operating on and through a concretely lived life in conditions of constrained desire and foreclosed reproduction, Ashby and Bates model how ontological disavowal and selective integration might appear (or not appear) to systems that manage life by rendering it abstract and to those persons who see the world as an assemblage of such systems.[77] These texts also show how forms of disposal shape and are shaped by explicitly economic concerns *and* conceptual systems that do not explicitly refer to value or its preconditions and outcomes. Framed in this way, the latter, which tend to appear at the emergence of new historical formations—whether early, industrial, or so-called post-Fordist capitalism—appear the proper objects of a history of science and technology grounded in the world- and subject-shaping tendencies of racial capitalism.

In seeking to mark these operations and their effects, I am guided by expressions of desire and expectation that exceed or remain indifferent to value's world-making protocols. If the placement of desires and expectations outside the field of legitimate need and the subsequent, partial, and burdened admittance of those who hold them into circuits of exchange are pushed forward by the formal (or, as I've hinted above and will argue more fully in the following pages, the *informatic*) logic of value, then the life-making practices that are pressurized by this logic but which cannot always be countenanced as bearing value or information (or value *as* information) represent critical sites of struggle. These practices do not point toward some ahistorical notion of matter, desire, or life as in themselves resistant or oppositional, but rather to collectivity without possession, or a future beyond the informatics of value.

I

THE INFORMATICS OF VALUE

1 THINGS COMMUNICATED

Messages, Persons, Goods

INFORMATION SYSTEMS TRANSMIT, STORE, AND PROCESS messages. Communication systems control "the traffic of persons and goods."[1] Friedrich Kittler makes this distinction in order to identify the conditions necessary for its dissolution. "If data make possible the operation of storage, addresses that of transmission, and commands that of data processing," Kittler writes, "then every communication system," by which he means every movement of bodies and things that can be represented and thus controlled through the alignment of these operations, "is an information system."[2] Whether the distinction holds or is dissolved is simply a matter of "whether the three operations are implemented in physical reality." When they are so implemented, the "triad of things communicated—messages, persons, goods" can be formulated according to the following schema:

- Firstly, messages are essentially commands to which persons are expected to react.
- Secondly, as systems theory teaches, persons are not objects but addresses which "make possible the assessment of further communications."
- Thirdly, as ethnology since Mauss and Levi-Strauss has taught, goods represent data in an order of exchange between said persons.[3]

Kittler's formulation abstracts the historical process through which commodity chains become intelligible as concatenations of what the American mathematician Claude Shannon diagrammed in 1948 as the general communication system. By applying information theory to the constituent operations of production and circulation, Kittler shows how information systems have come to signify a degree of control over labor and its products that makes it possible to treat "the traffic of persons and goods"

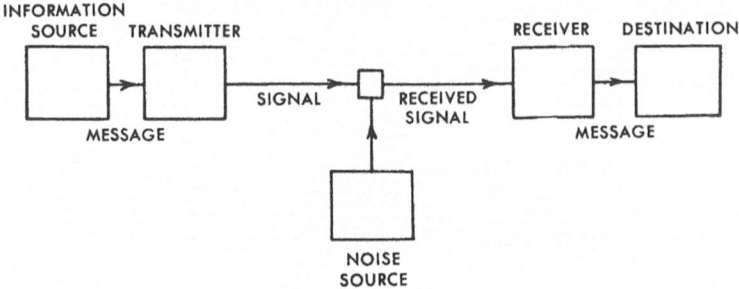

Figure 3. General communication system. Source: Claude Shannon, "A Mathematical Theory of Communication" (1948).

as equivalent to the transmission of signals in a technical communication system (telegraph, telephone, radio, computer network). How did this happen? Why did information theory prove so amenable to grafting with "the traffic of persons and goods"?

Although its practical roots can be traced to earlier histories of commodity circulation and its theoretical premises to knowledge systems such as the protocybernetic discipline of operations research (OR), the complex of infrastructural, organizational, and representational technologies most often named logistics should be understood as part of capital's response to declining economic growth after the late 1960s.[4] Technologies such as virtual supply-chain management software facilitate the increasingly granular forms of labor control and inventory tracking required to synchronize what Deborah Cowen identifies as "an astonishing cast of characters, multiple circulations of capital, and complex movements across great distances."[5] They do this by abstracting those people and processes, depicting them as reticulated symbols whose relationship to their material substrates is identical to that between logic and the automata that bear it in von Neumann's 1952 paper.[6] But, as Philip E. Agre has shown, these technologies don't simply represent entities and processes. They require the activities that comprise production and circulation to be reorganized in order to fit within the constraints of the technologies' representational schemes, producing new "grammars of action" and new mythologies according to which the activities in question are presented as always having corresponded to those grammars.[7]

In other words, grammars of action organize the movements of persons and goods as if they are data, addresses, or messages before those movements are represented as such in software. It is this prior organization that enables technologies such as supply-chain management software to depict and exert control over those movements. Together, the grammars of action and their mediated representation produce what Agre elsewhere describes as a *mirror world*, an abstract realm that remains separate from but nonetheless determines concrete operations of production and circulation.[8] In this realm, number dominates matter.

Once "optical fiber networks turn formerly distinct data flows into a standardized series of digitized numbers," Kittler wrote in 1986, "any medium can be translated into any other." And "with numbers, everything goes. Modulation, transformation, synchronization; delay, storage, transposition; scrambling, scanning, mapping."[9] Fifteen years later, Lev Manovich defined the new media object as "not something fixed once and for all, but something that can exist in different, potentially infinite versions" as a "consequence of [the] numerical coding of media."[10] Understood as an outcome of the conceptual synthesis Kittler sketches in his theorization of information and communication systems, logistics represents an assemblage of systems for bringing the emblematic promises of digital media—absolute fungibility, facilitated by numerical representation—to bear on the material world of production and circulation. This promise is crystallized in Jasper Bernes's characterization of logistics technologies as signifying a degree of control so complete that it can transform matter, turning "solids into liquids—or at its extreme, into electrical fields"—a description that clearly echoes the construction of information as "a kind of bodiless fluid that could flow between different substrates without loss of meaning or form" that N. Katherine Hayles identifies as one of the principal outcomes of cybernetics discourse.[11]

Of course, commodities only appear, flow, and transform like this in the visual and imaginative registers that logistics technologies crystallize.[12] The production and circulation processes those technologies depict are constantly interrupted. Vehicles break down or get held up by accidents, bad weather, and blockades. They are hijacked on land and sea. Accidents, strikes, and sabotage prevent materials from leaving extraction and processing sites and manufactured goods from leaving factories, sending delays reverberating along the supply chain until work resumes or another source is found.[13] The active interruptions—strikes, sabotage, blockades, and hijackings—might be motivated by the refusal of specific working conditions, resistance to colonial occupation or imperial expansion, or people's need to obtain the means of their subsistence. They might be the result of all of these things at once. Sometimes, disruptive events are carefully planned. At others, they can appear to arise directly out of the material effects of land dispossession, differential proletarianization, ascriptive racializing and feminizing regimes, and work discipline, as in the cases of spirit possession among women electronics factory workers documented by Aihwa Ong.[14] In every case, direct violence, intensified forms of work discipline, and new modes of dispossession are deployed in varying proportions to shrink the unbridgeable gap between the mirror world of logistics and the material world of people and things.[15]

Kittler's information-theoretical presentation of circulation as a triad of "things communicated" models the recursive historical relationship between social forms—interactions, subjects, and commodities—and the techno-scientific concept of information that shapes the logistics imaginary. On the one hand, Kittler's triad implies that the "traffic of persons and goods" has always functioned in ways amenable to the electronic metaphors of systems theory and information science. The black boxes of Shannon's system, Kittler insists, make "no claim to historicity," because they can represent anything able to receive inputs, process them according to some internal program, and transmit outputs. From this perspective, the cybernetic sciences simply provide a language for that which always was. On the other hand, Kittler's triad rests on a history of information systems that might be expanded to encompass a fundamental mode of socially synthetic mediation that remains absent from his account.[16] In Kittler's account, Shannon could only devise "a formal model of information" after "the start of the computer age, that is, when all operations of communication systems had been mechanised." The definition of *media* that Kittler wields here confines historical inquiry into this mechanization of social processes to transformations in reading and writing systems: the "decoupling of interaction and communication" in the passage from orality to writing; and the "decoupling of communication and information" in the transition from writing to technical media.[17] In this version of media history, the mode of social mediation that first decouples social synthesis from intent, and which surely informs the communication-theoretical representation and management of "persons and goods," remains unthinkable.

But the movement of persons and goods has always appeared as the movement of discrete abstractions—*for capital,* and within the imaginaries that take shape around and intensify the effects of its core dynamics. This is why Alfred Sohn-Rethel describes the realm of commodity exchange as a *second nature*—a "purely social, abstract, functional reality" that is separate from "material interchange with nature."[18] The superimposition of symbols and things that is facilitated by the treatment of "communication systems" as "information systems" reproduces in an explicitly symbolic and interactive form "the replaceability and interchangeability endemic to the commodity." We have already seen the different effects that the interpenetration of this "second nature" with material social life can produce in Equiano's narrative and in Marx's "atom of matter" remarks, as well as in the numerous passages in which the latter rigorously distinguishes the sensuous materiality of objects as use values from their abstract equivalence as exchange values.[19] The formal likeness of Agre's mirror world to the "abstract, functional reality" of commodity exchange may explain why so many of the practices that prefigure logistics—OR, system dynamics, marginal analysis, linear programming—depict production and circulation in the universalized cybernetic language of inputs and outputs.[20] It may also be why Marxian accounts focused on value tend to reproduce this language, as when Geert Reuten and Michael Williams describe production as a process that "necessarily requires inputs and outputs to be reduced to a universal, unitary form or common denominator."[21]

In other words, the representational and science-historical aspects of the logistics imaginary simultaneously rely on and occlude the contiguity of information systems with a social matrix whose possibilities and constraints are already circumscribed by the logic of capitalist social organization.[22] The former arise from the need to design more or less automatic systems of communication, and the latter optimizes the extraction of surplus value by shaping the social relations between individual producers in a manner that is not legible to them as coercion. The historical relationship between the two systems may explain why technological systems that are fundamentally about control so often appear to exemplify freedom.[23] As Moishe Postone observes, capitalism's defining characteristic is its capacity to function as a "system of abstract, impersonal domination" under which, "relative to earlier social forms, people appear to be independent" but "actually are subject to a system of social domination that seems not social but 'objective.'"[24] As a system of abstract domination, capital automated social relations long before the technologies of the so-called automation revolution came into existence. To use Kittler's terms, capital appears to induce action, render persons as discrete forms, and represent goods (including labor power) as data "in an order of exchange" between those forms. And it appears to do so not through direct coercion but through the transmission, processing, and storage of an abstraction that appears in mediated forms at each stage. This process—the organization of independent actors into a coherent system that tends toward the accumulation of capital—is often framed in terms of *forming* or *form-determination*, as in Diane Elson's analysis of value as "an historical process of forming what is intrinsically unformed."[25] The common imaginaries that congeal around capital and digitality, disclosing their conceptual and historical links, are shaped not by abstraction alone but by the animating role a specific abstraction plays in the synthesis of a specific kind of social form.

The social forms encoded in Kittler's triad of "things communicated"—messages, persons, and goods—model these historical processes of forming. The message, or the abstraction "to which persons are expected to react," effects social synthesis by compelling behavior without direct coercion. The person is an entity who is addressed by that abstraction and thus instantiated, made productive, and fitted for "further communications." Goods are the abstract-concrete forms of a person's labor after it has been deracinated as "data" and averaged in its products. The following chapters will work through these communicative and synthetic aspects of capitalist social form, developing the analysis I started to sketch in the Introduction through a close focus on information and value. Of course, as I started to show in the Introduction, the social processes that center on those abstractions and give form to the social and conceptual structures they constitute function through separation, exclusion, and differential inclusion. In the terms theorized by Hortense Spillers, they produce, hold apart, and connect body and flesh, or addressable personhood and the "seared, divided, ripped-apartness" that marks its denial.[26] Capital positions increasing numbers of people at the threshold of value-mediated sociality, oscillating between addressable and superfluous personhood in a state of precarious existence where what Saidya Hartman calls "the burdened individuality of freedom" is most keenly felt. These outcomes correspond to the two possibilities for racialized sorting that are informatically modeled by Ashby and Bates: ontological disavowal and qualified inclusion. I am interested in how the medium of social synthesis that precedes and makes possible the formulation of persons and goods in information-theoretical terms *produces* (rather than simply working around or finding and incorporating) those disavowed and precarious structural positions in order to maintain the circulation and expansion of value around the frayed edges of its circulation matrices. Part II will focus on these positions and their structural relationship to accumulation and digital-liberal personhood. In the rest of Part I, I focus on the informatic character of the processes through which capital constitutes social forms long before the emergence of the modern concept of information; the ways in which that concept subsequently cleaves to value, offering new ways to intensify and naturalize capital's control over labor; and the techniques of expulsion and differential integration that are central to informatic social mechanisms centered on the value relation.

As I have already suggested, forms of disposal are historically specific mechanisms that produce putatively self-regulating—which is to say, "free"—social formations through dialectical operations of abstraction, abjection, and differential integration. Such mechanisms undergird dominant modes of representation, technologies of structural determination, and clusters of promises—promises of transparency, formal coherence, and connection to economic, social, and political networks—that link a specific relationship to value with specific protections and privileges, if not to social existence as such. Considered against these dynamics, the contemporary synthesis of information and value in logistics exemplifies what Sohn-Rethel names "the general epistemological proposition" that the "socially necessary forms of thinking of an epoch are those in conformity with the socially synthetic functions of that epoch."[27] But how does such a precise technical intervention come to signify the socially synthetic power of abstraction more generally? Why information systems, and not simply maps or diagrams of moving persons and goods? In the following chapter, I aim to answer these questions by reading explanations and extensions of information theory alongside Marx's theorization of value as a mechanism of emergent connectivity, of social synthesis that appears (but only appears) to emerge and regulate itself without direct coercion. As I have already suggested, my wager is that it is this mode of connectivity, more so than the simple conversion of quality to quantity, that represents the most significant historical relationship between the two modes of abstraction.[28]

2 RELIABLE CIRCUITS, UNRELIABLE COMPONENTS

How Capital Connects

IN SEPTEMBER 1956, Claude Shannon published an article in the Institute of Radio Engineers' *Transactions on Information Theory* addressing the "wave of popularity" that had by the mid-1950s transformed a specific technical method into "something of a scientific bandwagon," leading to the appearance of information-theoretical concepts in "biology, psychology, linguistics, fundamental physics, economics, the theory of organization," and many other fields.[1] Although he admits that some of information theory's basic findings might prove useful in psychology, economics, and "other social sciences," Shannon cautions that integrating them into those fields would not be "a trivial matter of translating words to a new domain."[2] The sentiments expressed in "The Bandwagon" are consistent with Shannon's contributions to the Macy conferences, at which he regularly intervened—often with barely concealed irritation—when speakers used the concept of information in presentations that did not concern the kinds of engineering problems with which he was engaged in his writing and his work at Bell Labs. In the discussion following a paper by the British physicist Donald M. MacKay at the eighth conference, for example, Shannon snaps that "it seems to me that we can all define 'information' as we choose; and, depending on which field we are working in, we will choose different definitions." In communications engineering, he goes on to clarify, the only pertinent question is "How much channel do I need to transmit this information?"[3]

When Shannon was invited to contribute an article on information theory to the 1957 edition of the *Encyclopædia Britannica*, he evidently saw an opportunity to slow the bandwagon by circulating a precise account of the field's core concepts and applications.[4] He opens the entry by defining information theory as a broad application of communications theory concerned with the "mathematical laws governing systems designed to communicate or manipulate information." Its objects, he continues, are "quantitative measures of information and of the capacity of various systems to transmit, store and otherwise process information." Its applications are limited to "finding the best methods of utilizing various available communication systems, the best methods of separating signals from noise and the problem of setting upper bounds on what it is possible to do with a given channel."[5] Throughout these opening passages he repeatedly pins the scope of information theory to the questions with which he sought to separate it from other areas of inquiry at the Macy conferences and elsewhere: How much information does one want to send, and how much channel capacity does one need to send it?

After establishing the capacity and optimal use of the channel as the proper objects of information theory, Shannon defines information "in its broadest sense" as "the messages occurring in any of the standard communication mediums such as telegraphy, radio, or television, the signals involved in electronic computing machines, servomechanisms systems and other data-processing devices, and even the signals appearing in the nerve networks of animals and man."[6] The range of media is important, because Shannon is here establishing for the readers of the *Encyclopædia* how the semantic content of the message is irrelevant to the use of the concept of information in engineering problems. A message must be transmitted through the five stages of the communication system. In the case of radio: a person (information source) speaks (a message) into a system comprising microphone and "associated electronic equipment" (transmitter), which converts acoustic waves into electromagnetic waves (signal); the signal is then sent from a transmitting antenna to a receiving antenna (the space between them is the channel), received and converted back into acoustic waves by a home radio (receiver), and heard by a listener (destination). All other concerns belong to fields other than information theory. Once again: What do you want to send, and what is your channel capacity?

But strong beliefs about the legitimate and illegitimate uses of a particular form of knowledge do not necessarily lead to a grasp of the historical conditions that inform that area of knowledge and the imaginaries that take shape around it. A "homely analogy" that Shannon first used in a 1950 introduction to communication theory in *Electronics* magazine and then repeated in the *Encyclopædia* provides a glimpse of those conditions and their bearing on the modern concept of information.[7] In this analogy, which is intended to illustrate the theoretical treatment of information as if it were "a physical quantity such as mass or energy" in advance of more technical considerations of measurement, encoding, capacity, filtering and prediction, and cryptography, Shannon likens the communication system to "a lumber mill producing lumber at a certain point":

> The channel . . . might correspond to a conveyor system for transporting the lumber to a second point. In such a situation there are two important quantities: the rate R (in cubic feet per second) at which lumber is produced at the mill, and the capacity (in cubic feet per second) of the conveyor. These two quantities determine whether or not the conveyor system will be adequate for the lumber mill. If the rate of production R is greater than the conveyor capacity C, it will certainly be impossible to transport the full output of the mill; there will not be sufficient space available. If R is less than or equal to C, it may or may not be possible, depending on whether the lumber can be packed efficiently in the conveyor. Suppose, however, that we allow ourselves a sawmill at the source. This corresponds in our analogy to the encoder or transmitter. Then the lumber can be cut up into small pieces in such a way as to fill out the available capacity of the conveyor with 100% efficiency. Naturally in this case we should provide a carpenter shop at the receiving point to fasten the pieces back together in their original form before passing them on to the consumer.
>
> If this analogy is sound, we should be able to set up a measure R in suitable units telling the rate at which information is produced by a given information source, and a second measure C which determines the capacity of a channel for transmitting information. Furthermore, the analogy would suggest that by a suitable coding or modulation system, the information can be transmitted over the channel if and only if the rate of production R is not greater than the capacity C. A key result of information theory is that it is indeed possible to set up measures R and C having this property.[8]

Here, the concept of information is shown not only to abstract and thus afford the quantitative representation of a given content—here, the lumber—but also to determine the treatment of that content and the relations among the parts of a system that are animated by it. This example is intended to explain a communication problem and its solution by use of an analogy with the processing and transportation of lumber.[9] It is not intended to show what an automated lumber mill would look like. Nonetheless, is it not remarkable how clearly Shannon's analogy shows the information-theoretical representation of production and circulation to be in several essential ways identical to the value-mediated appearance of those phenomena?

Shannon depicts an array of what Marx called fixed capital: the mill, the conveyor, the sawmill, and the carpenter shop. And he sketches the processes required to move the lumber from source to destination most efficiently—the disaggregation and reassembly of the lumber at either end of the "channel." But his mill contains no workers, and it renders the consumer a destination (or address). This is not a vision of production and circulation augmented by communication technologies. It is a model of production and circulation *as communication*. It could just as well depict agricultural labor in sixteenth-century Britain or plantation labor in the Americas as the automated factories and supply chains of the present. The lumber appears in the mill, is cut into pieces whose size and arrangement are optimized for the conveyor, is transported from source to destination via a "coding or modulation system" that governs its movement by balancing rate of production with conveyor capacity, and is reassembled for transmission to the consumer, all without the presence of living labor. The whole process represents a production-stage counterpart to Marx's famous illustration of the form of wood that, in the course of its transformation into a commodity, a table, "changes into a thing which transcends sensuousness" and "evolves out of its wooden brain grotesque ideas, far more wonderful than if it were to begin dancing on its own free will."[10] For all of his attempts to limit the scope of information theory, and for all of his warnings about the too-easy application of that theory to fields such as economics and organization, Shannon's lumber mill reproduces the process through which, in Marx's words, "the value-sustaining appearance of labour appears as the self-supporting power of capital," so that "living labour appears to be put to work by objectified labour."[11] And it shows how that process finds a germane abstraction in the information theory it would later graft to in order to intensify its control over production and circulation.

Considered otherwise, the specific commodity that Shannon chooses as his "information," lumber, can point toward the histories that are erased in the abstract figuration of labor as communicated value.[12] As Evelyn Nakano Glenn has shown, these histories include the forced labor and the differential allocation of value and capacity facilitated by Alabama's adoption of the convict-leasing system in the 1890s, which led to a "state-operated slave market" through which black women, children, and the debilitated were sent to work in lumber camps.[13] Lumber similarly invites questions about the mill's geographical preconditions. Where does the lumber—not uncut trees, but prepared wood—come from? Where does it go after it leaves the carpentry shop? As John Perlin has shown, North American lumber merchants formed an eighteenth-century "trade loop" with planters in the British West Indies, slave traders in Africa and Europe, and manufacturers in England. Between 1771 and 1773,

> woodsmen had to cut far in excess of 240,000 trees to provide the West Indian market with the lumber. In exchange for the wood, Yankee traders, mostly Quakers and Puritans, obtained 3 million gallons of rum. With their cargoes of liquor, they headed to Africa to trade the rum for slaves or sell it to European slave merchants. They then returned to the West Indies with their human freight, and they bartered the slaves for sugar. The New Englanders shipped the sugar to England and traded it for manufactured goods which they sold in America. The money earned from those sales went to purchase more timber for another round.[14]

Timber turns into rum. Rum turns into slaves or cash. Slaves turn into sugar. Sugar turns into manufactured goods, which turn into cash, which turns into more timber. Or; timber turns into molasses, which turns into spirits, which turns into fur, which turn into cash, which turns into manufactured goods. Perlin says nothing of the labor arrangements or the conditions of dispossession that subtend these metamorphoses. Each exchange presupposes both the concrete deployment of labor and capital and a general equivalent which is sometimes expressed as money and at others as the direct exchange of one type of commodity for another. But not all of the exchanged goods are produced by the same kind of labor; Perlin's cycle mobilizes "free" waged labor, slave labor, and non-capitalist (or non- or indirectly value-mediated) modes such as that which produced the furs.

Connecting Shannon's imagined lumber mill to the historical conditions surrounding the production and circulation of lumber—land enclosure, colonial expansion, and resource extraction; market dependence and the differential allocation of value, capacity, and personhood—invites further questions about whether the concepts Shannon sought to illustrate rest upon, reproduce, and modulate those same preconditions. I suggest that they do, and that Shannon's "homely" analogy helps to make visible the abstract forms that shape and are shaped by capitalist social organization. In the same way, Shannon's earlier example of radio transmission encodes the historical conditions through which communicative personhood is allocated.

The self-moving commodities and the obfuscated preconditions of Shannon's lumber mill point toward an answer to one of the questions at the heart of this book: How did information technology come to exemplify the present iteration of a social system premised on abstract domination? I now want to pursue this question beyond the explicit representation of production and circulation, in order to think about how information theory became so amenable to conflation with value-mediated social relations.

In the opening sentences of "A Mathematical Theory of Communication," his signal account of the basic problem for which information theory offers a solution, Shannon writes:

> The fundamental problem of communication is that of reproducing at one point either exactly or approximately a message selected at another point. Frequently the messages have meaning; that is, they refer to or are correlated according to some system with certain physical or conceptual entities. These semantic aspects of communication are irrelevant to the engineering problem. The significant aspect is that the actual message is one selected from a set of possible messages. The system must be designed to operate for each possible selection, not just the one which will actually be chosen since this is unknown at the time of design.[15]

The irrelevance of "meaning" (or "the semantic aspects of communication") is among the most widely discussed techno-scientific principles in digital media theory.[16] Far less has been said about the problem that necessitates this indifference: "reproducing at one point either exactly or approximately a message selected at another point" in a communication system. This is significant, because the more Shannon abstracts his objects, severing them from the context, content, and effects that surround the statistics of transmission, the closer his system comes to reiterating the logic of value.

The approach Shannon takes to his core problem—the implementation of "pure" abstractions in material systems—was at the heart of his feted master's thesis twelve years earlier. In "A Symbolic Analysis of Relay and Switching Circuits," Shannon shows how the work of designing and constructing circuits able to "perform complex operations automatically" with the smallest possible number of switches and relays can be expedited by the use of a calculus "exactly analogous to the Calculus of Propositions used in the symbolic study of logic."[17] After the circuit has been diagrammed as an equation composed of logic symbols, Shannon writes, its physical implementation "may then be immediately drawn from the equations." Writing out the circuit in abstract, symbolic form makes it possible to build it more efficiently, albeit by limiting what can be materially constructed to "circuits containing only relays and switches."

The similarities between Shannon's thesis and von Neumann's subsequent description of automata as "ordinary logic" implemented in material components are clear, and reading the two accounts alongside each other emphasizes the centrality of synthesis to the informatic imaginary. In "A Mathematical Theory of Communication," Shannon decouples the form of the effect from that of the cause. In one of the most succinct accounts of what *is* essential to the engineering problems that information theory confronts, presented in the 1950 *Electronics* essay, he writes that "the thing that must be transmitted is a specification of the particular message which was chosen by the information source. If such an unambiguous specification is transmitted, the original message can be reconstructed at the receiving point."[18] In other words, what must be transmitted is not the content or substance that inhabits a given message but the rules governing the reconstruction of that message, which should make it impossible for a deviant outcome to occur at the receiver stage. This aspect of Shannon's theory is emphasized in Warren Weaver's "Some Recent Contributions to the Mathematical Theory of Communication," an introductory text published alongside Shannon's essay in 1949. Seeking to make Shannon's paper more accessible, Weaver supplements the "technical problem" of how accurately a message can be transmitted with two additional communication problems: the precision with which the transmitted message conveys "desired meaning" ("the semantic problem"), and the effectiveness with which the received meaning affects its recipient's conduct "in the desired way" (the "effectiveness problem").[19] Although he admits that Shannon is only really concerned with the first of these, Weaver insists that the technical problem "overlaps" the others to the extent that the theory of accurate transmission is "at least to a significant degree" also a theory of meaning and the determination of conduct.[20] As I suggested in my reading of von Neumann, the fantasy that coalesces around this aspect of information theory—the organization of the concrete by the abstract, which produces a reliable pattern across spatial and temporal boundaries—reiterates the basal logic of capitalist social organization. In Weaver's extension of Shannon's work, reproduction that occurs through the transmission of an abstraction rather than the direct physical manipulation of the receiver—writing, stamping, gauging, branding—comes to signify a knowable and controllable version of that which in most cases cannot be felt, let alone manipulated: the production of social form behind the backs of the individuals that compose it.

Put differently, the kernel of the informatic imaginary—"reproducing at one point either exactly or approximately a message selected at another point"—comes to restage in explicit rather than hidden form the mode of social organization without direct coercion that is (or appears to be) capitalism's *differentia specifica*. This explains why the concept of information, which in Shannon's work is largely confined to problems of channel capacity, encoding, decoding, and redundancy, takes on increasingly broad significance in a number of texts written between the 1950s and the 1970s before being installed as the cornerstone of social life and economic activity in the last decades of the twentieth century. Across these texts it is possible to observe a tendency toward abstract domination that clearly builds on the double inheritance of Shannon's information theory and Wiener's definition of information as "information, not matter or energy," but which in subtle and not-so subtle ways shifts this inheritance toward closer confluence with the logic of capital.[21]

This tendency is visible in J. D. Bernal's 1954 observation that "in the amplification effected by a valve, energy is fed in from the outside but the pattern can be *imposed* on it by one that is much weaker." "The valve," Bernal goes on to write, "is the type of device operating on *information* rather than on power. It was indeed the first fully flexible *cybernetic* device."[22] A near-identical definition appears in Karl Deutsch's *The Nerves of Government*, the first significant application of cybernetic concepts to political theory: "What has been transferred through [a] channel of communication," Deutsch writes, "is not matter, nor any one of the particular processes, nor any significant amount of energy, since relays and electronic tubes make the qualities of the signal independent from a considerable range of energy inputs. Rather, it is *something* that has remained unchanged, invariant, over this whole sequence of processes."[23] Deutsch's book extends the concept of informatics as the imposition of pattern without direct coercion beyond the technical capacities of the electronic valve and the general communication system, establishing it as a foundational concept for understanding the relationships between social actors and institutions. The same relationship of abstract determination recurs in an even more general form in Gregory Bateson's infamous claim that the basic unit of information is an "abstract matter," a "*difference that makes a difference*" within technological, biological, and social systems alike.[24] Through these extensions, information is invested with the capacity to effect transformations in material situations or substrates, ranging from communications systems to global politics, without the amount of energy required to produce such transformations via the direct application of force.

Although Shannon insisted that information was a generic descriptor for the purposes of modeling a possible transmission, a quantity of *something* that must be transferred along a channel of *some capacity*, several of his formulations imply a general mechanism of abstract, indirect form-determination—not a thing, but a relation—that by the middle decades of the twentieth century, following elaborations by Weaver, Bernal, Deutsch, and Bateson, became encoded in the information concept. This informatic relation *connects and shapes its material substrates*. It encodes the conditions of its own reproduction in the abstractions it transmits. And it makes possible situations in which *the abstract determines—or dominates—the concrete*.

The imaginaries that subtend and grow out of this informatic relation cleave to capital's linked modes of abstraction and organization. The concept of information, which emerged as an abstract designator for anything that might be encoded and transmitted and which was developed for the specific purpose of analyzing communication systems, ends up signifying the capacity of abstractions to inform material systems—which is to say, it ends up restaging the intangible but real social function of value. This convergence seems to support Sohn-Rethel's suggestion that the relationship between the exchange abstraction and "the formal constituents of cognition" is one of identity, not mere analogy.[25] But it does not result from a straightforward process of expressive causality through which the newer mode of abstraction simply takes on the shape and impetus of the older. In fact, this convergence reveals as much about the logic of value as it does about the centrality of information to contemporary social and economic imaginaries.

In a passage from the *Grundrisse* that directly follows a brief digression on the growth of "means of communication" such as telegraphy, Marx ironically observes that capitalism's "beauty and greatness" lie in its capacity for "spontaneous interconnection." Unlike earlier social bonds based on "blood ties, or on primeval, natural, or master-servant relations," Marx observes, capital fosters a "material and mental metabolism which is independent of the knowing and willing of individuals, and which presupposes their reciprocal independence and indifference." The resultant social form is one in which the "connection of the individual with all" constitutes a structure while maintaining "the independence of this connection from the individual."[26] The matrix of capitalist social relations, Marx here suggests, is a kind of information system in which individuals organize themselves without direct coercion into generative networks of production and reproduction.

This informatic language recurs across the various stages of Marx's critique of political economy. In an account of the synthesis of social structure from private activities in the *Second Draft of Critique of Political Economy* of 1858, Marx defines individual laborers as self-established, independent points "conditioned on every side in [their] connections with other individuals" by a "whole range of economic conditions."[27] The "economic conditions," this passage suggests, do not directly position the laborer but rather constitute the matrix in which individuals establish and position themselves. The same language remains central to the theorization of capitalist social relations ten years later, when, in an exchange with Ludwig Kugelmann following the publication of volume one of *Capital*, Marx defines capitalism as "a state of society in which the interconnection of social labour expresses itself as the private exchange of the individual products of labour."[28]

Spontaneous interconnection. Independent points conditioned by their connections with other such points. A reticular social system that emerges through private acts of exchange. The three descriptions cited above, each taken from a different stage of Marx's critique of political economy, present market-mediated social life as a distributed communication mechanism—an appearance that Ernest Mandel underscores in his 1976 introduction to *Capital* when he writes of "the cobweb of apparent 'exchange equality.'"[29] Since value is its mediating abstraction, this distributed system might be defined as a *value network*.[30]

Connection to this network takes place through the sale or purchase of commodities. Commodities—as computed quanta of abstract labor—circulate in it as exchange values. The frequency with which connections occur and the sequence in which they are arranged produce distinct social positions. Some buy both their means of subsistence and additional commodities and labor power, and they seek to extract profit from the latter. Others connect by selling their labor power, their only alienable property, in order to later connect as buyers of their means of subsistence. As these minimal sketches of capitalist and proletarian show, the value network is limned by dynamics of market dependence: subsistence and accumulation are secured through connection, so connection becomes a precondition for social validity, survival, and what passes for thriving under such a social system. "To state the case schematically," Robert Brenner writes,

> "production for profit via exchange" will have the systematic effect of accumulation and the development of the productive forces only when it expresses certain specific social relations of production, namely a system of free wage labour, where labour power is a commodity. . . . Only under conditions of free wage labour will the individual producing units (combining labour power and the means of production) be forced to sell in order to buy, to buy in order to survive and reproduce, and ultimately to expand and innovate in order to maintain this position in relationship to other competing productive units. Only under such a system, where both capital and labour power are thus commodities—and which was therefore called by Marx "generalized commodity production"—is there the necessity of producing at the "socially necessary" labour time in order to survive, and to surpass this level of productivity to ensure continued survival.[31]

The appearance of spontaneous interconnection is an effect, rather than a cause, of this system of market dependence.

When a majority of people are free from direct coercion but bound to seek participation in the value network in order to survive, value appears to function as the form-giving "content" of an interconnection that results from the independent actions of those individuals, who are computed as points within circuits of sale and purchase. Of course, the two alternatives—fully wage-mediated subsistence and successful accumulation—are not the only positions the value network produces, although they disproportionately populate the imaginaries that take shape around it. As Equiano, Smallwood, and Hartman (among others) have shown, value-mediated relations also produce forms of unfree labor such as those in which individuals are purchased, provided with a minimum level of subsistence, and worked under conditions of extreme coercion until no more labor power can be extracted from them. Such positions, along with those defined by structural underemployment, are necessary to secure the function and the meaning of the two "optimal" positions described above. I'll return in later chapters to the ways that the value network allocates form to those whom it does not fully constitute as either worker or owner. For now I want to note that, as Étienne Balibar has observed, humans "do not appear" in the network that produces these structural positions "except in the form of bearers for the connections implied by the structure, and the forms of their individuality as determinate effects of the structure."[32] The material particularity of those who connect to the value network is, to use Shannon's words, "irrelevant to the engineering problem." The "connections implied by the structure" constitute nothing less than an informatics of value.

To further emphasize the informatic character of the value relation, consider how the interconnections it appears to spontaneously effect might be mapped onto the stages of Shannon's general communication system. "Free" laborers appear as sources of the "signal" that in reality precedes and organizes (rather than emerging from) them. Labor—the transmission of this "signal"—then constitutes a "channel" between the "source" and its outcomes (goods, services). The aggregation of necessary and surplus labor with the costs of inputs and capital expended in the production process takes place at a "receiver" stage, at which point the value of the first is returned to the "source" laborer in the form of wages. Finally, commodities constitute the "destination" at which computed value is held until it is sold, after which it may enter another production process, circulate as money, or get exhausted in unproductive consumption.

In this informatics of value, each source "transmits" to the commodities in whose production it participates not an abstracted form of something specific to it but a number of generic units whose value is determined by the total socially necessary labor time (SNLT) required to produce the commodities in question. And socially necessary labor time is derived not from hours of actually expended time but through the reticulation of the individual producer with all others engaged in value-mediated labor. As Michael Heinrich puts it, "every hour of labor measured by a clock is an hour of a particular *concrete* act of labor," but abstract labor "cannot be 'expended' at all"; it is a "*relation of social validation*."[33] Abstract labor—the content of the abstraction "value"—is an "*element of the total labor of society*."[34] Or, privately exchanged concrete labor is mediated—or *informed*—by socially average labor in the course of its objectification as value. Value might be described as a form whose "content" is a portion of the "homogeneous mass" of socially average labor power that overwrites the individual producer's concretely specific activity in the process of transmission.[35] In this case, abstract labor, the "*common substance*" that allows commodities to appear "*qualitatively equal*" in the value network, might be understood as the "data" to value's "information."[36] If the "source" represents the stage at which these data are shaped into "information," the social relations through which concrete labor is converted into a determinate quantity of socially average labor before being transmitted as value then correspond to the "encoder" stage of Shannon's communication diagram. Mapping the value-mediated dynamics of this encoding process onto Shannon's diagram provides us with an informatic model of production that differs in significant ways from Kittler's "triad of things communicated." This mapping process shows how, under capitalism, something structurally analogous to Shannon's information appears to indirectly organize (rather than simply representing and facilitating direct control over) the traffic of persons and goods.

This brief account of the informatics of value should make it clear that value is no more a material substance that flows between laboring bodies and the commodities and services that result from their activities than information is a material thing that moves between source, encoder, channel, receiver, and destination. In both examples, the abstraction—value, information—only appears as content (or substance) within a specific technical relation that determines the form and constrains the prospects of its concrete bearers.[37] This abstraction may become most legible at the moment of exchange—to certain theorists, if not to the majority of participants behind the backs of whom it operates. But the systemic logic it informs determines other (and more fundamental) moments and processes. This is why Raya Dunayevskaya and Elson both insist that Marx pursued a "value theory of labor" over the labor theory of value already present in works of classical political economy. Whereas different versions of the latter uphold a notion of value as the substance of exchange, Marx emphasizes how the system in which value becomes intelligible as content entails particular ways of formatting, disciplining, and organizing the extraction of surplus value from labor.[38] As Elson puts it, Marx's specific intervention does not turn on a theory of the material transfer of "value" from a living being to an inert commodity. Rather, the idea of such a transfer is a mystification that Marx *describes* in accounting for the historically constituted relationship between the value abstraction, the impersonal domination of labor by capital, and the ideas of political economists. But in describing this relation, Elson argues, Marx is not attempting to track the movement of a real substance—*value*—from living bodies to commodities to market prices. He is not "seeking an explanation of why prices are what they are and finding it in labour" but rather pursuing "an understanding of why labour takes the forms it does, and what the political consequences are."[39]

Insofar as it "appears" at all, value appears to function as the immaterial "content" of the exchanges from which emerge a system that reliably tends toward its own expanded reproduction. And the reliability with which apparently independent acts tend toward that outcome suggests that the "content" in fact steers its bearers. Value is, to borrow Bernal's description of the informatic relation, a weak force that imposes pattern on a much stronger arrangement of matter and energy. Christopher Arthur provides a helpful summary of this imposition of pattern when he notes that, because only goods produced by capital count as value, and because the activity of production is an activity of labor, capital "makes that activity its own activity insofar as it thoroughly subsumes labour as a content penetrated through and through by the value form."[40] Responding to Arthur, Roberto Finelli notes that this process of formal determination constitutes a set of functions that "cannot ever be expressed by something material and finite, but organise and give sense to every material and finite content."[41] In other words, *the value relation connects and shapes its material substrates, encodes the conditions of its own reproduction in the abstractions it transmits,* and *makes possible situations in which the abstract determines—or dominates—the concrete.*

Marx sketches the emergent character of the value-mediated social system when he writes:

> In so far as the commodity or labour is conceived of only as exchange value, and the relation in which the various commodities are brought into connection with one another is conceived as the exchange of these exchange values with one another, as their equation, then the individuals, the subjects between whom this process goes on, are simply and only conceived of as exchangers.[42]

Marx's depiction of "subjects" rendered as "exchangers" captures the process through which value-mediated social relations constitute individuals as specific social forms and synthesize a structure from those forms. The abstraction of the individual producer—or the indifference of exchange value to the concrete character of this or that substrate, which clearly foreshadows the indifference of information to meaning—is both outcome of and precondition for this synthesis. Exchange value asserts itself through the direct comparison of more than one different thing, and thus both requires and tendentially multiplies the interconnection of persons, things, and relations. Heinrich illustrates this process by distinguishing it from commensuration on the basis of a common property such as color. A fire truck and an apple, Heinrich writes, can have the color red in common, but they remain red when they are isolated from each other. Value, by contrast, "is only obtained by things when they are set in relation with one another. . . . It's as if the fire truck and the apple were only red when they're actually standing alongside each other, and had no color when separated."[43] This system of abstraction and interconnection centers on the increasingly distributed computation of socially average labor for objectification in goods and services. As Marx puts it in the chapter of *Capital* on the form of value, "It is only the expression of equivalence between different commodities [in the network of value-mediated forms] which brings into view the specific character of value-creating labor, by actually reducing the different kinds of labour embedded in the different kinds of commodity to their common quality of being human labour in general."[44]

The reticular operations of value establish connection to the value network as the horizon of legitimate sociality. As Isaak Rubin explains, the status of a given activity as social labor only arises through the equalization of its output with that of all other producers.[45] Just as data and information constitute the systems in which they are operationalized, so too does value constitute a general and homogeneous exchange space that indifferently rules over material relations. Legitimate forms of individual and collective sociality are determined not by the abstraction of material life alone but by exposure to the seemingly automatic mode of interconnection and form-determination, this "grandiose system of spontaneous social accounting and comparison."[46] In Heinrich's words, value-mediated social relations "impose a certain form of rationality to which all individuals must adhere if they wish to maintain their existence within these conditions."[47]

Like the systemic relations that ground the modern concept of information, this spontaneous system of relational validation facilitates complex acts of distributed coordination in service of its overarching tendency toward accumulation and expansion. One example of this spontaneous coordination can be found in socially necessary labor time, the "level of average productivity" that is determined by the activity of "the entirety of producers of a use value."[48] Another occurs in the binding of wage levels to reproduction costs across the global field of production and circulation.[49] And still another can be found in the differentiation of so-called skilled and unskilled labor on the basis of their imputed reproduction costs—costs that can be "exceedingly small in the case of ordinary labor-power," and higher for that which requires "special education or training."[50] As Elson and Ruth Pearson have shown, one consequence of this differential rendering of skill is the systemic devaluation of racialized and feminized labor. Addressing the disproportionate employment of young women in garment factories in the Global South, Elson and Pearson note that such labor tends to be coded as unskilled, and remunerated accordingly, because the skills required to perform it are generally learned at home, passed down from "mothers and other female kin," and thus do not constitute additional education costs that must be returned in wages.[51]

Through value's reticular operations, which bind wages to reproduction costs, the optimal laborer is posited as a feedback loop in which outputs and inputs (sales and purchases, or production and reproduction) are perfectly balanced; the wage received in exchange for "freely" alienated labor power of a certain level of skill is high enough to maintain that labor power (and, in certain instances, to facilitate the reproduction of dependents and/or to pursue certain desires that are not directly connected to the production process), but is not high enough to allow its recipient to leave the network.[52] This homeostatic ideal is visible in Bernard Mandeville's insistence, in *The Fable of the Bees* of 1714, that, "in the interests of all rich nations," "the greatest part of the poor should almost never be idle, and yet continually spend what they get."[53] And it surely informs Lacan's remark that "living things" are homeostatic but slaves are not. The optimal capitalist, by contrast, is a positive feedback loop in which the cumulative effect of all sales and purchases (including the reproduction of capitalists and their dependents) is constant growth.[54] Regardless of the degree to which their manifestations in concrete reality correspond to their optimal, diagrammatic form, these loops produce a multitude of structural positions, relations, norms, and representations.[55] Yet in every case they enact the process through which, in Finelli's words, "the abstract occupies and itself invades the concrete, filling it according to the exigencies of its expansive-reproductive logic" and leaving only a "semblance, an exterior surface of concreteness."[56] This "*emptying out*" is central to the homeostatic appearance of value-mediated reproduction; it creates the impression of the "never-ending circle" in which mechanisms internal to the value network tend toward continuity of production and the accumulation of surplus value even as they make labor's reproduction increasingly impossible, devaluing and wearing down the lives of those they occupy and cutting increasing numbers off from even the minimal protections afforded by underemployment.[57]

For the vast majority, connection to the value network is associated with survival because that network mediates access to means of subsistence. But the promise of mere survival doesn't explain the fantasies and imaginaries that take shape around the value relation and its derivatives. It doesn't explain value's reticular and recursive aspects or its capacity to inform the techno-scientific visions of boundless possibility and immaterial accumulation that in different ways characterize the mercantile, industrial, and so-called information ages. To understand these, it is necessary to see how the informatics of value constitute—or impose as a pattern—a social actor that is characterized, as Hartman observes, by "will, mastery, autonomy, and volition." Encoded in this subject are the desires and reproductive practices that are legitimated by value-mediated social forms. And these legitimated desires and practices mediate between the abstract-concrete form of the person rendered as homeostatic loop and the forms of disposal that arise in its image.

Labor power, Marx writes, can enter the value network only when the individual who bears it sells it as a commodity. In order to do this, the seller must be the "free proprietor" of their own capacity.[58] The value network thus comes to embody "a very Eden of the innate rights of man." It posits capitalist social relations as the exclusive realm of "freedom, equality [and] property" in which buyer and seller

> contract as free persons, who are equal before the law. Their contract is the final result in which their joint will finds a common legal expression. Equality, because each enters into relation with the other, as with a simple owner of commodities, and they exchange equivalent for equivalent. Property, because each disposes only of what is his own.[59]

This passage shows how the emergent, self-regulating dynamics associated with value-mediated social relations inform the possessive individual, that exemplary legal and political-philosophical expression of modern personhood.[60] Responding to Sohn-Rethel, Theodor Adorno presents this forming process in even starker terms: the "reality" of the transcendental subject, he writes, arises not from some autonomous (or "narcissistic") elevation of the "I" but from the specific form of domination that is made possible by the generalization of market-mediated exchange.[61] The freedom, equality, and (self-)possession that characterize the liberal subject and demarcate its horizons of expectation result from capital's indifference to the lives it indirectly organizes, yet they come to signify the independence of those lives from direct domination and their resultant capacity for self-determination.[62] This capacity appears the prime mover of capital's emergent, noncoercive social structure. But its individual and collective expressions—formal independence and emergent structure—share the same cause: value mediation under conditions of market dominance. This chain of mediations surely leads to Bruno Latour's extraordinary idea that "emancipation . . . does not mean 'freed from bonds' but well-attached."[63]

When the possessive form of liberal personhood is understood as an effect of value-mediated social relations, the distinction between the posthuman (defined as a node in a network of informational processes) and the liberal humanist subject (defined in terms of its freedom from the wills of others) starts to dissolve.[64] Hayles follows C. B. Macpherson in identifying the latter's freedom with the equalizing functions of market relations and notes that its "notorious universality" results from its possession of a body rather than its status as a body.[65] But she does not go so far as to consider the possibility that the liberal humanist subject is already an effect of the informatic processes that constitute what Macpherson calls market society.

The liberal humanist subject is drawn in more explicitly informatic terms by Gunther Teubner, who posits law, rather than value, as its foundational matrix. Advocating for the continued importance of the legal person in deliberations about European social and economic policy after deindustrialization, Teubner defines that person as neither "flesh and blood" nor "spirit." The essence of legal personhood, he argues, is an element in an "internal dynamics system . . . with a capacity for self-organization and self-reproduction."[66] Like Macpherson and Hayles, Teubner insists that the status of legal personhood is not given in advance, as in the myth of possessive individualism as a state of nature. But unlike them, he describes the process through which this form of personhood is allocated in the reticular, communication-theoretical terms that Hayles uses to distinguish the posthuman. In Teubner's systems-theoretical account, legal personhood is allocated through a "sequence of meaningfully interrelated communicative events that constantly reproduce themselves."[67] It is hard to miss the similarities between this account of personhood and the value-mediated appearance of production and reproduction as a never-ending circle. In the network of self-reproducing communicative events, Teubner adds, there is a "cyclical linkage of identity and action via mechanisms of attribution." The network is composed of persons and their actions; it constructs participants as persons by allocating them to a self-created "communicative reality"; and it validates actions on the basis of this construction. Thus "events become system actions only once the communication network regards its participants or members as 'persons.'"[68] Although he mistakenly identifies law as the primary site of allocation, Teubner's system-theoretical account provides a fairly detailed diagram of the process through which liberal personhood is constituted by informatic processes. To be recognized as a person, it is necessary to connect to a communication network. This dynamic of "recognition by connection" legitimizes certain activities, placing limits on desire and expectation. From there it is only necessary to identify law as a second-order form of disposal—a space in which formal equality, freedom, and self-possession are most explicitly posited, and where their conditional and differential allocation is obscured—to see how Teubner presents a mediated image of the process through which liberal personhood is constituted by the informatics of value.[69]

Recall the full title of the Caltech paper in which von Neumann distinguishes "ordinary logic" from the substrates that bear it on the basis that the latter always contain "more" than—and thus impede the frictionless implementation of—the former: "Probabilistic Logics *and the Synthesis of Reliable Organisms from Unreliable Components.*" Following von Neumann, the value network's primary function might be understood as *the synthesis of reliable circuits from unreliable actors,* which is in the first instance to say, actors whose thoughts, feelings, intentions, or inclinations are not overtly directed toward the transmission of surplus value.[70] Viewed in this way, the informatics of value represent a system-level implementation of the promise that Charles Babbage found in industrial machinery: a check "against the inattention, the idleness, or the knavery of human agents."[71]

This mechanism for the synthesis of reliable circuits from unreliable actors informs many of the practices, fantasies, and imaginaries that cohere around value and information—practices, fantasies, and imaginaries that at least partly explain the more or less explicit conflation of those modes of abstraction in contemporary production dynamics and their attendant management sciences. And when one turns from the ideal form of this synthesis to its practical development, the double logic of disposal—as the deployment of abstraction *and abjection*—becomes clear. In the same year that von Neumann's talk was published in Shannon's *Automata Studies* collection, Shannon coauthored a response titled "Reliable Circuits Using Less Reliable Relays" with the mathematician and computer scientist Edward F. Moore. In their paper, Shannon and Moore elaborate on a principle that is left implicit in von Neumann's talk: a circuit "approaching perfect operation" can be constructed not only by the use of more reliable parts but also through the "redundant use of unreliable components."[72] In other words, the uninterrupted operation of a given organism or circuit under conditions that diverge from the optimal form of its representation in formal logic requires the inclusion of more components than will be "active" when the circuit is in operation. The circuit "approaching perfect operation" is premised on an excess that is unrepresentable as symbolic logic. In their concern for the unreliability of the concrete, both papers model the process of integrating devalued components that is a necessary but often overlooked element of value's socially synthetic operations. This triad of abstraction, devaluation, and synthesis is a principal site of continuity between the value-informatic and the digital form of disposal.[73]

The synthesis of reliable circuits from unreliable actors. The imposition of pattern onto the activities of "free" individuals without direct coercion. The distributed allocation of socially necessary labor, wage levels, and capacity. These formulations abstract capitalism's tendency to "reproduce itself in expanded form *as if* it were a self-equilibrating and self-sustaining system." This tendency, which Stuart Hall identifies in an essay on Marx's 1857 introduction to the *Grundrisse*, has at its core the "so-called 'laws of equivalence'" which function as "the necessary 'phenomenal forms' of this self-generating aspect of the system."[74] Hall's *as if* is as important as the language of interconnection and metabolism that he finds in Marx.[75] In the space between "*is* a self-equilibrating and self-sustaining system" and "functions *as if* it were a self-equilibrating and self-sustaining system" one finds the processes of separation and sorting that, while integral to the informatics of value, are not immediately legible in informatic terms. These processes operate across multiple scales, produce a range of articulated (but not always analogous) social formations, and shift in intensity depending on the systemic demand for labor power. At the atomic level of the individual producer, they effect what Federici calls a "*vivisection of the human body*" through which it is decided "which of its properties [should] live and which, instead [have] to die."[76] At the system level, they enact procedures for sorting populations according to the regularity and cost of their connection to the value network. In Part II, I consider how these processes—which, in Federici's account, are first identifiable in the religious and philosophical speculation of the sixteenth and seventeenth centuries—recur in intensified forms through cybernetic technologies, methods, and imaginaries. In the next three chapters, I focus on the processes that (1) make labor available for computation through connection to the value network and (2) devalue that labor in order to maintain rates of surplus value appropriation and ensure continuity of production. In so doing, I want to consider how racialized and gendered forms are instantiated and allocated capacity at the shifting threshold between abstraction and form-determined abjection.

3 THE INFORMATICS OF DISPOSSESSION

THE INFORMATICS OF VALUE—the sequence of processes through which capital reproduces its patterns without the direct application of force, synthesizing reliable circuits from a multitude of independent activities—are predicated on generalized market dependence. For surplus value to accrue, people must reliably present themselves for connection to the value network as buyers and sellers of labor and other commodities. For this to happen at the required distribution and frequency, those people must be left without any way to meet their needs that does not pass through connection to the value network. As Michael Denning writes in one of the most succinct formulations of market dependence as the motor of value-mediated social synthesis, "capitalism begins not with the offer of work, but with the imperative to earn a living."[1] This imperative requires processes of dispossession and expropriation that, while essential to the informatics of value, cannot be straightforwardly placed within the category of money-mediated exchange. Without them, capitalism cannot appear to function as a "self-equilibrating and self-sustaining system." Because it relies on them, it can only function *as if* it is such a system. The freedom from direct coercion that distinguishes capitalist social synthesis, and which recurs across the digital imaginary, is premised on the permanent threat of starvation and carceral violence. If we accept that the proliferation of digital imaginaries centers on a modern notion of freedom that emerged through the generalization of value-mediated labor, it is also necessary to observe, as Marx does, that "free" labor becomes so only when it has been "freed" from the possibility of living beyond the informatics of value.[2]

Marx uses the term *primitive accumulation* to name the processes through which the value network becomes central to the survival of large numbers of people.³ These processes are primitive, he suggests, because they form part of the prehistory of "mature" capitalism, preceding the "silent compulsion of economic relations" and receding once that mode of compulsion becomes dominant.⁴ But capital's self-regulating tendency requires the ongoing suppression of non-market-mediated reproduction, so the means by which that suppression is achieved cannot be confined to a moment of transition from precapitalist "extra-economic force" to self-regulating capitalist social relations. As Werner Bonefeld writes, primitive accumulation is neither an occasionally deployed means of disciplining labor nor a specific technique of imperialist expansion but rather the means of producing and reproducing "a certain historically specific mode of social labor, a labor divorced from its means of subsistence," which is "the constitutive presupposition of capitalist social relations."⁵ Additionally, the imperative of systemic expansion and the concomitant requirement to maintain profit levels through periods of faltering growth mean that even "in its full maturity" capital must expand into, connect with, or otherwise integrate noncapitalist social formations, imposing market dependence in ways that cannot be accurately described using the range of practices and the historical frame Marx provides.⁶ These processes of separation and integration mirror the appropriation and feminization of unwaged activity in the reproduction of labor power—processes that, because they are premised on the same separation of people from their means of subsistence, are more accurately described as indirectly waged or indirectly market-mediated.⁷ Finally, a narrow focus on proletarianization in Western Europe obscures the integration of slave trading, slave labor, and their afterlives with "silent" forms of economic compulsion and the use of settler-colonial occupation directed at the capture of land and resources over and above the "freeing" of labor power.⁸ For these reasons, Robert Nichols proposes the term *Enteignung*—dispossession or expropriation—as a "narrower and more precise term of art" that better names the ongoing, often violent operations required to implement, maintain, and guarantee the expanded reproduction of the dynamics that for Marx comprise "silent" compulsion.⁹ Nichols's terminological shift makes legible as dispossession a number of techniques and technologies that differ in significant ways from the transformation of agricultural populations into wage laborers in England that takes up the majority of Marx's account.¹⁰ With the analysis I am pursuing here I aim to contribute to the theorization of those techniques and technologies by identifying a common structure—a putatively abstract, self-regulating system maintained by externalized material conditions—that recurs across a range of modern social forms.[11]

Detached from the historical and geographical frame of Marx's primitive accumulation, dispossession and market dependence are revealed to connect a range of otherwise incommensurable social forms.[12] As Wynter and Smallwood have shown, the separation of people from their means of subsistence is as central to the protocols of Atlantic slavery and its afterlives as it is to the spontaneous interconnection of "free" individuals through the value network. The essential difference is that in the case of the enslaved, forced separation from the "wide variety of plant and animal foods" was conjoined to value-mediated social reproduction without the intermediate allocation of formal freedom that was elsewhere concomitant with dispossession.[13] The gap between the homeostatic reproduction and the horizon of desire Lacan allocates to "living things" and the dependency and foreshortened desire through which he defines slaves as analogous to machines represents an explicitly informatic formulation of this difference that is implemented through dispossession. The ongoing devaluation of black life and the attribution of a qualified self-possession that is most often recognized as criminal responsibility are similarly grounded in the linked protocols of dispossession, spontaneous interconnection, and the differential allocation of "free" personhood.[14]

This expanded historical and geographical scope similarly discloses recursive relationships between economic coercion and the expansion and granularization of the value network after the 1970s. In *Caliban and the Witch*, Federici shows how the structural adjustment program negotiated between the Nigerian government and the IMF/World Bank in the mid-1980s, ostensibly directed at stimulating international competitiveness after the economically deleterious effects of the 1970s oil crisis, in fact represented "a new round of primitive accumulation," a "rationalization of social reproduction aimed at destroying the last vestiges of communal property and community relations" in order to facilitate "more intense forms of labor exploitation."[15] In the same period, new kinds of debt relations function as technologies of dispossession at the individual scale. This is certainly the function of the microcredit technologies that capture the "work, energies, and inventiveness" of impoverished women in South Asia and Latin America, drawing informal life-making and survival practices into the formal economy of value-mediated relations.[16] The same is true of the predatory lending behind the subprime mortgage crisis of 2007–8 that Paula Chakravartty and Denise Ferreira da Silva identify as a "'relative' of crises that transformed the political economic horizons of Africa, Asia, and Latin America in the 1980s and 1990s." In each case, the techniques and technologies of dispossession-by-debt are directed at the extraction and distribution of labor power and resources in advance of their circulation in the value network. And, as Chakravartty and Silva show, these techniques draw upon, amplify, and repurpose earlier technologies of "conquest and slavery, along with the postcolonial apparatus of raciality."[17] Indeed, the histories of these coercive debt regimes, their geographical distribution, and their specific functions during periods of expansion and crisis all signal that colonial, racializing, and feminizing protocols are immanent to the informatics of value.

Understanding those protocols as immanent to the informatics of value brings into focus the latter's role in the production and differential valuation of social forms, much of which is obscured when the analysis of social reproduction is limited either to market-mediated acquisition of the means of subsistence (as it is in Marx) or to the positioning of unwaged activity and ascriptive protocols in exterior zones, linked but not essential to the core dynamics of capital accumulation.[18] In order to properly address these value-informatic processes of differential valuation and their role in constituting social forms, it is necessary to first identify an essential but invisibilized element of the system of dispossession, integration, and accumulation: the relative surplus population.

The relative surplus population encompasses a number of structural positions characterized by wagelessness or underemployment. Marx identifies four: floating, latent, stagnant, and pauperized. The floating surplus population comprises those who exist in a perpetual cycle of dismissal and integration as industries and sectors emerge, expand, and then shed living labor through increases in productivity.[19] The transfer of industrial workers to the multivalent service sector is a relatively recent example of this. In the latent surplus population one finds those who must wait "with one foot already in the swamp of pauperism" until it becomes possible to enter a new branch of employment. The classic example is that of agricultural workers "constantly on the point of passing over into an urban or manufacturing proletariat."[20] Those whose employment is so irregular that it furnishes only a fraction of the "average normal level" of subsistence form a stagnant surplus population exposed to "special branches of capitalist exploitation" characterized by "a maximum of working time and a minimum of wages."[21]

To clarify their determinate relationship to the informatics of value, each of these forms of the relative surplus population can be sketched as a variation on the homeostatic production-reproduction loop that anchors the informatics of value even when its material impossibility is plainly visible. For the floating and latent forms the loop functions intermittently; connection isn't always possible, so needs that are already tightly circumscribed are met inconsistently. For the stagnant form it oscillates wildly; even near-perpetual connection barely provides or fails to provide the wages necessary to meet basic needs. Below these forms is the "sphere of pauperism" into which fall those who outside periods of unusually rapid growth are unable to establish even intermittent or oscillating connections to the value network. If those consigned to the floating, latent, and stagnant parts appear within the value network as intermittent or oscillating loops, the pauperized are unconnected elements marked with higher or lower capacity and a greater or lesser chance of future connection.

As these descriptions should make clear, no part of the relative surplus population is external to capitalist social relations. Even the "lowest sediment" in the sphere of pauperism is directly connected to the positive feedback loop of expanded reproduction. In order to generate profit, market-dependent capitalists must introduce methods for reducing the cost of their inputs relative to the market-determined price of their outputs as soon as those methods become available. If they fail to do so they risk becoming unprofitable, losing their means of production to creditors, and ceasing to exist as capitalists. Simply lengthening the working day can increase the quantity of costs and outputs, but it leaves the ratio between them unchanged. The most reliable way to modify this ratio is to make labor more productive, extracting more output per unit of labor input through some combination of reduced wages, rationalization, and the adoption of new technologies. As a consequence, the process of capital accumulation under conditions of market dependence shifts the ratio of labor to constant capital in favor of the latter: as labor productivity rises, as competition dictates that the resultant profits are reinvested to expand production, and as additional facilities and machinery represent principal means of this reinvestment, the mass of labor employed in production shrinks relative to that of machinery and outputs.[22]

The relative surplus population is bound to the informatics of value by this cycle of accumulation, rationalization, expulsion, and differential integration. The size of the "relatively redundant working population" is in direct correspondence with the "energy and extent" of capitalist accumulation; since living labor is the only source of surplus value and thus of individual capitalists' accumulated wealth, the working population, organized by the informatics of value, effectively produces the means by which it is made superfluous.[23] This is one reason why the relative surplus population "belongs to capital just as absolutely as if the latter had bred it at its own cost."[24] But the relationship doesn't end with the creation and modulation of the relative surplus population. In fact, the latter performs a number of essential regulative functions, and must exist in order for the value network to function as if self-equilibrating.

First, the relative surplus population represents a mass of labor available for immediate incorporation into new and newly expanded branches of production. In this respect, it provides a reserve army of labor, "a mass of human material always ready for exploitation by capital in the interests of capital's own changing valorization requirements."[25] Second, this population functions as a lever of deskilling and intensified exploitation. It is structurally analogous to the "redundant" components that, as in von Neumann's and Moore and Shannon's accounts of logical automata, facilitate the synthesis of a reliable system from unreliable parts. Indeed, the relationship between working conditions and the size of the surplus population is a positive feedback loop: as "the over-work of the employed part swells the ranks of its reserve," Marx writes, "the greater pressure that the reserve by its competition exerts on the employed workers forces them to submit to over-work and subjects them to the dictates of capital."[26] Third, contrary to the classical economic dogma that links wages to absolute population levels, the cost of reproduction that is encoded in the value of labor is limited by the size of the surplus population.[27] The latter "weighs down the active army" during periods of stagnation and fetters its members' demands—"puts a curb on their pretensions"—during periods of rapid growth. In other words, the relative surplus population constrains expectation, ensuring that the limitless horizons encoded in value-mediated abstract personhood do not impair the extraction of surplus value by causing the cost of reproduction (and thus of labor) to rise.

If expanded reproduction is the objective toward which the informatics of value tend, then the relative surplus population is as important to the latter as Mandeville's homeostatic loops of production and reproduction. The informatic character of their relationship to value is underscored when Marx describes the latent as a "source" from which laborers "flow" into new and expanding branches along "distribution channels" whose capacity varies according to valorization requirements, being "wide open" only at exceptional times.[28] However, as this language of imbalanced redistribution from source to destination implies, the general tendency of the system of waged reproduction is not homeostatic. Rather, it shows how the self-sustaining and self-regulating aspects of capital accumulation tend toward the wearing down of life just as surely as the necessity of dispossession shows them to begin there. The homeostatic processes that the surplus population effects within the value network are secured by a negative feedback loop on the edge of that network in which income falls further and further from the cost of reproduction, leaving more and more needs unmet.[29]

As competition-driven increases in productivity shrink the mass of labor employed across the various lines of industrial production and manufacturing, the rate of profit falls while the surplus population grows. Because competitive expansion tends not to be limited by the material conditions it produces, and because there is not an infinite number of new lines of production ready to integrate labor that has been expelled elsewhere, a shrinking number of those who at least approximate Mandeville's self-reproducing worker, earning enough to return to the same job every day but not enough to even consider leaving the value network, are joined by increasing numbers of the floating, the latent, the stagnant, and the pauperized.[30] This tendency is intensified during the long downturn, as international competition pushes down the price of goods more quickly than the cost of labor inputs, leading to overproduction, increased un- and underemployment, and underconsumption.

On the one side, market-dependent capitalists are driven to expand their operations by maximizing their extraction of surplus value under conditions of global stagnation. On the other, masses of market-dependent people are forced to accept low wages, debilitating work, and insecure employment. Far from making possible entirely new (and newly boundless) forms of accumulation, electronic digital technologies primarily facilitate the intensified exploitation of the latter group by the former. This is exemplified in the techniques and technologies of logistics, whose sole purpose is to coordinate production and circulation processes that have been disaggregated in order to minimize labor costs. As Marx observes in volume 3 of *Capital*, the existence of a global value network with an equalized rate of profit requires on the one hand free trade and on the other "the abolition of all laws that prevent workers from moving from one sphere of production to another or from one local seat of production to any other." The latter is accompanied by a series of extralegal outcomes that are exacerbated by the growth of the surplus population: "indifference of the worker to the content of his work"; the "greatest possible reduction of work in all spheres of production to simple labour"; the "disappearance of all prejudices of trade and craft among the workers"; and, finally and especially, the "subjection of the worker to the capitalist mode of production."[31] In the age of technologically facilitated global coordination, absolute flexibility, that signature of the possessive individual, is repurposed in the absence of the latter's wage-enabled security as the imperative of continual movement between temporary jobs.

In addition to facilitating newly distributed forms of production and circulation, the overt convergence of value and digitality during the long downturn intensifies the conditions under which people are employed on low wages in jobs that are by nature difficult to rationalize.[32] In 1867, Marx argued that growth of "domestic industry" was concomitant with that of the stagnant surplus population. Today, the convergence of value mediation and mobile digital platforms makes possible forms of service labor that combine the constant movement required of the floating, the deskilling and intensified exploitation imposed on the stagnant, and the separation of wages from the cost of reproduction that characterizes the latent and the pauperized. These forms of labor scrape small quantities of surplus value from increasing numbers of those who, dispossessed, market dependent, and unable to access sufficiently waged work in a single area, must piece together the money they need to reproduce themselves and their dependents by working excessive hours on a task-by-task basis. As Marx anticipates, when the "connection between paid and unpaid labour is destroyed" it becomes possible to "annihilate all regularity of employment," to "make the most frightful over-work alternate with relative or absolute cessation of work" according to "convenience, caprice, and the interest of the moment," and to "abnormally lengthen the working day."[33] This disarticulation of production and social reproduction is only possible when large swathes of labor are marked by superfluity in a context in which the drive for accumulation remains unchecked. The same factors explain the emergence of biopolitical techniques for maintaining life in the absence of sufficient waged labor, the vertiginous growth of consumer debt, and the "management" of the surplus populations in the fully or partially privatized prisons, detention centers, and other carceral sites that represent substantial and growing parts of the global service sector. In combination with logistics, these techniques and technologies represent some of the principal ways that "redundant" and "unreliable" components are deployed in the synthesis of reliable circuits of surplus value extraction.

What I am hoping to show here is that dispossession, integration, reproduction, the production and modulation of the surplus population, and the generalization of the latter's conditions during periods of crisis constitute invisibilized but internal operations of the informatics of value. Units of socially necessary labor time, the data to value's information, do not naturally occur and spontaneously enter the value network through individual living components.[34] The entire process requires populations be sorted, integrated, valued, and disciplined in accordance with shifting structural demands. The techniques and technologies of sorting, integration, valuation, and discipline are value-extractive counterparts to the procedures through which materials are refined before entering the production process proper—where forests become lumber, in the case of Shannon's "homely analogy." It is in the interactions between these processes and the construction of more or less balanced loops of production and reproduction that the informatics of value give rise to social forms that carry higher and lower value.

Because the value network represents an internally self-regulating logical system that functions as if independent of the material conditions it rests on and shapes, the processes that invisibly subtend it can be revealingly compared to those which produce the appearance of frictionless instantaneity upon which digital culture relies.[35] As Nicole Starosielski has shown, electronics-grade copper and silicon do not "exist in the earth" as raw materials but must be "cut from other elements by means of pyrotechnical processing." In the same way, she argues, the techniques required to turn extracted matter into electronics-grade materials are "not merely a chain of natural chemical transformations but a set of thermocultural processes intended to differentiate pure elements from polluting ones, and signal from noise." These processes of separation and differentiation "produce a digital order defined by speed and precision."[36] Dispossession might be understood as the range of more or less overtly violent procedures of extraction, separation, and processing required to produce components for the circuit of capital accumulation. In the case of dispossession, though, the relationship between the extraction, sorting, and integration of the components and their marking as pure or impure is inverted. Individual producers appear within the value network as components with higher or lower levels of reliability and purity. But those levels of purity and reliability do not precede or exist independently of those individuals' encounter with the informatics of value. Rather, they are assigned on the basis of their regularity of connection and the price of maintaining it. Workers are coded as high-value and high-reliability on the basis of the cost of their education and training—which forms part of their reproduction cost and must be included in their wage—and the regularity of their connection to the value network—which implies a stable demand for their labor, suggesting that it cannot be easily deskilled or rationalized. The relative and consolidated surplus populations represent stores of components whose purity and thus reliability is coded as too low to be consistently usable, but which might allow them to serve as redundant units when the value network rapidly expands or when new technologies make it possible to extract value without the requirement to facilitate reproduction.

What are race, gender, and capacity if not registers of the reliability and purity imputed to living bodies? The ascriptive processes that function in concert with the differential valuation of social life might thus be understood as producing the necessary forms of appearance of an informatic logic that structures the historical arc and geographical span of capital accumulation, and that includes shifting relations of dispossession, freedom, integration, and reproduction.[37]

4 DIFFERENTIATION AS REGULATION

IN THE PREFACE TO *Aberrations in Black,* Roderick Ferguson writes that subject formations arise out of "an economy of information privileged and information excluded."[1] Ferguson is here addressing what is left out of canonical sociological and historical engagements with segregation and its afterlives, but the structural dynamics he identifies behind those exclusions point toward a more fundamental "information" that shapes both the differential valuation of racialized and gendered populations and the senses of historians and social scientists. The economy of inclusion and exclusion, Ferguson writes, connects the allocation of abstract personhood to the production of those "superfluous and indispensable" populations that "fulfil *and* exceed the demands of capital."[2] If the freedom and self-possession associated with the optimally self-reproducing social unit—the homeostatic person—are promises whose partial fulfillment is conditional on wage-mediated connection to the value network, then surplus populations represent less a site of "information excluded" than a site in which the flow of "information" is attenuated or rendered intermittent by the value network's regulatory mechanisms.[3] What does Ferguson's observation that "normal" and "deviant" subject positions are formed at the shifting threshold of the surplus population make legible when each position is understood to be constituted by and constitutive of the informatics of value?

Processes of "gendered criminalization and racialization," Ruth Wilson Gilmore writes, accompany and mask the structural character of the "ordinary destructive violences" that make premature death likely in "regions that have been abandoned by capital and state."[4] Gilmore's observation that gendering, criminalization, and racialization are linked ascriptive processes that cohere around precarious reproduction crystallizes the relationship between the procedures required to install the value network as the dominant mechanism by which means of survival are allocated, the value-informatic distribution of more or less stable and sufficiently waged connections on the basis of shifting structural requirements, and what Gilmore elsewhere calls the production and exploitation of "group-differentiated vulnerabilities to premature death."[5] Capital only functions *as if* it is an autonomous, self-regulating system, and in order to maintain the *as if* it is necessary to separate people from the possibility of living without the value network *and* to maintain populations that can barely live or cannot live on the wages the value network affords them. Race, gender, and capacity are the necessary forms of appearance of these regulatory mechanisms as they play out across "distinct yet densely interconnected political geographies."[6]

This relationship between ascriptive processes and the value-informatic allocation of regular and sufficient connection is implied in Marx's observation that the sphere of pauperization is a site of outlawed social reproduction whose emblems are distinctively racialized and feminized: "vagabonds, criminals, prostitutes."[7] And it can be underscored by triangulating Gilmore's definition of racism, the operations of the value network, and Alexander Weheliye's account of racialization as "a conglomerate of sociopolitical relations that discipline humanity into full humans, not-quite-humans, and nonhumans."[8] If "full" connection to the value network designates lower vulnerability to premature death and the attribution of fully human status, nonconnection or partial connection map onto greater vulnerability and withheld or partially allocated humanity.

Lisa Lowe has argued that although abstract labor grounds the "formal political equality granted through rights and representations by the state," capitalism as a total system operates by "creating, preserving, and reproducing the specifically racialized and gendered character of labor-power."[9] Exposure to the homogenizing logic of exchange does not render all who connect to the value network equal. Lowe's intervention points toward two ways in which the extent of a given person's connection to the value network appears as social difference: as the degree of belonging to civil society extended to that person; and as the essential characteristics and collective histories with which they are associated. The first is foreshadowed in Marx's elaboration of the logical sequence through which labor power appears on the market only as the freely disposable property of its citizen-bearer, and the second goes beyond that elaboration in suggesting that the freedom of disposal and the value imputed to that labor power are differentially allocated and give rise to racial and gendered forms. Building on Lowe's theorization, Iyko Day shows how the uneven distribution of the privileges associated with the "full" bearer of abstract labor is encoded in the process of abstraction. The "principal violence of capital accumulation," Day suggests, lies in "the very way it abstracts (or renders homogeneous as commensurable units of labor) highly differentiated gendered and racialized labor *in order to create value*."[10] Capitalism, she goes on to clarify, "is a representational (and misrepresentational) regime."[11] When representation and misrepresentation are understood as effects of the separations and equalizations required to compute surplus value, the relationship between value and social difference starts to appear co-constitutive rather than linear.

These theorizations of how difference is encoded in abstract labor lead me to the claims I want to make here: that the informatics of value effect a distribution of more or less reliable and more or less costly components; and that the processes through which those components are formed and distributed are co-constitutive with racialized and gendered social forms. The processes of sorting and encoding required to make this distribution work—to synthesize a reliable circuit—can be clearly seen in the binding of lower reproduction costs to populations marked with lower levels of "development." Marx explains that in general wages must be sufficient to maintain a person's "normal state as a working individual" and, in some cases, to sustain their dependents. He also notes that the determination of sufficient means of subsistence and the "normal" state of a working population occurs on the basis of differential calculations. The "number and extent" of a given worker's "so-called necessary requirements" and "the means through which they are satisfied" are "products of history, and depend to a great extent on the level of civilization attained by a country." And the "level of civilization" primarily indexes "the conditions in which, and consequently on the habits and expectations with which, the class of free workers has been formed." In contrast to other commodities, Marx concludes, "the determination of the value of labor-power contains a historical and moral element."[12] Building on this passage in Marx, Heinrich observes that the value of labor power "is determined differently not just in different countries, but also within the same country for different sections of the working class . . . and that asymmetrical gender relations and racist discrimination lead to differences in the value of labor-power."[13] And Raji C. Steineck notes, albeit in an account that downplays the relationship between these dynamics and the structural logic of racialization, that these variations should be understood as structurally comparable to the deployment of new technologies to increase relative surplus value extraction. Although technical innovation is the most commonly stated means of increasing relative surplus value, Steineck writes, the latter can "also be increased by diminishing the value of labour power through other means, such as forcing the labourers to accept a lower standard of living. This is simply the application of the same principle under different circumstances—relative surplus-value now is increased by coercively lowering the value of labor. More appropriately, one may say that technical innovation and degradation of the standards of living are two sides of the same coin."[14] The racial-capitalist dimensions of this process are marked in volume 3 of *Capital*, where Marx observes that profit rates can be stretched in colonies because of the "lower degree of development" and the intensified exploitation of labor through "the use of slaves and coolies."[15]

In "Black Metamorphosis," Wynter tracks the process through which the differential allocation of value operates in concert with the production of racialized social forms to Atlantic slavery. Wynter writes that "it was [the] devaluation of the labor power of the black, a devaluation carried out through exchange, rather than slavery per se—since slavery was only its first form, the first mechanism by which his labor power would be devalued—that led to the devaluation of his humanity." This process anchors the "racism intrinsic to the capitalist system," which is determined not by ideology but by "the economic infrastructure."[16] In developing this analysis, Wynter recounts how Portuguese slave traders used *pieza* (piece) for "the African who functioned as the standard measure" of optimal labor productivity, "the general equivalent of physical labor value against which all the others could be measured—with for example three teenagers equalling one pieza, and older men and women thrown in a job lot as refuse."[17] The *pieza* denoted not a single person but a unit of socially average capacity tallied to abstracted bodily characteristics. The social average is shown here to function not only as a virtualization of labor but also as a mechanism for differentially allocating capacity in order to optimize the extraction of surplus value.

The racialization and feminization of labor through the allocation of differing levels of capacity occur at the threshold of the value network. This allocative process produces different structural positions in different historical moments and geographies. It organizes what Lowe calls the "'coloniality' of modern world history," not a "brute binary division, but rather one that operates through precisely spatialized and temporalized processes of both differentiation and connection."[18] The same process connects (without conflating) a range of social arrangements: chattel slavery and the colonial production and management of indentured and "free" labor in the Americas, Asia, and Africa both before and after formal abolition; the post-1960s proliferation of outsourced, deskilled, and devalued manufacturing labor; the global distribution of services, including what Kalindi Vora calls "life support" labor—domestic work, gestational surrogacy, call center work, technical support, IT, and the sale of organs; and the forms of platform-mediated gigwork and microwork that, in Tadiar's words, convert the time of unemployment into the "time of waiting on others."[19] In each instance, racialization and feminization are recursively bound to (but not entirely reducible to) the informatics of value—a system of accumulation based on "spontaneous" interconnection, dispossession, and differential integration. In each instance, the informatics of value effect a distribution of lives whose reproduction is more or less assured, and who can expect to circulate more or less freely. The interconnection and mutability of the resultant social forms are evident in Chris Chen's observation that "the surplus capital produced by fewer and more intensively exploited workers in the Global North" generates growing relative surplus populations in which racialized groups are substantially overrepresented, "scours the globe for lower wages, and reappears as the racial threat of cheap labour from the Global South."[20]

In a critique of developmentalist accounts of export manufacturing as a means of overcoming gendered subordination, Elson and Pearson identify the feminizing dynamics that are interlaced with this "racial threat of cheap labor." First, Elson and Pearson counter the developmentalist fantasy with the structural reality of logistics: to enter into the value network via export oriented manufacturing, "*Female labour must either be cheaper to employ than comparable male labour, or have higher productivity, or some combination of both; the net result being that unit costs of production are lower with female labour.*"[21] They then list the ascriptive processes that cohere around this value-informatic principle. The overrepresentation of women aged between fourteen and twenty-five in garment, textile, and electronics factories tends to be justified through an equation between productivity and "concrete" racialized and feminized characteristics, as in the attribution of "nimble fingers," docility, and discipline to South and East Asian women workers. The intermittent employment of those workers is then "rationalized as an effect of their capacity to bear children," which makes them appealing hires for "firms which periodically need to vary the size of their labour force so as to adjust to fluctuating demand for their output in the world market."[22] And these workers enter the value network without additional reproduction costs derived from paid education and training, and are thus "already determined as inferior bearers of labour."[23] At each stage, the ascription process entails a chain of mediations that is animated by the informatics of value. In order for geographically disaggregated production to be profitable, labor must be both cheap and easy to acquire and discard; Global South women's labor is regarded as both because of its association with freely acquired skill and capacity for motherhood; the work women coded as such are able to access is thus marked as both unskilled and intermittent.

The authors of "The Logic of Gender" present a similar argument while developing a systematic theory of gender under capitalism. Imagining a scenario in which employers do not ascertain the gender of an applicant but only reward "those who have 'the most mobility' and those who are 'the most reliable, 24/7,'" they note that "gender bias would reappear as strong as ever." As signatures of the "reliable" component whose reproduction costs will not impede surplus value accumulation, degrees of mobility, availability, and reliability are allocated by (rather than arising outside) the informatics of value. Because the value of labor indexes the reliability and quality attributed to a given component, and because reliability and quality are only assigned on the basis of regular, high-value connection, racialized and feminized characteristics represent forms of appearance of "the commodity labour-power with a cheaper price" that can be used "in short spurts and at cheap prices."[24]

Gendered and racialized differences do exist within the value network, then. But they appear abstractly, as intermittent connection or higher or lower levels of imputed capacity. Understood in relation to von Neuman's account of reliable circuits and Starosielski's analysis of extraction and purification, racialized and feminized forms take shape around components that can be cheaply integrated but whose use is associated with "a sacrifice of both speed and reliability," and which are consequently marked as less refined or "pure."[25] The abstract-concrete processes that are disclosed in this analysis clarify the stakes of Ashby's fraught exchange with Bates. Inferiorized biology and the faulty component are different forms of appearance of the connection that is registered by the informatics of value as intermittent and/or bearing a weaker (or noisier) signal.

The ascriptive processes that shape and are shaped by this value-informatic distribution of capacity can be revealingly mapped alongside Denise Ferreira da Silva's theorization of modern racializing protocols. The usefulness of this mapping is signaled by the informatic character of the language and the conceptual frame Silva uses in articulating the distinction between subjects and "affectable things."[26] For Silva, the transparent "I" names "Man the subject, the ontological figure consolidated in post-Enlightenment European thought," while the affectable "I" is the outcome of "the scientific construction of non-European minds."[27] The latter, Silva writes, connotes susceptibility to "outer determination."[28] According to the onto-epistemological assumptions governing modern European thought, the affectable "I" encounters the world of people and things as a collection of material forces that bear directly upon its thoughts, feelings, and actions. The transparent "I," by contrast, "seeks to decipher the regularities" it sees in the world, "but it is not determined by nor does it determine what it seeks to know." Its encounters, including its self-reflections, are mediated by "abstract (formal) tools" that ensure that its relationship to the world remains one of information received and information transmitted—or pattern reproduced without direct contact.[29] Underscoring the protocybernetic character of the transparent "I," Silva later describes it as existing in a state of *autopoiesis* that is maintained through the mediating function of conceptual abstractions.[30] Following the theorization set out above, I want to suggest that these conceptual abstractions and the forms of personhood they distinguish are elements of a value-mediated perceptual economy.

Silva's interrogation of the "analytics of raciality" is in large part motivated by the need to show how the allocation of transparency and affectability goes beyond a simple logic of exclusion. Central to her theorization is the claim that "the scene of (self-)regulation," the "ordered world" of self-determining subjects, requires the affectability that inheres around and haunts those subjects to be externalized.[31] The living bearers from which abstract labor is computed and the material compulsion that, while often hidden, nonetheless exists behind every instance of market "freedom" might be understood as principal sources of this affectability. Their ubiquity under the capitalist mode of social organization explains the modern emergence of racialization as a means of projecting affectability onto the non-European populations encountered through the expansion of the modern world system. From this perspective, modern racialization emerges conterminously with the designation of the idealized, political-philosophical form of the subject, whose proximity to the homeostatic loop of production and reproduction indexes its capacity for self-regulation. Understanding the allocation of transparency and affectability as a function of the informatics of value helps to explain why the relationship between the two states so closely resembles that of the commodity's "natural form" to its "value form."[32] If affectability describes a state of direct dependence, transparency is the optimal experiential state of the subject "ruled by abstractions" that are "nothing more than the theoretical expression of those material relations which are their lord and master."[33] In every case, the former must be both preserved and abjected so that the latter may continue to function as a basic element of the value network.

By linking Silva's theorization of transparency and affectability to the processes of reduction and construction through which the informatics of value take hold of concrete social relations, it becomes possible to more clearly understand the role of racialization in the allocation of capacity, formal freedom, and liberal personhood. Like the invisibilized processes that precede and make possible value's socially synthetic function, affectability is positioned "before (in front of) the ethical space inhabited by the proper national subject."[34] Or, one might say that affectability is the *abjected bearer of transparency,* marked upon certain bodies and relations in order to externalize transparency's material causes and constraints. The ideas and feelings that arise as a result of this externalization are the media through which promises of freedom, security, and disembodiment are encrypted in digitality. The mode of "modern thought" that informs and belongs to the transparent "I," Silva summarizes, is characterized by a triad of "determinacy," "separability," and "sequentiality"—or the primary characteristics shared by value and digitality.[35] Like the idealized fiber-optic cables of the digital imaginary, the universality that is actualized in "Europeanness/whiteness" is predicated on a "*formal determination.*"[36] Or, universality is an effect (rather than the source) of informatic transmission.

Finally, linking the attribution of transparency and affectability to the value-informatic distribution of prospects emphasizes how the latter produces and is modulated by a range of social forms. As components in the value network, informatically "free" persons should be understood as both transparent *and* affectable, reliable *and* faulty. Transparent because they are configured, from the "point of view" of the value network, as nodes through which value is transmitted in higher or lower levels and with higher or lower frequency. Affectable because this transmission is predicated on dispossession and market dependence and modulated by structural demand and imputed reproduction costs. These variations produce and are produced by racialized and gendered forms that exist in more or less precarious—or affectable—conditions. In each case, the compulsion to strive toward a more transparent state indexes not some ontological superiority of the transparent "I" but rather the indissoluble link between that state and less precarious conditions of reproduction.

In these opening chapters I have engaged at length with the informatics of value: the spontaneous interconnection and expanded reproduction toward which they tend; their dispossessive mechanics; and the differential allocation of social forms that takes place through and secures the productive interplay of their basal processes. I have done this in order to show how thoroughly the informatics of value inhabit the cybernetic formulations of personhood and social life that shape the digital imaginary. Before more closely analyzing those formulations and their logics of disposal in Part II, I want to restate and complicate my concerns through a reading of Samuel R. Delany's *Neveryóna,* a novel that superimposes cybernetic machines with the informatics of value, the long downturn with the emergence and maturation of capitalist social relations, and the transparency and self-regulation attributed to "free" persons with slavery and the burdened individuality of "freedom."

5 TWO MODELS

Samuel R. Delany's Neveryóna

IN THE EIGHTH CHAPTER OF Samuel R. Delany's *Neveryóna*, the merchant Madame Keyne shows two models to the novel's protagonist, Pryn. In so doing, she completes a series of lessons on value, capital accumulation, and social synthesis that has taken up the majority of the preceding two chapters. The first model, which was built by the inventor Belham four decades before the events depicted in *Neveryóna*, is a miniature representation of Madame Keyne's mansion and gardens. At the actuation of a lever, water pours in through a gate at the top of this miniature, runs through streams and tributaries, crashes over a vertical drop, and erupts from a series of fountains.[1] The second model was constructed by Venn, an inventor and theorist who first appears in a tale about the imbrications of abstraction, imperialism, and gendered violence in the preceding volume of the Nevèrÿon series. Venn's model consists of an upper bowl filled with set plaster into which a pattern has been gouged and a lower bowl filled with loose sand. When water passes from the upper bowl to the lower (again, at the operation of a lever), the pattern gouged into the plaster above is transferred with it, becoming imprinted in the sand below (*N* 219–20). The pattern left in the sand is an almost perfect reproduction of that gouged into the plaster, and the transfer leaves displaced sand streaked across the bowl's sides and piled in a filter tray below. "Not only does the water remember its height in the top bowl," Madame Keyne remarks, "it remembers the entire shape within the bowl, remembers it all the way down the length of the tube through which it runs, remembers it well enough to recreate that shape when it runs into conditions that allow it to demonstrate what it remembers" (*N* 220).

78 ·

Belham's model functions at a low level of representational abstraction. Its fidelity to the objects it depicts is such that Pryn is drawn to imagine "two diminutive female figures [who] had just stepped over its threshold, one of whom, even now, at a miniature table's edge, leaned over a tinier rise, atop which stood a tinier hut, its tinier door ajar, and over whose tinier threshold had just stepped—" (*N* 216). In consonance with its mode of representation, this model's dynamic element is effected by the direct transfer of energy through the streams and tributaries, down the waterfall, and into the fountains from which water spurts powerfully "instead of merely dribbling out in an uninteresting spill" (*N* 217).[2] What does Venn's model represent? As she shows it to Pryn, Madame Keyne recalls Venn's boast that while "any barbarian can look at the bottom of a falls and see in the rising splash the principle of the fountain," *she* had devised a way to show something that would "remain a wonder until the globe of the world and the globe of the sun meet in their common center, and the one consume the other" (*N* 220–21). Belham simply replicated a natural force—one that even affectable "barbarians" can sense. Venn gave concrete form to something that cannot be so easily perceived.

What are the characteristics of this wonder? If Venn's device models the dynamics of a specific material process, it does so without directly reproducing the appearance of the space, objects, or bodies that shape and are shaped by that process. And it is clear that the transfer of the pattern from the higher to the lower bowl functions according to principles quite different from those observable in the tributaries, waterfall, and fountains of Belham's model and the social space it represents. Whereas Belham's model functions through the simple transfer of energy (or force), Venn's transmits a relatively complex pattern though a medium—the water that flows from the upper to the lower bowl—that does not appear to have the capacity either to "remember" or to impose such a pattern.

In this chapter I take Delany's presentation of Madame Keyne's models as an occasion to rehearse and more closely engage with the complex of value, dispossession, and differential sorting. Delany maps this informatic complex across three levels of abstraction, each of which makes legible specific material implications of value-mediated social organization: the models themselves; the lessons on value and economic determination that Madame Keyne delivers against a backdrop of concrete labor and material immiseration; and Pryn's subsequent encounters with surplus populations, "free" and slave labor, and the modes of racialized

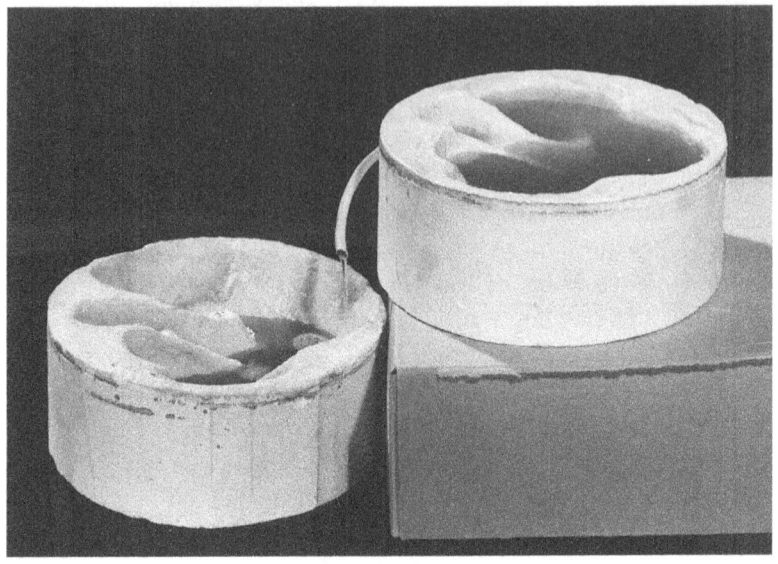

Figure 4. Pattern transfer models. Source: René Thom, *Structural Stability and Morphogenesis* (1973).

and gendered differentiation that shape and are shaped across the boundaries of those structural positions.³

The chapter in which Madame Keyne demonstrates the two models opens with a passage from the French mathematician René Thom's *Structural Stability and Morphogenesis* that reads: "Usually, when we speak of 'information,' we should use the word 'form'" (*N* 215).⁴ This epigraph provides a clue to the provenance of Venn's model, which is clearly based on a series of photographs that appear in Thom's book to illustrate the transfer of features through genetic inheritance.⁵ But the version of this model that appears in *Neveryóna* does not illustrate genetics, and neither the concept of information nor that of form appears in the passages in which Madame Keyne unveils it, demonstrates it, and describes its impact on her. Instead, Venn's model is associated in Madame Keyne's conceptual and social imaginary—and, consequently, through her economic practices—with the prospect of a self-organizing social form that is animated by an abstraction and oriented toward accumulation. As she explains to Pryn toward the end of her lessons on capital, her fascination with social synthesis and quasi-automated reproduction began with Venn's model, which she has always regarded as her property even though it was built for her father (*N* 212). Her first encounter with the model, she remarks, "was the beginning of my interests in magic of the sort you have seen me engaged in" (*N* 221).

The patterns of Belham's hydraulic model are materialized through the direct transmission of energy. But Venn's device transmits a pattern without such direct (or mechanical) causation. This difference cleaves to the distinction Wiener cements when he defines information as "information, not matter or energy" and the process described by Bernal as the imposition of pattern on an energy system "by one that is much weaker." Simply put, Venn's model is a water-and-sand-based version of the cybernetic arrangement of electronic components through which an apparently weak force can reproduce form or pattern within—or determine, or dominate—a given material system. Why is there a cybernetic machine in the middle of Delany's sword-and-sorcery rendering of racial capitalism? In the context of the Nevèrÿon series' historical-geographic diagram of the emergence and effects of capital accumulation, Delany's counterposing of two informatic devices—Venn's model and the abstract form of Madame Keyne's economic activities—emphasizes the continuity between the generalized idea (or fantasy) of informatics and the synthetic operations of value.

Madame Keyne's understanding of those operations becomes apparent in the lessons on accumulation that lead up to her demonstration of the models. Over the two chapters in which she delivers these lessons, it becomes clear that Madame Kenye has a deep commitment to the ideal of value-mediated social relations, which she plans to optimize through the construction of a space called the New Market.[6] Pryn encountered a less developed form of these relations earlier in the novel when she met the slave liberator Gorgik in the Old Market—a site in which geographically and qualitatively disparate modes of production and circulation are equalized through money-mediated exchange. This mode of mediation, Pryn learns from Gorgik, makes production and circulation appear part of a single system; the market becomes "a particularly complicated inscription of the nation around it," a site at which the goods for sale "are *signs* of the great distilleries, piggeries, religious festivals, and diligently hoed fields about the nation" (*N* 74–75; emphasis added). Madame Keyne intends the New Market to provide these mediations with "air, light, [and] room for commercial growth," leading to "the encouragement of true diversity amongst products, marketing methods, competition, and profits" (*N* 185). Or, she regards it as a site at which the relations of production and reproduction can become fully value-mediated, or really subsumed.

The effects of this generalized value mediation can be glimpsed in the differences in labor organization across the two markets. Whereas direct producers or their apprentices come to the Old Market with "country wares, country skills" (*N* 73), those in the New Market are subject to new (and newly gendered) systems of work discipline under which male workers perform rationalized manual labor on the site while women pass through with drinking water and buckets into which "anyone who has to may relieve himself." Under this system of organization, Madame Keyne triumphantly notes, "there should be no need to leave till we say so" (*N* 186). To her, the direct purchase of labor power and the maximization of efficiency are necessary corollaries of a system of production that appears automatic and self-regulating: *the synthesis of reliable circuits using less reliable actors*. The appearance of such a system, we quickly learn, is built on the racialized allocation of capacity. Recalling her early attempts to develop a system of labor management, Madame Keyne tells Pryn that "our first crew of barbarian loafers did more sipping and pissing and splashing of water over their heads than they did digging—*and* expected to get paid for it! But we've finally managed to locate a better breed for our wants here" (*N* 186). When the informatics of value are taken as expressions of a natural order, reliability and quality appear as embodied properties that afford particular expectations (such as being paid sufficiently for labor performed). Those who do not carry those associations of reliability and quality are marked as *affectable*—unable to defer their wants and needs, doing more sipping, pissing, and splashing than digging, and introducing more "noise" than "signal" to the production process.

In the New Market, self-regulation equates to the efficient performance of tasks and thus to the "clean" transmission of value. Immediately after marking the distinction between "barbarian loafers" and the "better breed" she now employs, Madame Keyne models the link between market dependence and surplus value, the relation upon which the "whole system of enterprise, profit, and wages" is premised, by staging an encounter in which she pays a worker a single iron coin for immediately and voluntarily—automatically—retrieving a gold coin of a higher value from the ground (*N* 199). From her value-informatic perspective, abstract domination entails both a self-regulating (and thus nonbarbarian) workforce and the automatic, frictionless return of surplus value.

Madame Keyne learned this notion of an abstract mechanism that dominates and determines (or forms) social activity from Venn's model. It was from that model that she came to understand a logic of form-determination that shapes and is shaped by a complex of self-regulating production and self-expanding value. The emergence of this logic through the development of value-mediated relations is elaborated and shown to link connection to a certain idea of freedom in the text from which Delany took the epigraphs to and much of the content of the chapters on the New Market. That text, Fernand Braudel's *Afterthoughts on Material Civilization and Capitalism*, is marked by the recurrence of images that resonate in telling ways with Latour's remarkable, network-theoretical insistence that to be emancipated is to be well attached—an insistence that assumes market dependence and equates freedom with access to market-mediated relations. In language that foreshadows the recent digital-cultural dissipation of distributed network into cloud, Braudel observes that the marketplaces at the "frontier" or "lower limit of economy" form a "vast layer," a "cloud of tiny dots" that represents the "numerous starting points [with which] begins what we might call the exchange economy."[7] The emergence of the private market, or exchange relations that are not constrained by "supervision or control by haughty officials," extends this "cloud" through "very long, autonomous commercial chains that acted freely and, moreover, that evidenced no qualms about profiting from this freedom."[8] The "longer these chains become," Braudel continues, "the more successful they are at freeing themselves from the usual regulations and controls and the more clearly the capitalistic process emerges."[9] As Robinson has shown, the ideals of freedom as volitional mobility that accrete to market-mediated social relations first appear in the mobility and "capacity to capitalize on frequent ruptures and breakdowns of the reproduction of populations sunk into the manorial soil" that marked eleventh-century merchants as a "class of deracines."[10] Through this association with mobility and capacity, market-mediated connection starts to connote freedom from "natural" and social bonds. It is already possible to identify in this emergent market "freedom" the workings of Venn's model, in which the connection between higher and lower bowls is neither effected nor constrained by direct force, but rather functions through the "soft" form of the water that flows between them.

Braudel shows how the network in which connection and freedom become conflated is formed through relations of money-mediated exchange. This network overlays and determines aspects of "material life" and provides the precondition for the informatics of value. "Above the enormous mass of daily life," Braudel writes, "the market economy cast out its nets and kept the network alive. And it was usually above the market economy itself that capitalism prospered."[11] In other words, the logic of free circulation as interconnection whose emergence Braudel tracks both foreshadows and provides the form and logic of, but has not yet been generalized to constitute, the informatics of value.

In *Neveryóna,* Thom's comments on information and form appear directly after the chapters that begin with epigraphs from Braudel and contain Madame Keyne's explanations of the economic "magic" she engages in. The demonstration of Venn's device, the form and function of which Delany derived from Thom, immediately follows these explanations. The trajectory strongly suggests that Venn's model and Madame Keyne's lessons depict at different levels of abstraction the generalized form of the relation that elevates Braudel's market freedom to a mechanism of social synthesis, reproducing the "pattern" of surplus production without direct coercion. Like Braudel's emerging capitalist in the cloud of markets and Latour's "emancipated" subject, the independence of the "node"—in this case the bearer of labor power—is both precondition for and outcome of connection to the value network. This emancipating connection thus becomes the medium for the mode of "social domination in capitalism" that Postone states "cannot be apprehended sufficiently as the domination and control of the many and their labor by the few."[12] The "magic" that Madame Keyne begins to understand after encountering Venn's device models precisely such a mode of domination—the mode that, as Sianne Ngai observes, appears as the "synthetic action of an abstraction-like value—the way it palpably shapes the empirical world of collective activity to which it belongs and in which it acts."[13]

Recall that the Thom epigraph does not simply define the modern concept of information. If that were all Delany needed, any number of earlier (and clearer) definitions would have sufficed. The epigraph reads: "Usually, when we speak of 'information,' we should use the word 'form.'" By placing this epigraph immediately after Madame Keyne's lessons on subsumption and self-regulation and directly before her demonstration of the device from which she derived the substance of those lessons, Delany connects the modern concept of information to older dynamics whose exemplar may be value's function as a form-reproducing mechanism. Put differently: by placing Venn's cybernetic device and Thom's insistence that information really just means the transmission of form alongside Braudel's account of the emergence and generalization of value-mediated social relations and Madame Keyne's celebration of those relations, Delany emphasizes the striking continuities between value's socially synthetic logic and the capacity that tends to be associated with the modern concept of information. And by placing Venn's model, the knowledge Madame Keyne derived from it, Nevèrÿon's emerging commercial networks, and the deployment of "free" labor alongside the visible presence of dispossession, direct violence, and slavery, Delany foregrounds the structural obfuscation of the racialized, feminized, and debilitating violence that grounds and is motivated by value's apparently self-regulating dynamics.

As I argued in the previous chapter, the subject whose political-philosophical form Silva names the transparent "I" constitutes a node in the emergent matrix of value-mediated spontaneous interconnection. The affectability that is externalized in the course of this node's production must appear elsewhere. The independence of reticulated individual producers and the opacity of the processes through which each is given social form require the affectability that necessitates their waged activity be consciously projected onto populations marked as unwaged or underwaged. Delany rigorously positions Madame Keyne's understanding of capital, Braudel's history, and Thom's informatics in relation to those populations in order to show how the informatics of value effect dispossession and differential valuation as a condition of their ongoing functionality. These logics of separation and differentiation are visible long before Madame Keyne demonstrates the models, and they are fully elaborated through Pryn's subsequent travels in Nevèrÿon.

In other words, what Venn's device really demonstrates is the logic of a process that operates *as if* self-reproducing and self-equilibrating by externalizing its material preconditions and effects. This is emphasized when, in an appendix to *Return to Nevèrÿon*, the final book of the Nevèrÿon series, Delany reveals that the images on which he based the device are "photographs of prepared models—not of real experiments."[14] In Thom's book, the "fluid containment replication" machine uses an analogy between hydraulics and informatics to visualize a genetic process that cannot be directly observed. The model that serves as the inspiration for Venn's "demonstration machine" might work "in principle," but building one in physical reality would require physical materials with the weight and texture of abstractions. Delany writes:

> For the real "demonstration machine" to operate as I described it . . . the upper container would require flooding with some ideally non-turbulent liquid, possibly a very light but very dense polymer oil (if there were such a thing). With most real liquids, however, the entrance into the pipe, the trip

down, and the exit from the spigot at the bottom would add so much "noise" to the "message" that, in practical terms, little or none of that "message" would enter the bottom basin intact. Similarly, the imprint medium in the bottom tub would have to be almost weightless. Nor could it mix with the incoming liquid. Rather, it would have to be immediately and ideally displaced. (*RN* 399)

Similarly, the "magic" Venn's machine demonstrates requires material conditions to be treated as logical relations. The sand and water that overflow the lower bowl and pile up in the trays and filters below grant no insight into the mechanism through which the "message" is transferred, but they register (however faintly) the violent separations and the processes of abjection upon which the transmission of form is predicated. Madame Keyne may understand them as opposites, but Venn's informatic model derives much of its significance from the prior demonstration of Belham's energetic one and all of its basic functionality from the flow of water that both models share, even if the mechanisms through which the pattern is transferred from upper to lower level remain opaque.

The dispossessive and ascriptive processes that must be externalized in order to maintain the appearance of spontaneous interconnection surround value-mediated social relations in *Neveryóna*. In the New Market, the backs of Madame Keyne's laborers run with sweat "like the falls in Madam Keyne's garden" (*N* 192). The analogy subtly undermines the subsequent distinction between Venn's and Belham's models by linking the rationalized working conditions Madame Keyne imposes as a result of her understanding of the former to the material and energetic character of the latter, which was built to provide measurements for the falls' construction and which is supposed to stand in for the matter and energy that information is not. Following this initial subversion of the "magic" that makes Venn's device so distinctive for Madame Keyne, the informatics of value are shown throughout *Neveryóna* to both rest on and determine the survival chances of bodies that are fully or partially excluded from their channels. The inextricability of those unequal prospects from value-mediated reproduction becomes evident just before the appearance of the two models, as Madame Keyne's market monologue reaches a crescendo against a backdrop of dispossession to which she never refers. To facilitate the New Market's construction, "a whole, impoverished neighborhood of Kolhari has had to be torn down."[15] But Madam Keyne barely recognizes the cause of this destruction or its structural relationship to the streets "filled with poverty" (*N* 180) that surround the site. In her celebration of the homeostatic processes that value facilitates, she says nothing about the foreclosed reproduction that is internal to but obfuscated by those processes. And she says equally little about the ongoing presence of slavery or the explicit signs of what Hartman has shown to be the modes of racialized subjection that extend out of that baleful institution into the age of so-called freedom. Yet it is these forms of material determination and racialized subjection that Pryn repeatedly encounters as she travels Nevèrÿon's world system with Madame Keyne's lessons on the informatics of value ringing in her ears.

Nevèrÿon's geography doubles in compressed form the colonial spatiality whose most recent expression is a world system in which logistics technologies reticulate without undoing the distinct spheres of Global North and Global South. The fictional preface to the series' first volume states that Nevèrÿon simultaneously resembles the Mediterranean, Mesopotamia, North Africa, the Middle East, and 1970s San Francisco.[16] However, in Nevèrÿon the dominant populations—the aristocracy, the merchants, and the "better breed" of apparently self-regulating workers—are black and brown, while the "'barbarians' from the [Global] South," and consequently the vast majority of slaves in Nevèrÿon, are "blond and blue eyed."[17] This inversion emphasizes the structural production and modulation of racialized forms, while the economic dynamics and externalization processes crystallized in Madame Keyne's understanding of Venn's model locate these processes of production and modulation at the threshold of connection to the network of value-mediated relations.[18]

Madame Keyne discloses a wholly informatic understanding of these dynamics and their attendant processes of ascription and abjection when she voices her fascination with and anxiety about the growing influence of Gorgik, the liberator. As she travels to the New Market with Pryn, an encounter with one of her associates reveals that she has been paying assassins to mount "under-equipped, under-manned" attacks, enough to "give the liberator some trouble" but not enough to succeed in killing him (*N* 179). Her ambivalence arises from uncertainty about the effects abolition will have on her economic activities. And this uncertainty is grounded in an understanding of the relationship between slaves, "free" workers, and surplus populations that is fully enclosed by the directly value-mediated elements of the informatics of value. Initially, Madame Keyne defines slaves as "men and women who labor for no pay" and surplus populations as groups of "men who do no labor for no pay." "The similarity is enough," she continues, "that they might make the mistake themselves"

(*N* 187). Should such a situation lead to alliances between the populations consigned to those two quite different positions, she reckons, the informatic mode of social synthesis and surplus accumulation would be degraded. "If the Liberator makes the same mistake," she muses, "I may well have to pay the full twelve and six to the next fanatic who asks" (*N* 187). Later, she speculates that "just as a man who has no work and gets no money for it may think himself a slave, so a man who has work and gets only very little money for it may think himself the same" (*N* 190). According to her understanding of value-mediated social dynamics—reinforced by assurances from her foreman, Ergi, that "nobody wants any liberator on *this* [the waged, 'free'] side" (*N* 189)—such a situation is held off by the visible presence of surplus populations. The workers she employs are, appear, or pretend to be content "because they have the discontented example of the barbarians on the other side of the fence to instruct them" (*N* 193).

In these speculations, Madame Keyne misrecognizes slavery and surplus populations as holdovers from a suboptimal era of social management whose current function is limited to deterring recalcitrants. In fact, they are structural elements of the informatics of value—two instances of life whose reproduction cannot or will not be accommodated within value's recursive computations, but which remain bound to the productive deployment of the processes that subtend those computations. It is dispossession, not directly market-mediated social relations, that subtends the apparently homeostatic system of slaves, surplus populations, and "free" workers, making possible their differential integration into circuits of accumulation. As an enslaved man puts it in the course of resisting his liberation by one of Gorgik's accomplices, "you free the labor pens into a world where, at least in the cities and larger towns, a wage-earning populace, many of them, are worse off than here. And an urban merchant class can only absorb a fraction of the skills of the middle level slaves you turn loose from the middens and smithies" (*TN* 291–92).

The liberal capitalist Madame Keyne can only imagine each of these social forms abstractly, which is to say, through an optic that is conditioned by and attuned to the logic of self-equilibrating value. In this informatic optic, slaves, "free" workers, and surplus populations can only understand their existence and their positions relative to each other through the possibility of entering into or dropping out of participation in the network of money-mediated exchange. In other words, Madame Keyne understands the homeostatic functions of the enslaved and surplus populations, but she grasps neither the dialectical production of the enforced desire for membership in the pseudo-universal category of the "free" worker nor the structural impossibility of extending such membership to the entirety of Nevèrÿon's population. And she can only faintly grasp the ways in which racial and gendered forms emerge from, maintain, and modulate this relationship between connection-as-freedom and the impossibility of full connectivity. Although her assistant, Jade, pushes her to hire "more women and barbarians," the thought of doing so fills Madame Keyne with "stabs of fear," the feeling that "something terrible might happen," although she cannot think what (*N* 193–94).

This "terrible" thing that Madame Keyne cannot imagine might be nothing less than the collapse of a system of accumulation that requires the structural externalization and differential integration of racialized, feminized, and debilitated life in order to maintain rates of relative surplus value extraction. Difference, in Madame Keyne's view, only exists insofar as it can be configured as one or another level of the communication system whose informatic "content" is value. The system she celebrates cannot accommodate the perpetual dispossession that is its condition of possibility. In other words, Madame Keyne takes the lesson of Venn's model to be an ontological one. *A slave is simply a person who labors for no pay*—a definition that renders invisible the specific histories of conquest, commodification, abjection, legal and political-theoretical codification, natal alienation, resubordination, resistance, and fugitivity, as well as the particular dynamics of gender and sexuality, that are integral to the structural logic of Atlantic slavery.[19] These histories appear toward the end of Pryn's journey through Nevèrÿon's reticulated modes of production, accumulation, and governance in the form of Bruka, an enslaved woman who has just been beaten. Far from and too close to the abstract processes that Venn's model represents, Bruka marks the most unthinkable point within the liberal-capitalist optic: the figure whose labor, reproductive capacities, and dreams and practices of freedom have "proven difficult, if not impossible" to assimilate within narratives of value production *and* those of rebellion and radicalism.[20]

Unable to recognize these dynamics of subordination, differentiation, and abjection as integral to the informatics of value, Madame Keyne nonetheless understands the formal relationships among slave, free worker, and surplus as somehow homeostatic, and in so doing she severs value-mediated social relations from the violence that produces and maintains them. Her commitment to the logic of value as the basis of an optimal, self-regulating, form-determining system means that she can only understand this logic as historical in terms of linear progress: away from violent coercion, and toward freedom, autonomy, and self-responsibility. The dynamics of fantasy and material impossibility that surround this progressive teleology are encoded in the histories attached to Belham and Venn, and thus to their models, across the Nevèrÿon series. Immediately after illustrating the mechanism of quasi-automatic surplus value accumulation through the example of the gold and iron coins, Madame Keyne proclaims:

> No wonder the Empress and the Liberator both decry slavery, when *this* is such a far more efficient system. You know where most of the iron for these little moneys comes from, don't you? It's melted down from the old, no-longer used collars once worn by— (*N* 199)

This passage suggests that the medium of exchange upon which "spontaneous interconnection" is premised succeeds and transforms the substance of direct, racialized domination. But the history of the collar, which is sketched earlier in the Nevèrÿon series, discloses a historical relationship between slavery and market-mediated "freedom" that does not correspond to the linear progress narrative Madame Keyne imagines.

In "The Tale of Dragons and Dreamers," Gorgik is told that the lock and key were invented by the same Belham whose model exemplifies matter, energy, and force in Madame Keyne's demonstration (*TN* 302). In *Neveryóna*, Pryn learns that before the invention of those technologies, slave collars were "permanently welded closed" (*N* 435). The relationship between the unlockable collar and money, the medium of market-dependent "freedom," shows Belham's and Venn's models to be inseparable. The inventor of the former set in motion the chain of transformations that subtends the process materialized by the latter. Formal freedom is neither the opposite nor the continuation of slavery, but its racialized modulations figure what Hartman calls "the shifting and transformed relations of power that brought about the resubordination of the emancipated," or the transition from the "pained and minimally sensate existence of the slave to the burdened individuality of the responsible and encumbered freed person."[21] The "far more efficient" system of "free" labor and its attendant mechanisms of surplus value extraction are built on, require, and maintain relations of material violation and differential integration whose forms of appearance are constantly shifting.

Perhaps Venn intended her model to illustrate not abstract domination alone but the inseparability of that form of domination from the relations of violation and differentiation that ground it. In "The Tale of Old Venn," which is set some time after her construction of the model shown in *Neveryóna*, she teaches a series of lessons about the violence that shapes and is shaped by nested modes of formal abstraction to the children of the Ulvayn islands, a fishing community in the early stages of its absorption into Nevèrÿon's emerging world system. Her first lesson concerns symbolic systems and centers on the uses of writing. But her lesson does not equate to an endorsement. "We must stop this," Venn tells the children,

> Or we must curtail it severely. I did not invent this system. I only learned it—when I was in Nevèrÿon. And I modified it, even as you have done. And do you know what it was invented for, and still is largely used for there? The control of slaves. If you can write down a woman's or a man's name, you can write all sorts of things down next to that name, about the amount of work they do, the time it takes for them to do it, about their methods, their attitudes, and you can compare all of this very carefully with what you have written about others. (*TN* 104)

In this strict rejoinder to the unmarked equation between literacy and civilization, Venn not only illustrates the centrality of abstraction to the differential allocation of labor value but also, and more importantly, gestures at the aggregating and comparative mechanism that makes it possible to coordinate that allocation across a global network. Curtailing the former may mean a broken link, a breakdown in the value-mediated aggregation and recursive intensification of racialized violence.

Later, Venn teaches the same children about the transformation of the Rulvyn—a group of tribes farther to the periphery than the Ulvayn islands—through forms of market dependence and gendered differentiation that had already become naturalized elsewhere in Nevèrÿon (*TN* 113–28). In elaborating these value-mediated transformations, Venn identifies a series of effects, including phallocentric psychoanalysis and gratuitous patriarchal violence, that cannot be connected directly to economic interests. This lesson is comparable to the one Federici teaches in *Caliban and the Witch*. It concerns a wave of dispossession that not only sets "free," differentiates, and disciplines "productive" labor power but also feminizes and racializes un- and underwaged practices of social reproduction. The internalization of these processes by those who are shaped by them is marked when, in the months following Venn's death, a ship crewed entirely by women—"tall ones, short ones, brown ones, black ones, fat ones, blond ones—every kind of woman you could think of!"—weighs anchor in front of one of the Ulvayn villages (*TN* 158). After several young women express a desire to run away and join the ship's crew, the men of the village burn it to the waterline, killing everyone on board (*TN* 158–71). And after the men burn the ship, the village children encode this episode of violent gender regulation in a game (*TN* 167).

Rather than an illustration of the reality and supremacy of value-mediated freedom, Venn's device might instead be placed at the start of this series of lessons on abstraction and violence—in front of the lessons concerning the use of writing to catalog, differentiate, and exert disciplinary power over the productive capacities of "free" and enslaved labor, the value network's destructive global expansion, and the link between market dependence, rationalization, and gendered differentials. This sequence emphasizes the processes through which what might be called secondary forms of abstraction—writing, money, information, identity—are shaped by value-mediated relations in the manner that Sohn-Rethel elaborates. By modeling a world in which all of these forms arise at the same time, Delany emphasizes how the abstract imaginaries that take shape around each can be understood as mediations of the informatics of value. The anachronistic presence of Venn's cybernetic device underscores the way that these relations eventually shape the modern concept of information. Before the information age, there are the informatics of value.

Finally, by materializing the informatics of value in Nevèrÿon's spatially and historically compressed model of racial capitalism, Delany shows how ascriptive processes allocate form differentially, producing bodies and populations marked by varying degrees of form and formlessness. The fictional preface to *Tales of Nevèrÿon* locates the world in which the tales take place "beyond the borders of history," on the edge of an "*unrectored chaos* out of which grew (and we watch grow page on page) the *techne* that make history recognizable: money, architecture, weaving, writing, capital" (*TN*, 10; first emphasis added). The temporal claim—that the growth of these *techne* marks the beginning of history as a movement away from "unrectored chaos"—reveals the kernel of what Silva calls affectability in an implied nonrelation to formal systems that simultaneously connotes formlessness and incivility. Those marked with this nonrelation are positioned outside history, which is to say, without agency. In what appears to be the only appearance of the phrase before Delany's preface, W. H. Auden's commentary on *The Tempest* includes a passage in which Caliban is described as the child of a mother whose name is not uttered but who is in quick succession described as "that envious witch" and "the unrectored chaos."[22] So the term Delany uses to describe that which appears to lie before and outside informatic systems is identical to an ontologizing description of the witch Sycorax who, for Federici and for many others, emblematizes the ascriptive dynamics that have remained essential to the reproduction and regulation of capitalism from the moment of its emergence to the present.[23] The history of this phrase, its direct connection to colonial processes of feminization and racialization, shows that the construction of "unrectored chaos" happens within the history of value-informatic mechanisms. It is here that the true historical stakes of information and form come into relief. Directly or indirectly mediated connection to the value network separates people from the "unrectored chaos," giving them a form by situating them within a form. Under conditions of generalized value-informatic sociality, to fail to establish such a connection is to be marked as *formless*. What this should make clear is that formlessness is not an ontological state. It is an abstract property that is bound to protocols of form-determination. The "unrectored chaos" is not a historical precursor to the emergence of formalizing social dynamics. It is brought into being by and abstracts those dynamics' externalized conditions. Insofar as it is a direct outcome of informatic processes, formlessness should be understood as a class of outlawed or abject form.

By mapping these dynamics across Nevèrÿon's compressed racial-capitalist world system, Delany also makes it clear that the people whose structural positions and chances of survival are marked by the differential allocation of form and formlessness are not reducible to the inert abstractions that, from the perspective of the value network, appear to spontaneously circulate, reproduce themselves, and generate surplus value. Exposure to the violence of enslavement, Gorgik tells Pryn, affords knowledge of the "flow and form" of accumulation and dispossession about which "free" people remain ignorant (*N* 85). Venn fled from the Rulvyn village as the gendered enclosures took shape in order to teach the Ulvayn children how not to aspire to "civilization" (*TN* 104). Some of the young women from the Ulvayn village attempt to join the red ship to escape the same enclosures—an act whose threat to the value-mediated social matrix can be measured in the magnitude of the violent response. Venn's student, Norema, travels Nevèrÿon attacking slavers and freeing slaves. An unseen member of the surplus population pelts Madame Keyne with mud as she celebrates the logic of value—and this act leads her to admit the fragility of the putatively homeostatic relationship between "free" worker, slave, and surplus population. The most precarious workers at the brewery in which Pryn is employed toward the end of *Neveryóna* devise ways to maximize the appearance of constant work while minimizing their productivity, and Pryn devises accounting tricks to help them. By freeing Bruka, Pryn distorts the social form afforded by her knowledge of reading and writing, her employment as a skilled worker at the brewery, and her education in the logic of value.

These acts do not take place at a level of abstraction whose visualization requires a device such as Venn's. Each cuts across the layers of the informatics of value, revealing and undermining the intricated dynamics of dispossession, market dependence, spontaneous interconnection, and differential valuation. Each shows how the abstract dynamics gouge out the concrete, always leaving a remainder that must be abjected. And each reveals how the relationship between the informatics of value and material life is not unidirectional; action at the level of the latter produces effects in the former. On one hand, they show the mutuality of form and formlessness—how the one is conditional on the other and how close the mobility, flexibility, and self-possession associated with form are to the precarity and burdened individuality of formlessness; it is the need to externalize and recuperate this mutuality that animates the fantasies of immateriality and distributed sociality that anchor digital culture. And on the other hand, they gesture toward collective practices that are not reticulated by value, and which entail different kinds of connection. In Part II, I turn my focus to these phenomena: the cybernetic reformulation of value-informatic personhood; the externalization, recuperation, and intensified disavowal of formlessness; and the possibility and the abjection of refusal.

II

MEDIA HISTORIES OF DISPOSAL

6 HUMAN USE, OR THE DIGITAL-LIBERAL PERSON

IN A PASSAGE FROM THE 1950 FIRST EDITION of *The Human Use of Human Beings*, Norbert Wiener writes:

> We ordinarily think of a message as sent from human being to human being. This need not be the case at all. If, being lazy, instead of getting out of bed in the morning, I press a button which turns on the heat, closes the window, and starts an electric heating unit under the coffeepot, I am sending messages to all these pieces of apparatus. If on the other hand, the electric egg boiler starts a whistle going after a certain number of minutes, it is sending me a message. If the thermostat records that the room is too warm and turns off the oil burner, the message may be said to be a method of control of the oil burner. Control, in other words, is nothing but the sending of messages which effectively change the behavior of the recipient.[1]

Although it maintains a distinction between human beings and "pieces of apparatus," Wiener's description of message-mediated interactions limns the value-informatic production of "free," self-possessed humans as components in an automatic, self-regulating system. The processes he describes function through the transmission of differences that make a difference. The human being is both positioned in a network of informatic relations and defined as a uniquely self-possessed component of that network. The language of command and control Wiener deploys thus makes legible the cybernetic sciences' encounter with the informatics of value's principal contradiction; the person shaped by informatic relations they cannot grasp is depicted as the agent who is able to determine the behavior of other people and things. But what of the difference that makes no difference? What of the recipients who are not affected, who do not alter their behavior, or who respond with behavior that differs from that encoded in the message? What of those who appear to neither send nor receive messages? Wiener makes no reference to these possibilities. He writes nothing of the non-message.

In his 1989 introduction to *The Human Use of Human Beings*, Steve Joshua Heims notes that Wiener extensively revised the book in 1954 to produce a second edition "where the framework is more philosophical and less political."[2] What does "more philosophical and less political" mean? And what does the more political version reveal about the objects and horizons of the political as formulated in Wiener's book? Answers to these questions start to become legible when one looks at the first of the major revisions. In replacing the first chapter, "What Is Cybernetics?," with an entirely new one titled "Cybernetics in History," Wiener excised a reflection on industrial machinery through which the book's title is explicitly posited as a protest against the "inhuman use of human beings" when they are "reduced to the level of effectors for a supposedly higher nervous organism."[3] His aim, he writes toward the start of these comments, is to make industrial machinery secondary "in all matters of value that concern us to the proper evaluation of human beings for their own sake and to their employment as human beings, and not as second-rate surrogates for possible machines of the future."[4]

Wiener's account of the inhuman use of human beings is striking for its similarity to Marx's formulation of the "*automatic system of machinery...* consisting of numerous mechanical and intellectual organs, so that the workers themselves are cast merely as its conscious linkages."[5] In this respect, Wiener joins a long and heterogeneous list of writers concerned with the devaluation of uniquely human traits as an effect of technological change. What I am concerned with here are the terms in which he posits the optimally *human* use of human beings. As Hayles points out, Wiener saw cybernetics as an extension of liberal humanism, not a means of dismantling it.[6] In contrast to the "inhuman" uses exemplified by factory labor, Wiener proffers "human beings" functioning "in conjunction with all types of automata which participate in a two-way relation with the world about them."[7] This two-way relationship, he writes, should be understood in terms of the exchange of messages. Which is to say, returning to the definition with which I opened this chapter, the uses that most closely align with human being are those involving the exchange of *signals that change the behavior of their recipients*. More communication—more exchange—equals more freedom. And *this* definition is remarkably close to Marx's ironic claim about capitalism's capacity for "spontaneous interconnection," its configuration of the human as an "independent point . . . conditioned on every side in his connections with other individuals and in his own mode of existence."[8]

This image of homeostatic communication as the sign of full humanity is reinforced in the sixth chapter of the 1950 edition of *The Human Use of Human Beings,* which bears the remarkable title "The Individual as the Word." There, Wiener writes that although "earlier accounts of individuality were associated with some sort of identity of matter, whether of the material substance of the animal or the spiritual substance of human soul," it had become necessary to recognize the human person "as something that has to do with the continuity of pattern, and consequently as something that shares the nature of communication."[9] In the final chapter he reiterates this definition of "man" in terms of "variability" and "integrity" in order to map the gradated allocation of personhood onto capacity for communication. "For man to be alive," he continues, "is for him to participate in a world-wide scheme of communication. It is to have the liberty to test new opinions and to find which of them point somewhere, and which of them simply confuse us." To "be less than a man," he concludes, "is to be less than alive."[10] Although defined against the constraining character of industrial labor, Wiener's account of unconstrained humanity as the maximal exchange of messages reproduces in overtly cybernetic terms the image of emergent social synthesis and connectivity whose origins lie in the informatics of value. Which is to say, the human is formed by relations that systematically tend toward its inhuman use.

For Wiener, "automation" names a tendency that, if left unaddressed, would continue to constrain all that is "of moral worth in the human being" by limiting the possibilities for free communication in a global network of bodies and things.[11] But by grounding his critique in a definition of the human as constituted by informatic interactions with other entities, he reproduces in explicitly information-theoretical terms the form of the possessive individual whose capacities are allocated through the informatics of value. If there is a critique of automation in the opening passages of *The Human Use of Human Beings,* it is one that detaches the specific techniques and technologies employed in industrial production from the structurally determined drive toward intensified efficiency through abstract domination—the same drive whose underlying social matrix produces multiple iterations of self-possession, including those which anchor the digital imaginary. The image of unimpeded communication that more or less explicitly grounds these iterations of self-possession exemplifies a mode of social synthesis that is relatively indifferent to (and in fact informs, rather than being shaped by) the desires of the "Fascists, Strong Men in Business, and Government" with whom Wiener exclusively associates the inhuman deployment of "human beings."[12]

This identity between the ideal human he celebrates and that which is formed through the informatics of value explains why Wiener can critique certain aspects of automation, white supremacy, and settler colonialism while at the same time elevating and calling for the intensification of those phenomena's logical and imaginative foundations—the dynamics that reproduce optimal personhood as abstract, communicational form. Indeed, Wiener's liberal antiracism, like his concerns about mechanized industry, is premised on the ideal of universal, untrammeled communication. He rails against white supremacy, but does so because while it continues to "belong to the creed of a large part of the country" he can "not say that [his] ideal of communication is attained in the United States."[13] In characterizing racialized abjection as an *impediment* to informatically "free" personhood rather than that ideal's *precondition,* Wiener crystallizes the mode of communicative political rationality that emerges through the informatics of value to constitute one of its principal contemporary effects: the digital-liberal person.[14]

When he identified the second edition of *The Human Use of Human Beings* as "more philosophical and less political" than the first, Heims surely had in mind the removal of the more strident claims about automation and white supremacy. But "political" may instead name the symptomatic disclosure of the human's value-informatic character that recurs in so many of the passages Wiener excised in the course of his revisions. Reading the first edition of the book in this way reveals how the liberal-humanist critique of dehumanizing protocols, exemplified by certain kinds of bad feelings about automation and white supremacy, seeks to resolve the increasingly visible contradiction between "free" person and more or less reliable component by associating the former with intentional control over a network of objects. Put simply, this association, the nucleus of the digital-liberal subject, externalizes and inverts the value-informatic determination of personhood into information-technological mastery.

In January 1951, Wiener traveled to Paris to present a paper on "one of the leading questions" of early cybernetics research: "whether machines could recognize form, or the generalization of form which is known by the German psychologists as gestalt."[15] Wiener's examples in this talk included the vocoder, television, and early experiments in what would become known as optical character recognition. In each case, the process of machinic form-recognition centers on the notion of information as relation, as transmitted pattern. In the early conversations about machinic form recognition, Wiener notes, "the idea was introduced of a process of scanning not so much of a set of energies as a group of transformations of an energy. In this way, it seemed to be possible to abstract from the individual orientation of the energy concerned and to recognize a figure independently of its orientation."[16] It is this notion of form, always the outcome of a relational transformation, that computing machines may or may not be able to recognize.

When read alongside the definition of messages in the first edition of *The Human Use of Human Beings*, these comments on form disclose an epistemological mechanism whose implications extend far beyond the capacity of a machine to identify and transcode spoken phonemes, written signs, and so on. If the book posits the elevated form of the self-possessed human as a node in a "world-wide scheme of communication," the Paris paper diagrams the process through which that human is recognized and given form by the communication system that constitutes it. The "generalization of form" that a machine might recognize is, after all, another way of naming those abstractions that are constituted through connection to the value network. Wiener's insistence that computational figuration abstracts "transformations of energy" from individual orientations of energy may as well deploy the language of concrete and abstract labor, use value and exchange value, or affectability and transparency that in different ways describe the relational process through which the informatics of value allocate and valorize social form. Read together, the texts set out the two sides of the process through which the informatics of value shape perception—the process that Marx in 1844 called the "forming of the five senses."[17]

According to the digital-liberal optic reproduced in Wiener's "political" version of *The Human Use of Human Beings* and his comments on computational perception in the Paris lecture, to be in the realm of form, or to become legible through an informatic relation, is to receive, process, and transmit messages, or signals that "effectively change the behavior of the recipient." The process of scanning, of allocating something a form, abstracts that thing from its material context in order to locate it within a specific system of relations, as in Wiener's example of the computing machine's capacity to "recognize an ellipse apart from the ratio of axes and their orientation."[18] To be allocated a social form is to be in the realm of value, separated from prior social relations and placed in new, value-mediated relations with people and things. The "behavior" that is effectively changed by certain messages may here be taken to mean either regular connection to the value network as a more or less reliable component or the constant pursuit of expanded reproduction. But, as we have already seen, those behaviors and the social forms they give rise to result not from some message encoded in the signal "value" but from dispossession and market dependence. The "message" is material necessity. This arrangement foregrounds the contradiction that must be sustained in capital's pursuit of accumulation through spontaneous interconnection. Transparency, or the capacity for untrammeled communication that defines the "free" human as a mediated form of appearance of value-mediated social relations, is only evidenced by a change in behavior that is externally determined. Self-possession can only be confirmed by affectability.[19]

Which means that self-possession as transparency requires affectability, opacity, and formlessness be either revalorized or externalized onto persons marked by nonconnection or partial or low-value connection. Delany identifies the latter when he connects the production of racialized and feminized states of "unrectored chaos" to a logic of abstraction he later characterizes through explicit references to information and form. Ralph Ellison evokes the same set of processes when his narrator observes that he is "not only invisible but formless as well."[20] The other possibility—that certain kinds of formlessness might be elevated, as in the heightened mobility and flexibility that distinguish the digital-cultural iteration of the possessive individual—becomes increasingly visible in the years following the last of Delany's Nevèrÿon texts.[21]

I have already started to argue that the threshold between the value network and its putative outside is an *interface*. I use *interface* here in the sense that Alexander Galloway formulates it, as "that moment where one significant material is understood as distinct from another significant material," not a "thing" but an "effect."[22] This differential relation crystallizes the dynamic through which value-mediated self-regulation, spontaneous interconnection, and social synthesis are produced, maintained, and modulated by social formations that appear to be independent of but are in fact externalized constituents of their formal processes. The value interface produces on one side the network of "messages" that paradoxically allocate full or partial self-possession by determining behavior, and on the other what Frantz Fanon calls the "zone of nonbeing," that "incline stripped bare of every essential from which a genuine new departure can emerge."[23] This zone of nonbeing appears in expressly informatic terms in the conversation about analog and digital I discuss in the Introduction. Following von Neumann's elaboration of the digital as a simulation of discrete processes on a background of continuous ones, the engineer Julian Bigelow states that a proper definition of the digital requires not only "two or more discrete levels" but also "a forbidden ground in between and an agreement never to assign any value whatsoever to that forbidden ground, with a few caveats on the side."[24] If the "forbidden ground" articulates Fanon's zone of nonbeing in relation to the digital abstraction, the caveats are the interface effects through which an entity wholly or partially moves between the space of the non-message and that of the message.

Put differently, rather than marking a simple distinction between ontologically given spaces of form and formlessness, the interface between value and non-value produces and populates both states through a constantly shifting assemblage of conceptual and practical apparatuses.[25] These interface effects facilitate responses to shifting valorization requirements by opening up new spaces and relations of accumulation. And they appear concretely as shifts in the relative necessity and superfluity of labor power and as the differentiation of bodies marked as productive from those marked as aberrant. In the preceding chapters, I focused on showing how value, as "an historical process of forming what is intrinsically unformed," comprises a set of informatic relations. Now, I turn my focus to the historical process of allocating and exploiting formlessness as a necessary stage in the valorization of formal relations.

7 ELEMENTAL SPACE

Coloniality and Flexibility

THE RETICULATED OPERATIONS of differential valorization and abjection at the interface of the value network can be glimpsed in an extraordinary passage from "Progress and Entropy," the second chapter of the first edition of *The Human Use of Human Beings*. Seeking to illustrate the tension between techno-scientific progress and the constraints presented by a fully mapped world of finite resources, Wiener writes:

> After the disaster of the Stone Fleet and the destruction of the whalers in the Great Freeze at Point Barrow, New England capital left the sea, never to return. Why did it leave the sea and where did it go? On the one hand the period of adventure which characterized the New England of Colonial and Federal times had exhausted itself in a generation of *epigonoi*. On the other hand, the geological discoveries of Alexander Agassiz had opened the new copper mines of the Northwest, and many Boston fortunes which had sailed the seven seas now found a safe berth in the stocks and bonds of Calumet and Hecla. New England, from being a community of merchant adventurers, became a community of rentiers, of absentee landlords....
>
> ... Let us not forget that owner of gilt-edged bonds is prone to deny any contact with the source of his income, and any responsibility for the means by which it is obtained. In this rentier heaven, the prospect of floating through eternity on a continual magic carpet of other people's inventions seems no more remote than any realty of life....
>
> Besides this comfortable and passive aspect of the belief in progress, there is another one that appears to have a more masculine, vigorous connotation. To the average American, progress means the winning of the West. It means the economic anarchy of the frontier and the vigorous prose of Owen Wister and Theodore Roosevelt. Historically, the frontier is, of course, a perfectly

genuine phenomenon. For many years, the development of the United States took place against the background of empty land that always lay further to the West. Nevertheless, many of those who have waxed poetic concerning this frontier have been praisers of the past. Already in 1890, the census takes cognizance of the end of the true frontier conditions, and the geographical limits of the great backlog of unconsumed and unbespoken resources of the country have been clearly set.

In this connection, the career of Theodore Roosevelt invites many interesting comments. He was the prophet of the Vigorous life in the open air and the irreconcilable enemy of the Nature-Faker. Nevertheless, the very red-blooded outdoor life to which he devoted himself had already begun to partake of the quality of a myth. His Wild-West Youth in the Dakotas was exactly the section in which last remained an enclave of the frontier, when the great frontier of the United States has passed beyond it. His adventures as a hunter in Africa belong to the period when the big game had already begun to be confined to great reserves, established to perpetuate a dying sport, and to serve as an outdoor museum for the naturalist of the future. There are not any regions of Brazil now available for exploration after the fashion of the River of Doubt.[1]

In contrast to the animated rejection of the "inhuman use of human beings" in industrial labor that precedes it, this depiction of settler- and franchise-colonial expansion and their extractive afterlives does not center on the destructiveness of those baleful (and ongoing) procedures.[2] Later in the same chapter, Wiener does counter the idea of "the virtuous rapidity of progress" with an account of "the modern period" as an age of the "consistent and unconstrained exploitation" of natural resources, "conquered so-called primitive peoples," and "the average man." But the declension narrative that begins from New England's "merchant adventurers," the "perfectly genuine phenomenon" of "empty land" and "unbespoken resources" to the West of the frontier, the possibility of "adventures" in Africa, and a Brazil still "available for exploration" imbricates a concern for resource exhaustion with a sense that the shift from expansion to extraction impedes human flourishing by limiting new possibilities for "communication."

Read alongside Wiener's foregoing definition of capacity for participation in "a world-wide scheme of communication" as the mark of the fully human person, this narrative appears to rest on an implied continuity between those who are maximally open to communication with the "world around them" and merchants, settlers, hunters, and explorers engaged in colonial "adventure." Wiener's elevation of "economic anarchy" over sedentary labor and fixed capital maps the freedom that is value's promise onto an abstract capacity for movement in an emergent—"spontaneous"—network of persons and things. Given the conceptual and terminological endowment contemporary information-economic fantasies draw from cybernetics, it is hardly surprising that this image of circulation and exploration as the unimpeded movement of productively homeostatic bodies closely resembles the spatial and temporal imaginaries of supply chain management and platform-mediated flexibility.[3] Whatever else it does, the passage from "Progress and Entropy" valorizes a specific form of mobility—frictionless, emergent, and constantly renewable—over propertized land, fixed extraction sites, and low-risk financial instruments ("gilt-edged bonds"). The passage prototypes a disrupters' manifesto.

In this respect, Wiener's celebration of the "merchant adventurers" of New England, which grounds the human use of human beings in abstract ideals of flexibility and mobility, foreshadows Bernhard Siegert's claim that the techniques of Iberian colonial expansion turned ships into "cybernetic machines."[4] These machines, Siegert suggests, foreshadow the digital operation because they function through a homeostatic mechanism—"a loop comprised of measurement, adjustment [and] commands to the rudder and rigging"—that renders "the elemental space of the sea" legible and navigable.[5] The critical difference is that where Siegert's cybernetic formulation of transatlantic shipping emphasizes technical processes in order to undermine the notion of untrammeled agency that continues to demarcate the conceptual parameters of modern personhood, Wiener's installs the process of steering—the feedback loop between entity and environment—as the basis of that agency. The difference might be resolved by observing the process through which the human subject is produced *as autonomous* by an informatic mechanism that *conditions* and *sets limits on* its autonomy. But neither Wiener nor Siegert identifies the informatics of value that precede and condition the cybernetic conceptualization of shipping as a physical procedure for the transmission of abstractions. Consequently, neither can account for the "message" that determines the actual practices of shipping that lie behind their conceptualizations, which is to say, neither includes in their cybernetic diagram of shipping the accumulation drive that animates circulation and the practices of colonial expansion. If the ship is a cybernetic machine, then it is so before the feedback loop of map and shipping route, rudder, and rigging facilitates its triangular movement between Europe, Africa, and the New World. Before the movement of value-bearing bodies and things there is always already the movement of values around the quasi-autonomous space of a network that must constantly expand and increase its granularity. Before the possibility of imagining the ship as a cybernetic machine are the informatics of value.

Wiener's utopian prescriptions, which elevate a perpetually moving (or adventuring) human actor in an open mesh of possibility, show how the digital inheritor of liberal personhood emerges from linked histories of dispossession and racialized differentiation. By mapping concrete practices of exploration, occupation, and expropriation onto abstract ideals of communicative mobility, he shows how human flourishing is premised on the perpetual renewal of conditions that require transparent humanity's affectable others to be either differentially integrated into networks of communication or rendered literally nothing, as in Wiener's account of the "empty land" beyond the frontier.

This should make it clear that the relationship between form and formlessness is nonlinear. As Wynter observes, the fifteenth-century Portuguese integration of "areas of West Africa into a mercantile network and trading system, on the basis of the exchange of their goods for gold or slaves" was a "necessary and indisputable prelude, not only to Columbus's own voyage but also to the specific pattern of relations of which Cerio speaks between Christian Europe and the non-Christian peoples of the world to which Columbus and his crew had newly arrived."[6] In this exemplary case, the integration of people into networks of exchange—as merchants and as commodities—requires market-mediated reproduction in West Africa be rendered formless; the resultant accumulation of capital makes possible a subsequent imposition of formlessness onto unpropertized land and non-market-dependent people in the New World; and this imposition of formlessness makes possible the formalization of bodies, land, and resources through their integration into networks of accumulation; and so on. To flourish, Wiener's human requires the perpetual renewal of this arrangement. Both the informatics of value and the colonial imaginary they inform require the conceptual implementation of elemental spaces (the sea, unconquered land) and bodies (natives, slaves) through and across which the value network can expand and intensify its operations. And this relationship between form and formlessness, as an outcome of that between value-mediation and its externalized preconditions, is recursive. Formlessness is constructed as the outside of formal, value-mediated processes; and the demands of capital accumulation often lead the form that has been allocated through value-mediated processes to be either rescinded through ejection or rendered intermittent through flexibilization.

Fanon diagrams this reticulated construction of "empty" space, "affectable" bodies, and value-informatic personhood when he writes of a "becalmed zone" in which "the sea has a smooth surface, the palm tree stirs gently in the breeze, the waves lap against the pebbles, and raw materials are ceaselessly transported, justifying the presence of the settler." In this realm of frictionless circulation, Fanon ironically remarks, "the settler makes history" while native populations "form an almost inorganic background for the innovative dynamism of colonial mercantilism."[7] This "innovative dynamism" perfectly describes the development of techniques and technologies for constituting and differentially integrating unformatted space and bodies. Raw materials and land are the materialized forms of this integration, the measures of the value network's content and reach. And the processes of constitution, integration, and materialization tend to reproduce a double projection through which those spaces and bodies marked as formless simultaneously connote sites of limitless possibility and sources of limitless danger, both of which require the invention and deployment of regulatory techniques.[8]

Equiano underscores the quite different opportunity for self-possession that the smooth sea offers the enslaved. "One day, when we had a smooth sea, and moderate wind," he recounts, "two of my wearied countrymen, who were chained together (I was near them at the time), preferring death to such a life of misery, somehow made through the nettings and jumped into the sea . . . and I believe many more would soon have done the same, if they had not been prevented by the ship's crew."[9] Yet even this mark of circulation's violence can be remapped according to the logic of value, appearing as the risk of lost cargo and diminished returns that animate financialized forms of insurance. James Wallace captures the trader's sense of financial risk in his 1795 history of Liverpool, writing that "the African commerce holds forward one constant train of uncertainty, the time of slaving is precarious, the length of the middle passage uncertain, a vessel may be in part, or wholly cut off, mortalities may be great, and various other incidents may arise impossible to be foreseen."[10] So the "becalmed zone" is also that about which there is nothing "automatically propitious." It is a space in which "one single storm" can turn a shipowner or merchant from "a rich man into a beggar," and which thus necessitates the constant production of new technologies—from the nets and the readiness of the crew Equiano observes to new navigational techniques and instruments of insurance—to maintain and inflate the notion that values circulate and expand in an autonomous and frictionless manner.[11] In the same way, when measured against modern, legal forms of property (whether as self-ownership or the ownership of external objects), the putatively inorganic background composed of "natives" presents an obstruction to productive land use that is evoked to naturalize and inflate the value that can be "set free" through occupation. This construction gives rise to all manner of "improper" forms of use, which is to say, social practices that appear non- or not-quite-human when measured against the value-informatic parameters of the possessive individual.

This projection of a value-mediated sense of possibility against a racialized backdrop of affectable bodies informs settler-colonial technologies that precede and anticipate the modern formalization of biological racism.[12] Beginning from William Petty's *Political Anatomy of Ireland* and *Political Arithmetick*, Brenna Bhandar shows how, in seventeenth-century Ireland, land measured by cadastral survey was plotted against value calculated through the allocation of productive capacity to individuals, leading to the marking of populations that did not propertize land or engage in "marketized forms of cultivation" as inherently criminal, underdeveloped, and savage.[13] Through Petty's (and subsequently Locke's) property-based justification of occupation, "emergent concepts of race and racial inferiority were smuggled into new forms of value, constructed, ostensibly, on logics of measurement and quantification."[14] Bhandar goes on to show how this double movement, comprising the racialized attribution of formlessness and the subsequent, gradated integration of people and land into value-mediated social forms, recurs across geographically distinct instances of settler-colonial occupation, constituting "racial regimes of ownership."[15] In each, the projection of empty space available for improvement by propertization requires existing occupants be marked as incapable of operating as transparent components within reliable circuits of accumulation, and thus as a "continual threat to civilization and security."[16] In these methods, it is possible to observe the deployment of the "unrectored chaos" as a spatializing technology. As Katherine McKittrick puts it, the equation that produces colonial-racialized form "presumes—and fundamentally requires—that subaltern populations have no relationship to the production of space."[17]

What Bhandar names racial regimes of ownership might be posited in value-informatic terms as the feedback loop through which formlessness is ascribed so that form can be differentially allocated, its promises amplified for some and extended to others only tentatively, tied to the burden of assimilation, and indexed to the reproduction cost imputed to already devalued (because affectable) lives.[18] Reading the scenes of coloniality Wiener sketches in "Progress and Entropy" as a narrative of the waxing and waning of conditions in which the "full" communicative human can thrive reveals an additional stage of this loop. If capacity for untrammeled communication appears the measure of self-possession, and if connection to the value network is the real basis for that measure, then the expression of full human capacity requires a degree of affectability—exposure to external conditions in pursuit of opportunity—that cannot be attained through a repetitive job in a fixed location. Indeed, this is the kernel of Wiener's definition of inhuman use; work "which demands less than a millionth of [a person's] brain capacity" is a "degradation to a human being."[19] Once again, the value-informatic allocation of personhood is shown to require exposure to the allocating mechanism's putative outside. The maintenance of the individual person as a "continuity of pattern" requires a continuous feedback loop of production and reproduction that only steady and sufficiently waged work can maintain; but such work impedes the full expression of human capacities that is value-mediated personhood's promise; but the absence of steady work both attenuates personhood and increases the likelihood of premature death. Connection is inseparable from dispossession. Transparency is inseparable from affectability. Form is inseparable from formlessness. We have already seen how these contradictions surface in the racialization and feminization of labor, which really mean devaluation and precaritization for the purposes of lowering costs, intensifying surplus value extraction, and weathering system-level fluctuations. As Kyla Schuller shows, mid-nineteenth-century impressibility discourse represents an attempt to manage the same contradictions through a series of racializing and feminizing bifurcations; the capacity to turn exposure to natural conditions into abstract knowledge came to distinguish "the civilized state of impressibility from the racialized quality of being easily moved and yet unable to retain the effects of those movements."[20] Wiener's account of colonial "adventures" shows how the racializing and feminizing processes required to manage this contradiction extend into the social relations and digital imaginaries of so-called post-Fordism, which are thus revealed to recode the inhospitable (or "elemental") sea, the doctrine of *terra nullius*, and the savage ("inorganic," "affectable") native as a global space of flows in which mobility, flexibility, and responsivity prosper. Those social relations and imaginaries valorize formlessness in deracinated form—as the signature of optimally "free" personhood.

How else could images of natives, nomads, and the conquest of frontiers proliferate so widely in accounts of digital freedom and its concomitant forms of optimally human use? Perhaps the most striking examples of this phenomenon can be found in the name of the cyberlibertarian Electronic Frontier Foundation and in its founder's suggestion that lifelong internet users are "natives" in a world in which their parents will always be immigrants.[21] In 1996, John Perry Barlow insisted that, as a world without bodies, cyberspace leaves race behind. But note the substitutions that take place between Wiener's prototype and Barlow's more developed form of the digital-liberal imaginary. In Barlow's "Declaration," "native" is not opposed to "settler." Instead, it stands in its place, deployed in deracinated form to trope maximum connectivity and frictionless mobility. And to function in this way, it must be weighed against another racialized form: the cheap, intermittent connection signified by "immigrant."

Equally remarkable is the claim, found in promotional materials for Panasonic's Wear Space technology—essentially a set of horse blinders for use in co-working spaces—that "as open offices and digital nomads are on the rise, workers are finding it ever more important to have personal space where they can focus."[22] The Wear Space advertisement promises to maintain the specifically deracinated form of nomadism attached to freelance and other precarious workers by minimizing the possibility of affection by external forces. In each of these examples (and in many others) the deracinated forms of native and nomad are positioned *after* and in a *state of greater freedom than* the settler, who by definition settles into sedentary dwelling.[23]

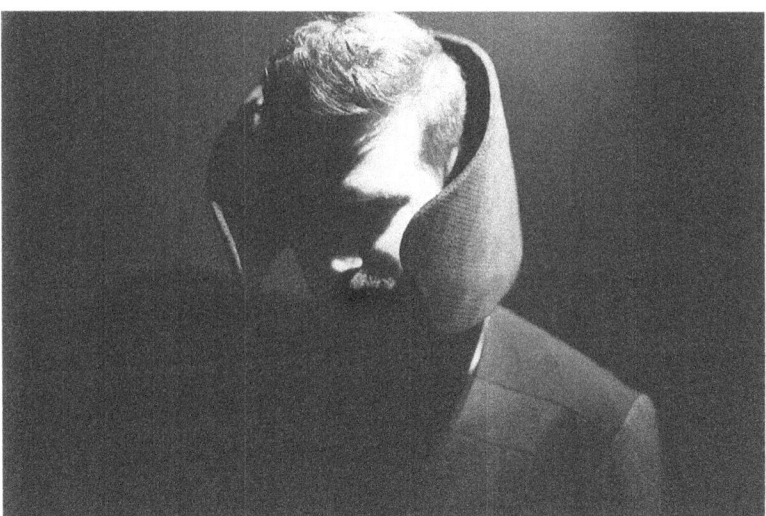

Figure 5. Panasonic Wear Space.

8 DEPLORABLE ALTERNATIVES

"Mechanical Slaves" and Upgradable Labor

WIENER FIRST ENGAGED THE PROBLEM of industrial automation as a fetter on human capacities in 1948, in a brief aside toward the end of the introduction to *Cybernetics*. In that discussion, he employs an extraordinary definition of automatic machinery as a form of labor that "has most of the economic properties of slave labor" without the "direct, demoralizing effects of human cruelty."[1] Wiener's use of this analogy clearly gestures to Karel Čapek's inaugural use of "robot," derived from the Czech *robata* (forced labor), in his 1920 play *R.U.R.* But Wiener's brief discussion of machines and slaves—four paragraphs at the end of a long survey of the technological and intellectual developments that shaped and were shaped by the cybernetic sciences—is more significant for the way it underscores the unmarked centrality of value mediation to the figure of the human as communicative agent that, as we have already seen, grounds *The Human Use of Human Beings*. In both books, the human-as-laborer constitutes the horizon of Wiener's analysis. In the later book, Wiener subordinates labor to communication, evaluating the former on the basis of its capacity to constrain or facilitate the latter; in the earlier, he posits labor *and its racialization* as technologies of humanization. Although Wiener considers the possibility that the "new and most effective collection of mechanical slaves" will spare "humanity" the "need of menial and disagreeable tasks," he worries about how coexistence with those "slaves" might impinge on the value of human labor. Any form of labor that accepts "the conditions of competition with slave labor," he warns, "accepts the conditions of slave labor, and is essentially slave labor." And "the key word of this statement," he concludes, "is *competition*."[2]

What exactly does Wiener mean by "*competition*" here, and why does he posit it as the most significant implication of the new "conditions of slave labor" represented by automation? On one hand, his claim that accepting *conditions of competition* with slave labor is tantamount *to* slave labor is consistent with his subsequent account of the inhuman use of human beings, in which he names work in a mechanized factory an almost equivalent degradation to being chained to an oar and used "as a source of power." This is an equation that remains all too common in Marxian and liberal accounts of waged work.[3] But when the preceding reference to "mechanical slaves" is taken into account, it appears that Wiener is using "slave labor" as a synonym for automatic machinery, in which case his claim is simply this: accepting conditions of competition with machinery means accepting working conditions equivalent to those of machinery, which means accepting a situation in which one is treated as machinery. If the force of Wiener's claim rests on the moral implications of treating people like machines, the "mechanical slaves" analogy appears inessential. It is not necessary to posit an equivalence between slaves and machinery in order to say that the same equivalence is reproduced upon "free" labor once machinery becomes the dominant element of the production process. It would be more straightforward to simply say that workers are treated like machines when they are used as effectors of a machine. Indeed, this is the analogy that appears in the penultimate chapter of *The Human Use of Human Beings*, where Wiener writes that when workers are used "as cogs and levers and rods, it matters little that their raw material is flesh and blood. *What is used as an element in a machine, is an element in the machine.*"[4]

So why does Wiener have to place humans in competition with "mechanical slaves" in order to emphasize the perils of subordinating workers to machinery? Louis Chude-Sokei has argued that these passages show that Wiener was "quite cognizant of the social history behind [cybernetics'] metaphors and analogies."[5] But this does not explain Wiener's need to analogize machines and slaves in order to strengthen his message about the threats posed to "free" labor by automation. The key to resolving this conundrum, I think, lies in the basic fact that the institutions and afterlives of Atlantic slavery did not threaten the formation or the livelihood of the "free" person in the way that Wiener suggests "mechanical slaves" do.[6] Slavery *secured* the formation, reproduction, and capacitation of that form of personhood—both economically and conceptually. What appears in the shift from machine to "mechanical slave," then, has to do with the dissolution of those conditions through which personhood is secured, which is to say, it has to do with the racialization of capacity that underwrites the "free" human person. Being treated as equivalent to a machine while retaining "free" status and a sufficient wage to reproduce oneself might just mean having a boring job. But becoming equivalent to a "mechanical slave" implies devaluation, foreclosed conditions of reproduction, and self-responsibility in the absence of wage-mediated access to the means of meeting basic needs. Although Wiener briefly acknowledges slavery's "human cruelty," he overwhelmingly deploys the slave as a rhetorical figure in order to evoke sympathy for the future "free" persons whose "potential"—but really whose *value* and *prospects of regular connection*—will be constrained by shifting organic composition in a manner that may feel tantamount to abjecting racialization. Or, he foreshadows James Boggs's argument that cybernation, or subordination to automatic machinery, would eliminate "the ladder, by means of which white workers moved up, leaving the dregs behind to the Negroes," but does so in order to defend the ladder as an indispensable technology of human flourishing.[7]

In this respect, Wiener's rhetorical deployment of slavery shows digital-liberal automation anxiety to share a conceptual foundation with the liberal humanism that sanctioned the abolitionist John Rankin to imagine himself and his family as slaves in a written appeal to his slaveholding brother. As Hartman has shown, Rankin's "good intentions" and "heartfelt opposition to slavery" notwithstanding, the ease of his "empathic identification" results not from some common language of humanity but from "the fungibility of the captive body."[8] Although this fungibility is ascribed through the same value-informatic processes that constitute the "free" person, there is a racialized bifurcation that renders the enslaved person "an abstract and empty vessel vulnerable to the projection of others' feelings, ideas, desires, and values." This procedure grounds the processes through which "the dispossessed body of the enslaved" becomes "the surrogate for the master's body," guaranteeing his "disembodied universality" and acting "as the sign of his power and dominion."[9] The material operations that constitute the slave—kidnapping, natal alienation, captivity, and strictly constrained reproduction—secure the quite different dynamics that constitute and valorize the "free": universality, mobility, transparency, and wage-mediated self-reproduction. The liberal abolitionist Rankin amplifies the protocols that inform the institution of slavery and its afterlives. And the digital-liberal humanist Wiener externalizes the informatic logic of those protocols as communication.

Wiener is correct when he senses that the racialization of labor is linked to its devaluation. But because he cannot trace that devaluation to the same informatic mechanisms that produce, reproduce, and allocate value to "free" persons—mechanisms he can only apprehend in mediated form, as universal communication—he rends the structurally inseparable categories of human, slave, and machine into a pair of opposed categories. This rending exemplifies the processes of racial ascription that take place in the context of value-informatic sociality. For the human to exist as the bearer of a range of capacities that can be more or less fully utilized, its devalued others must be rendered as machines, objects capable only of performing repetitive tasks. And because capacity is allocated value-informatically, the prospect of falling out of the value network gets coded as the prospect of falling into that second category. Of course, this distinction does not originate with Wiener, whose opposition between humans and "mechanical slaves" maps directly onto the distinction Ian Baucom finds in the minute book for the Lords Commissioners of the Admiralty for July 1783, which records lifelong compensation packages for named, "far-flung workmen of the empire whose bodies had been wounded in the service of the [British] crown" and singular values for the 440 unnamed slaves, "valued at 30 pounds a head," who were murdered and then presented to insurers as lost to ill weather and disease by the captain of the slave ship *Zong*.[10] Where self-possessed, value-transmitting humans are allocated degrees of capacity and autonomy that can be degraded, evaluated, and compensated, slaves, like machines, are valued as single commodities, bearers of a fixed value. They can be "lost," damaged, or destroyed, but they cannot be incapacitated. Wiener's formulation of humans in competition with "mechanical slaves" is significant, then, because it explicates the informatic logic of this bifurcation and models its rearticulation in the context of deindustrialization.

In a 1953 text on "The Future of Automatic Machinery," one of a spate of talks and articles on that subject from the years surrounding the original publication of *The Human Use of Human Beings*, Wiener describes industrial labor as a filter applied to human capacities. The employees of a mechanized factory may "eat and drink, love and hate, enjoy and tire, like other human beings," he writes, "but from the point of view of their job alone, these outside faculties and necessities of their lives are nothing more than so much tare, so much useless baggage, perhaps inseparably connected with the pair of hands for which the employer pays, but of no direct value to him." Consequently, "the question of replacing these workers by automatic machinery is not the question of replacing of so many men, but rather half-men or quarter-men or even hundredth-men."[11]

This account of reduction in the process of construction is the closest Wiener comes in any of his writings on labor to grasping the logic of value mediation through which activities associated with reproduction—eating and drinking, loving and hating, degrees of enjoyment and tiredness—can appear only abstractly, in mediated form, as costs that may or may not have to be factored into the wage and thus into the computation of surplus value. That said, what is most striking about this passage is the way Wiener assumes the universality of the figure whose full range of capacities *might* be incorporated into value-mediated social relations. His dismay at the exclusion of phenomena such as loving, hating, and enjoyment from the valuation of labor implicitly posits a post-Fordist fantasy in which the human use of human beings entails the value-mediated integration of those phenomena into the process of capital accumulation. And, as Wiener's earlier comments on "mechanical slaves" show, this digital-liberal fantasy represents the afterlife of the bifurcation of "free" workers from those who, in Marx's words, were subjected to the "maxim of slave management in slave importing countries, that the most effective economy is that which takes out of the human chattel in the shortest space of time the utmost of exertion that it is capable of putting forth."[12] By positing the extent of value mediation as the measure of the human use of human beings, Wiener's comments on the devaluation of the human by automation show how connection to the value network functions as a precondition for and modulator of human status. To achieve the latter, one must want and be able to subject one's full bodily, affective, and cognitive capacity to value mediation. And, since capacity is allocated by the informatics of value in a manner that is co-constitutive with ascriptive processes, the human use of human beings is subtended by differential protocols. Wiener's list of half-, quarter-, and hundredth-persons makes differential valuation visible, but in a manner that inverts the process through which that valuation is actually effected. In his account, the communicational "full" human precedes and is more or less fully integrated into the value network.

The racializing implications of Wiener's humanly used human become explicit in an untitled piece on automatic factories from 1954 in which he turns to the question of "the upgrading of proletarian labor." The same concern appears in *Cybernetics* immediately after the comments on "mechanical slaves." There, Wiener observes that although "the skilled scientist and the skilled administrator" may retain a place in labor markets after automation, just as "skilled" carpenters, mechanics, and dressmakers "survived" the Industrial Revolution, the worker of "moderate achievements or less," with "nothing to sell that is worth anyone's money to buy," will not be so lucky.[13] This aside rests on a distinction between "skilled" labor and that marked as of "moderate achievements or less," which hints at the differential protocols encoded in the communicational definition of the human and the idea of automation as a filter preventing that human from channeling its full capacity into circuits of accumulation. The untitled 1954 text makes those racializing dynamics and their structural implications more or less explicit: that "the upgrading of proletarian labor" is possible, Wiener writes,

> is shown convincingly by the training of specialists in the military services. That such an upgrading is universally possible is too much to hope. For the people who simply cannot be upgraded, we are left only the two deplorable alternatives: They must suffer or they must be carried by the community as part of the socially necessary burden of caring for the sick, the weak, and the other socially ineffective. To some extent we may have the good luck to be able to breed them out of our society, but a complete success along this line is too much to hope for.[14]

Wiener's predictions are very similar to those Boggs sets out in "The Challenge of Automation" nine years later. But where Wiener assumes the perspective of the "community" that must "carry" or eliminate those who cannot be "upgraded" and projects a passive mass of the "socially ineffective," Boggs forecasts antagonism between those who regard themselves as part of that community and those who "are forced to struggle for a society in which there are no displaced persons."[15] On the one hand, the distinction between upgradable labor and that which must suffer, be carried as a "burden," or be biopolitically eliminated exemplifies the logic of disposal that implicitly subtends Wiener's informatic model of the "free" subject, that "continuity of pattern" which "shares the nature of communication." The concept of upgradable labor underscores the centrality of value mediation to the specification of the human use of human beings, while the "deplorable alternatives" and the presentation of a market-mediated eugenics as the best possible outcome—an outcome so ideal that "a complete success along this line is too much to hope for"—disclose the racial-capitalist character of that mode of mediation. The proximity of that which can be upgraded to that which must be eliminated evokes what Sylvia Wynter identifies as the modern, Darwinian/Malthusian reformulation of the human. Under the informatic logic that grounds this reformulation, specific "behavior programming schema" are informed by and reproduce a logic of dysselection based on "a dual mode of Natural Scarcity—that is, a scarcity of full genetically selected human beings, on the one hand, and of material resources on the other."[16] Within this scheme, unupgradable labor might as well be called obsolete labor. It might as well be called obsolete life.

But Wiener's formulation of upgradable and "socially ineffective" labor doesn't only make legible the continuities between two iterations of disposal—the ascriptive and civilizational dynamics of racialization that recur across settler colonialism and Atlantic slavery, and the ostensibly race-blind differentials that are intensified under so-called post-Fordism.[17] It also reveals how each iteration informs a different kind of human-machine analogy.[18] Where the enslaved were imagined by planters as "man-shaped ploughs" and rendered by financial technologies as endlessly fungible value, the idea of upgradable labor makes explicit the formatting of the "free" person as a putatively self-regulating recipient, processor, and conduit of the message "value" whose abstract universality can only be replicated by a universal machine, the idealized form of the electronic digital computer.[19] The emergence of this human-as-information-processor, which follows the generalization of cybernetic concepts and accompanies the waning of capital's capacity to sustain the reproduction of those it makes dependent on it, produces the "user" as a dominant expression of agential personhood. As Orit Halpern writes, the latter "is not consolidated in identity but rather operates through the logic of units of attention, and bandwidth, consisting of roving populations of action in the network."[20] Identifying the trope of the human-as-information-processor as an effect of value-mediated personhood under conditions of deindustrialization connects plantation to post-Fordism, manual to "creative" labor, hardware to software, and racialized subjection to the freedom of the (ostensibly raceless) digital-liberal person.

Wiener's brief comments on white supremacy in *The Human Use of Human Beings* are immediately preceded by a definition of the ideal social structure as a "moderately loose social community, in which the blocks to communication among individuals and classes are not too great."[21] The mode of relationality that produces this structure, Wiener continues, would be a "*formless democracy.*"²² *Formless* here describes the association of humanly used humans, which is to say, those whose relationship to the informatics of value is one of full integration and homeostatic reproduction. Halpern's network of users shows how this ideal and the optimal form of the human person that grounds it persist while connection and the allocation of "bandwidth" become simultaneously literalized and separated from the meeting of needs. But, as Wiener's viciously casual remarks on those who "simply cannot be upgraded" show, this "free" system of relations requires the production and circulation of a second valence of formlessness. This second valence manifests in value-informatic terms the Darwinian-Malthusian reformulation of evil whose emergence Wynter locates in the synthesis of scientific racism and liberal political economy that from the middle of the nineteenth century functioned to elevate a newly "degodded" conception of man.²³ This reformulation is bound to mechanisms of selection and dysselection under which "those relatively few selected were now to be seen as being as naturally scarce as the resources for which they all had to compete" in order to rationalize the positions of the growing part of the global population situated around the threshold of the value network.²⁴ The *formless democracy* of "full" humans is both enabled and naturalized by this second valence. Abject formlessness is posited as an outcome of natural selection—the residue from the elevation of "upgradable" populations— and efficient resource allocation—the dysselection of the "obsolete"— rather than of the racialized protocols of value-mediated freedom and capacity that instantiate and manage the ever-shifting distinctions between those who remain necessary to capital accumulation and those who do or will not. Such are the dynamics of the message and the non-message, or (value-)form and formlessness.

9   THE DIGITAL ATLANTIC

Sondra Perry's Typhoon coming on

THE VALUE-MEDIATED DISTRIBUTION of prospects is mapped across the Atlantic and the computing machine in Sondra Perry's *Typhoon coming on*. The version of that work displayed at the Serpentine Sackler Gallery in London in early 2018 includes a single-channel digital video composed of two animated seascapes that the artist created using the Ocean Modifier tool in the 3D graphics suite Blender and projected in series around the gallery's perimeter. The first of these seascapes is colored purple to match Blender's "missing texture" warning. The second is based on a high-resolution scan of J. M. W. Turner's *Slave Ship* (originally titled *Slavers Throwing Overboard the Dead and Dying—Typhoon Coming On*) of 1840, from which Perry extracted and animated the parts of the canvas that depict the "empty" ocean.

Turner's *Slave Ship* is in part based on the infamous 1781 massacre in which the crew of the slave ship *Zong* murdered more than 130 enslaved Africans by throwing them overboard after a series of navigational errors led to a shortage of potable water. The insurance policy taken out by the Liverpool-based Gregson slave-trading syndicate in advance of the *Zong*'s journey covered the value ascribed to "cargo" lost at sea, but not that of enslaved people who died onboard due to illness, dehydration, or malnutrition. Hence the decision to throw them overboard. As Baucom and Bhandar have both argued, in addition to exemplifying the violence of Atlantic slavery and serving as a cornerstone of liberal abolitionist narratives, the *Zong* massacre and the subsequent legal case *Gregson v. Gilbert* represent key moments in the history of economic abstraction and racialized violence that continues to unfold in the present.[1] By projecting Turner's ocean around the gallery, Perry extends and intensifies

Figure 6. Sondra Perry, *Typhoon coming on.*

his spatialized emplotment of the spectator in the afterlife of the Middle Passage.[2] And by removing the ship, the manacled, drowning bodies, the fish and birds, the sky and sun, and the distant storm, she underscores the structural separation of modern, computational forms of personhood and finance from the direct racialized violence that birthed them and that continues to modulate them. But *Typhoon coming on* doesn't only consist of the *Slave Ship* animation, and to focus on this brilliant sequence in isolation is to risk missing the informatic ground of the piece's two "empty" oceans and, by extension, the connections those oceans make between digitality, value, and racialized violence.[3] Indeed, Perry has insisted on the centrality of the Ocean Modifier software to the conceptual and political armature of *Typhoon coming on;* for her, the tool "encompasses so many things that are true," most significantly "the ocean, ocean-as-modifier in the African diaspora, the thing that changed, or flipped everything over."[4] The ocean-as-modifier that changed "everything" is an ocean that has already been conceptually and practically formatted as a "smooth" space for the circulation of value and an "elemental" space for the risk-based calculations of possession and speculative finance. Which is to say, it is an ocean that has already been rendered formless and then digitized. This is why the techniques of scanning, editing, animation, and modeling are as important to *Typhoon coming on* as the presence of Turner's *Slave Ship*. Together, the two animations link the informatics of value and the digital imaginaries they precede and inform to chattel slavery, coloniality, and the differential production of upgradable and obsolete life that grounds the most recent iterations of the digital-liberal subject.

In the *Slave Ship* sequence, computational tools make legible the interface between abstraction and concreteness. By removing the ship and the drowning bodies, leaving only animated waves constructed from the light-dappled water of Turner's canvas, Perry figures modernity's foundational technologies of abstraction through the digitized and manipulated form of the painting. If the erasure of historical violence becomes manifest through the explicit, software-enabled absence of the ship and the bodies—as Nora N. Khan has pointed out, we do not see them, but we know they are there—the scanned, digitized, edited, animated, and projected appearance of Turner's ocean stages the loss inherent to abstraction, the exclusions that always occur when a concrete thing is computed.[5] It makes visible the reduction that occurs every time a body or thing is computed as a commodity, every time a box is computed as a byte, and every time labor power is computed as socially necessary labor time. At the same time, it shows how this reduction is a precondition for the manipulability—or *fungibility*—of the now digitized object, which can be edited, composited, and animated precisely because it has first been rendered numerically, just as the fungibility that adheres to chattel slaves, as commodities and as the basis of financial speculation, relies on their prior rendering as exchange value.[6]

The network of relations through which these processes of reduction and transformation are enacted appears in mediated form in the purple wave sequence. Here, the animated ocean does not begin with the capture of a preexisting object. It originates in the computer. If the ocean in the *Slave Ship* sequence is the outcome of a series of computational abstractions from a concrete object, the purple ocean appears a model with no such "original" referent. To paraphrase Galloway's formulation of the difference between photography and computation, the purple wave images are not *of* the world but *on* the world.[7] In this respect, the relation of the modeled waves to any actually existing body of water, or to an actually existing painting of water, is analogous to that between the value network and the world of concrete social relations. In this realm, the ships and the bodies of the shipped aren't excluded, cut out of representation with editing tools like the "unupgradable" labor that is cut out of the valorization process in Wiener's account of shifting organic composition. In the ontology of the model, if it is not generated in the software, *it does not exist.* To exist in this realm, a concrete body or thing must be digitized and thus subject to exchange, transformation, and animation.[8] By saturating the modeled waves with the color of the missing texture warning, Perry deploys Blender's operational grammar to make legible the value-informatic processes of dispossession, differential integration, and the intermittent allocation of prospects. The texture that is missing might be that of the non-value-mediated social weave that, as in Édouard Glissant's formulation, is obscured by the liberal-capitalist optic with its fixation on making transparent the "nature of its components."[9]

Baucom's close reading of *Slave Ship* centers on his claim that Turner appropriated a specific synthesis of "actuarial and melancholy historicism" from the diagram of the *Brooks* slave ship that follows a passage on the impossibility of directly representing the suffering of those imprisoned in the hold in one of his sources, Thomas Clarkson's *History of the Rise, Progress, and Accomplishment of the Abolition of the African*

Slave-Trade by the British Parliament of 1808.[10] What Turner takes from the *Brooks* diagram, Baucom argues, is not a pictorial style but a specific technique for addressing viewers whose senses have been conditioned by the mediated outcomes of economic abstraction. In other words, the diagram is directed at the complex of sympathy and technocratic rationality that comprises the liberal-humanist subject. And, consequently, so is Turner's painting. What *Slave Ship* makes visible, Baucom argues, is not the *Zong* massacre as such but "the very mind of romantic liberalism, contemplating such things" as that massacre and the institution whose violence it exemplifies.[11] Its rendering of fact as sentiment connects the "high solitary mind of the artist" to that of the viewer.[12] I'd like to suggest that this makes *Slave Ship* a digital image long before it became possible to remediate it with digital camera or scanner. It was digital from the moment of its conception, produced by and for a sensorium whose parameters are shaped by the informatics of value.

And this is why neither diagram, nor painting, nor close reading of the painting can visualize the informatic processes connecting the subjectivity that produces them and their projected audiences to the technologies of coloniality and slavery.[13] In its alternating presentations of the "pure" space of informatics and the eliminative process through which concrete objects are captured and represented in that space, *Typhoon coming on* insists upon a history of digital abstraction that is grounded not in the computer but in the informatics of value, or the differential computation of living labor and its reproduction. Rather than measuring the gap between the value network's abstract form and its concrete effects against the communicational ideal of the humanly used human, as Wiener does, Perry's projections underscore the differential valuation of life through which the informatics of value produce a range of racialized, gendered, and capacitated forms that includes but is not limited to that of the "full" human. Each sequence figures one "level" of the system through which difference is produced and deployed by the informatics of value: as capacity calculated against "the anticipated and capitalized surplus-value or profit that is to be extracted," and as dysselection, abject formlessness, and vulnerability to premature death in the concrete space that is determined by but not representable within the value network.[14] By wrapping these alternating sequences around the spectator, *Typhoon coming on* does two things. It presents the selected, digital-liberal, "upgradable" person—the contemporary iteration of the "mind of romantic liberalism," standing in or walking around a digital media art exhibition at a gallery sponsored by an exemplarily predatory pharmaceuticals company—with the conditions of its formation and maintenance. And through the tangibility of omission and the visible mark of the missing texture it attests to the persistence of those who "simply cannot be upgraded" in spite of and against conditions of value-informatic personhood.

10 REDUNDANT LIFE

Intellectual Workers and Street Nuisances

ALONGSIDE THE DISRUPTIVE CAPITALIST and the startup entrepreneur, the linked figures of the user and the upgradable laborer are exemplary manifestations of the digital-liberal person in the context of so-called deindustrialization. From the conjoined perspectives of the computer network and the value network, these figures demonstrate the capacity to connect reliably, to "transmit" with a high "bandwidth," and to traverse the open mesh of possibilities that Wiener names formless democracy. Those "who simply cannot be upgraded," which is to say, those whose reproduction is not reliably facilitated by the informatics of value, are collected into discrete, interlinked categories, each of which connotes proximity to an abject formlessness that threatens the transparency, autonomy, and spontaneous interconnection upon which formless democracy thrives. What I hope to show with this formulation is that the explicitly informatic complex of connection, flexibility, and freedom that shapes contemporary digital imaginaries emerges historically through racial-capitalist dynamics. And to do that, it is necessary to sketch a genealogy of value-informatic formlessness.

Processes of colonial expansion and exploitation, in Fanon's words, required natives be represented as "not only the absence of values, but also the negation of values," as a "deforming element" that operated upon "all that has to do with beauty or morality."[1] And, as Peter Linebaugh and Marcus Rediker show in their comprehensive study of the "dispossessed commoners, transported felons, indentured servants, religious radicals, pirates, urban laborers, soldiers, sailors, and African slaves" collectively depicted between the seventeenth century and the nineteenth century as an uncontrollable hydra, this "disfiguring element" attests to the problem of disciplining populations that cannot or will not be accommodated by directly value-mediated social relations.[2] By collapsing the groups it encompasses into a "chaos" that must be overcome in the creation of "social order," the hydra analogy superimposes and reveals the structural relationships and divergences between a social division of labor that must encompass multiple practices, skills, products, and regions and the taxonomical production of "different creatures, of gender, of race, of ethnicity, or geography, and of species."[3] At times the formless chaos is associated with intentional refusal and rebellion; as Cedric Robinson writes, "the forms that Black resistance assumed were incomprehensible" to European witnesses of slave rebellions, who "fell easily into whatever language was on hand to evoke mystery: the participants in Black resistance were seen as having reverted to savagery; were under the influence of satanic madmen; had passed beyond the threshold of sanity."[4] Elsewhere, it is understood to arise from a kind of malevolent stasis; consider, for example, the indignant letter to the *Times* dated November 21, 1857, gleefully reproduced in the *Grundrisse*, which attributes a monstrous destructiveness to the "free blacks of Jamaica" who "content themselves to produce only what is strictly necessary for their own consumption," "regard loafing itself . . . as the real luxury article," "don't give a damn about sugar and the fixed capital invested in the plantations," and "react with malicious pleasure and sardonic smiles when a planter goes to ruin."[5] In each case, enforced, intentional, or accidental deviation from value-mediated social relations gets represented as a corrosive formlessness that requires the application of plantation management, work discipline, state power, colonial governmentality, carceral violence, and a range of other formalizing technologies.[6]

Georges Bataille writes that the formless thing "does not, in any sense whatever, possess rights, and everywhere gets crushed like a spider or an earthworm."[7] But if the processes that give rise to abject formlessness are located within the informatics of value, those marked as formless are equally likely to exist in a state of suspension or oscillation, not crushed but maintained in a condition of precarious subsistence through underemployment, biopolitical management, consumer debt, or incarceration. In this respect, abject formlessness mirrors the information-theoretical concept of noise. As Weaver shows in his précis of Shannon's "Mathematical Theory of Communication," the quantification of information as "freedom of choice" from a field of possible alternatives constructs noise not as the opposite of information but as an increase in the size of the total information field that entails a greater chance of error or distortion in the transmitted message. Every message is a selection from the field of alternatives that noise comprises.[8] But noise can distort the message, introducing the possibility of errors at the receiver stage. Put simply, noise is a precondition that threatens clean transmission. Or, it is integral to the synthesis of reliable circuits from unreliable elements.[9] The threshold between noise as precondition and noise as threat precisely reproduces the dispossessive bifurcation of formless democracy and abject formlessness, or selected and dysselected life. Like noise, the formlessness of the non-value-mediated population connotes the possibility of future integration and expansion even as it is filtered and marked as deviant in the determination and elevation of form.[10] Perhaps this identity between value-informatic formlessness and information-theoretical noise explains why surplus populations are so often associated with excessive, discordant sound.

In 1864, Charles Babbage—advocate of labor rationalization, designer of computing machines, and early exponent of digital philosophy—published a twenty-five-page pamphlet on the street musicians he regarded as a "positive nuisance to a very considerable portion of the inhabitants of London."[11] Street music, Babbage complains, "robs the industrious man of his time," "annoys the musical man by its intolerable badness," "irritates the invalid," "deprives the patient, who at great inconvenience has visited London for the best medical advice," and "destroys the time and energies of all the intellectual classes of society by its continual interruptions of their pursuits."[12] His public campaign against street musicians had by the time of his writing only increased his "celebrity" and thus the frequency and vigor of performances in front of his London home.[13] "Street Nuisances" comprises an exasperated report on that turn of events, a detailed taxonomy of the instruments, musicians, and audiences associated with street music, an estimation of work hours lost to sonic distraction, and an appeal for protection in the form of doubled police numbers. If the "intellectual classes of society" represent an early iteration of upgradable labor, Babbage's pamphlet amounts to a historical record of how the formlessness attached to surplus life has been positioned as a direct threat to that labor since the earliest years of digital machine computation.

In 1829, Babbage purchased a house in Dorset Street, in Marylebone, with the intention of developing his analytical engine. The "extensive plot of land" that came with this house would accommodate the necessary

1. Air gun	1
2. Window sash warping	1
3. Frost	1
4. Crowd	1
5. Frame badly made	1
6. Dog	1
7. Slate from roof	1
8. Bottle of soda water burst	1
9. Cart shaking window	1
10. Door opening causing package to fall	1
11. Iron bar falling	1
12. Board falling	2
13. Shutting window	2
14. Rioters	2
15. Dressing shop window	2
16. Men repairing the road	2
17. Thieves entering premises	3
18. Stones kicked up by horses or cattle	3
19. Persons throwing various things	3
20. Sash rope of window breaking	5
21. Opening shop	5
22. Package in window falling	6
23. Cord or hook of fanlight giving way	6
24. Settlement of building	7
25. Horses, sheep, or cattle running against	7
26. Blind falling	9
27. Opening door too wide or violently	9
28. Cart, carriage, or truck ran against	10
29. Wilfully (three imprisoned)	12
30. Slamming door or window	12
31. Drunken men, women, or boys	14
32. Gas	15
33. Cleaning windows	16
34. Boys throwing stones at each other	16
35. Men fell through	18
36. Pushing against it	19
37. Violence of wind	32
38. Shutter falling	43
39. Pair of steps or other things falling against	50
40. Persons throwing stones	55
41. Unknown	68
Total	464

Figure 7. Charles Babbage, "Table of the Relative Frequency of Occurrence of the Causes of Breaking Plate Glass Windows." Source: *Mechanics' Magazine* 66 (1867).

offices and workshops, and the "very quiet locality" would enable him to conduct experiments and produce drawings undisturbed. A little over fifty years earlier, Marylebone had been one of the principal locations of the impoverished lascars and formerly enslaved or indentured Africans collectively named in liberal relief efforts as the "black poor." The disastrous 1787 attempt at "resettlement" in Sierra Leone partly explains the abundant space, low property prices, and quiet atmosphere Babbage found in 1829. Perhaps it was these same conditions that from the early 1850s saw the area "invaded" first by a hackney-coach stand and then by "coffee-shops," "beer-shops," and "lodging-houses," all of which attracted a "new population" whose character "may be inferred from the taste they exhibit for the noisiest and most discordant music."[14] Even this very brief history of the area reveals that, among other things, "Street Nuisances" belongs to a genealogy of the feelings, sentiments, and expectations that subtend and are reshaped by tech-driven gentrification; three years later, Babbage would apply comparable methods in an article on the causes of broken plate glass that might similarly be placed in the genealogy of broken windows policing and the computational methods of predictive policing that build on it.

Although Babbage notes in passing that the "new population" of Marylebone had reduced the value of his property, he is more concerned by the "one hundred and sixty five instances" across eighty days in which his work on the analytical engine—including times when he "was giving instructions to . . . workmen relative to some of the most difficult parts"— was interrupted by street music.[15] Overall, he estimates that a full quarter of his working power "had been destroyed by the nuisance." And 25 percent "is rather too large an additional income-tax upon the brain of the intellectual workers of this country, to be levied by permission of the Government, and squandered upon its most worthless classes."[16] It is this capacity to transfer the affectability of the "worthless classes" to the minds of "intellectual workers" that makes street music a threat significant enough to warrant a doubling of police numbers. The tables of people that Babbage presents in "Street Nuisances" with the same mathematical certainty as his calculation of "lost" work hours show how the externalization of that affectability onto bearers of devalued social reproduction both marks surplus populations as formless and produces discrete racialized and gendered abstractions.

To enumerate the facts of his case, Babbage first presents a table of the "*Instruments of torture permitted by the Government to be in daily and nightly use in the streets of London.*" Recall that a taste for the "discordant music" produced by those instruments functions for Babbage as a measure of the defectiveness of Marylebone's "new population." Value-informatic form fosters a taste for certain aesthetic forms. The formless only derive pleasure from aesthetic formlessness. And who are the formless? Although intolerable to "intellectual workers" such as inventors of computing machines, Babbage observes to his chagrin that the "discordant noises" found "great encouragers" among "the lower classes of society," "people from the country," and "ladies of elastic virtue and cosmopolitan tendencies, to whom it affords a decent excuse for displaying their fascinations at their own open windows."[17]

Babbage's description of street music's pauperized, feminized, and criminalized "encouragers" is notable for its similarity to the extraordinary depiction of the "public, common, or tramping gang" that appears three years later in the first volume of *Capital*. Largely composed of children and young adults recruited by a gang-master to perform piece work for "large scale farmers," the gang exhibits features of the stagnant and the pauperized parts of the surplus population. In Marx's description,

> Coarse freedom, noisy jollity and the obscenest kind of impertinence give attractions to the gang. Generally the gang-master pays up in a public house; then he returns home at the head of the procession of gang members, reeling drunk, and propped up on either side by a stalwart virago, while children and young persons bring up the rear, boisterously, and singing mocking and bawdy songs. On the return journey what Fourier calls

Instruments of torture permitted by the Government to be in daily and nightly use in the streets of London.

Organs.		Bagpipes.
Brass bands.		Accordions.
Fiddles.		Halfpenny whistles.
Harps.		Tom-toms.
Harpsichords.		Trumpets.
Hurdy-gurdies.	The human	Shouting out objects for sale.
Flageolets	voice in	Religious canting.
Drums.	various forms.	Psalm-singing.

Figure 8. From Charles Babbage, *Passages from the Life of a Philosopher* (1864).

Encouragers of Street Music.

Tavern-keepers.	Ladies of doubtful virtue.
Public-houses.	
Gin-shops.	Occasionally titled ladies;
Beer-shops.	but these are almost in-
Coffee-shops.	variably of recent eleva-
Servants.	vation, and deficient in
Children.	that taste which their sex
Visitors from the country.	usually possess.

Figure 9. From Charles Babbage, *Passages from the Life of a Philosopher* (1864).

"*phanerogamie*" is the order of the day. Girls of 13 and 14 are commonly made pregnant by their male companions of the same age. The open villages, which supply the contingents for the gangs, become Sodoms and Gomorrahs, and have twice as high a rate of illegitimacy as the rest of the kingdom. . . . Their children, when opium does not finish them off entirely, are born recruits for the gang.[18]

This image is not derived from experience. Marx directly lifts it, and in several instances the exact language in which he paints it, from the sixth report of the Children's Employment Commission, published in March 1867. Although the passage establishes a foundational relationship between partial connection or nonconnection and the attribution of bawdiness, impertinence, unproductive consumption, and pathologically aberrant sexuality, it does so by reproducing (rather than dissolving) norms of moral and sexual propriety that are grounded in that same relationship.[19] In other words, Marx is able to forensically locate the production, the structural function, and the social positioning of the surplus population vis-à-vis the informatics of value, but he is unable to grasp the ways in which the norms the gang appears to transgress are determined by those mechanisms. Coarse freedom and noisy jollity, boisterous movements, and "mocking and bawdy songs" might otherwise be understood as life-making practices that take place beneath or outside the network that differentially allocates value to living "components."

Babbage's lists of instruments and "encouragers" show how the noise exemplified by street music connotes underemployment, pathological sexuality, outlawed reproduction, and frivolity, all of which threaten the productive activities of the "upgradable" intellectual worker. The next

MUSICAL PERFORMERS.

Musicians.	*Instruments.*
Italians . . .	Organs.
Germans . . .	Brass bands.
Natives of India . .	Tom-toms.
English . . .	Brass bands, fiddles, &c.
The lowest class of clubs	Bands with double drum.

Figure 10. From Charles Babbage, *Passages from the Life of a Philosopher* (1864).

table shows how the characteristics associated with formlessness are encoded on the bodies of the surplus population, producing racialized distinctions. A comparison between Babbage's list and the accounts of street musicians in Henry Mayhew's *London Labour and the London Poor* suggests that the last of these classifications, "the lowest class of clubs," denotes not African musicians but blackface performers, or "Ethiopian serenaders."[20] One of Mayhew's interviewees reports that the "Westminster school" of serenaders performed with kettledrums and never sang. Given the location of Babbage's property, this would have been the form of minstrelsy he most often encountered—and this likely explains his reference to the "double-drum" rather than the ensemble of banjo, tambourine, fiddle, and bones associated with "Ethiopian serenaders" elsewhere.[21] An article on minstrelsy in the *Saturday Review* three years earlier states that following the success of Thomas D. Rice's blackface shows in the mid-1830s, "a band of black musicians became as necessary an appurtenance of the London streets as Punch's show or a barrel organ, much to the discomfiture of lovers of quiet in general, and of Dr. Babbage in particular."[22] The same article notes how blackface performers "lost no time in publishing portraits of themselves, with the white faces bestowed on them by nature" and "styled themselves 'Ethiopian Serenaders'" in order to distance themselves from slavery and thus from the "suspicion that they had the least drop of black blood in their veins." But it appears that these efforts, which are clearly animated by the "well-established doctrine that to call a white person 'Black' is to defame" them that Harris identifies as "the direct manifestation of the law's legitimation of whiteness as reputation," made little difference to Babbage.²³ By deviating from the national designations through which he itemizes the "English" who often performed the "Ethiopian serenader" role and the "Natives of India" who accompanied the formerly enslaved in the liberal-reformist category of the "black poor," he deploys blackface—and, by extension, blackness—as a metonym for absolute dispossession. Which is to say, he deploys it as a sign of the "lowest form" of affectable life and thus the greatest threat to those who seek to use their "time and energies" productively.

For Babbage, "street nuisance" is the sonic mark of a racialized and feminized urban surplus, a category of disordered sound that is intolerable to intellectual workers but finds enthusiasts among pauperized immigrants, sex workers, drunkards, beggars, and street children. Or, it is an aural manifestation of attenuated social reproduction. Read in the context of his work on computing machinery, Babbage's disgust at this sound and the populations it indexes represents an early trace of the connection between digital-liberal imaginaries and the longer history of ascriptive processes grounded in the informatics of value.

Even before he moved to Marylebone, Babbage wrote with great enthusiasm of how his intellectual labors would render other forms of labor superfluous. In an 1822 letter to Sir Humphry Davy, the president of the Royal Society, he sets out the now-familiar argument that machinery could substitute for the "lowest operations of the human intellect," mitigate some of the "evil" represented by errors arising from "persons employed," and free those with the capacity for higher pursuits from "intolerable labour and frightful monotony."²⁴ But there is a sleight of hand here, as there is in the recent spate of automation-as-luxury-communism fantasies. Freedom from some practical element of work does not mean freedom from the obligation to work in order to meet basic needs. And, with this imperative to earn a living in mind, recall Babbage's comments, presented ten years after the Davy letter in *On the Economy of Machinery and Manufactures*, that machinery, the kind of machinery whose design was interrupted by the sound of the street musicians, represents a check against the manual and moral imprecision inherent in the labor of dispossessed persons. As I have argued above, dispossession and market dependence—the phenomena that produce and maintain the imperative to work—represent a form of social automation. On the one hand, automatic machinery militates against and thus rests on assumptions about the deviations inherent in living labor; on the other hand, dispossession and market dependence militate against the desire on the part of actual or potential living labor to run away, to live otherwise, beyond productive and reproductive respectability, without the need for wages or indirectly mediated connections to the wage. If machinery automates a greater or lesser part of the labor process, the complex of dispossession and market dependence automates the supply of abstract labor.

Babbage's missive against street music reveals how ascriptive processes take place in the space that is torn open by dispossession but not fully stitched back together by the value-mediated integration of living labor. And it shows how fantasies of upgradable labor stand at the hinge of those interdependent but not entirely aligned value-informatic mechanisms. With that said, the complaint he sets out in "Street Nuisances" is worth reiterating in a longer historical trajectory. Babbage's text represents the imagined interests of a class of intellectual workers against the sensory affront posed by the existence of racialized and feminized surplus populations—populations whose spiraling growth and presence in cities will be metonymically figured (if not directly caused) by the automatic machinery that results from the intellectual workers' activities. Placed in this trajectory, "Street Nuisances" clarifies the genealogical relationship between the figure of the "intellectual" laborer, the emergence of digitality, and the abjection of bodies whose capacity to reproduce themselves has been attenuated by the same processes that form others as upgradable. The music of "intolerable badness" that appears in Babbage's text might be understood as the *sound of unupgradability,* the sound of the dysselected, the sound of the redundant, or the sound of those positioned beyond productive and reproductive respectability.[25] And its capacity to destroy the productive time of intellectual or upgradable workers might be understood as a refusal of the historical conditions that inform such workers by dividing them from their affectable others.

Which is to say that there is another way to understand the sound Babbage finds so intolerable: as a register of the social-reproductive practices that, whether by desire or compulsion, fall outside the conditions of transparency, self-possession, and upgradability that the informatics of value differentially allocate. Tadiar has compellingly formulated the range of "bodily, perceptual, affective, and imaginative capacities and practices of life-making" that occur "beneath the level of the field of exchange on which the abstract value of life-times is determined and negotiated."[26] Such capacities, practices, and occurrences are weighed upon but not fully determined by the informatics of value. They are too often abjected in critiques of the conditions that produce them. But their suppression does not amount to their obliteration. Aspirations "that are wildly utopian, derelict to capitalism, and antithetical to its attendant discourse of Man" tend to be "in excess of legibility and of the law." But this doesn't mean that they did or do not exist.

Echoing Tadiar's theorization of the capacities and life-making practices that obtain around life-times of disposability, Hartman warns against the overly rapid assimilation of these aspirations that are "in excess of legibility and the law" as instances of "revolutionary longing."[27] Instead, she identifies them as "forms of care, intimacy, and sustenance" that are both necessitated by and exploited under racialized capitalism, but which remain neither "reducible to or exhausted by it." The impossibility of assimilating such practices to "the template or grid of the black worker," she continues, is as important as the ways that they "nourish the latent text of the fugitive."[28] This impossibility makes it clear that living "in excess of legibility and the law" means living beyond value-mediated connection and, as a result, in close proximity to the violence required to balance the informatics of value. Hartman emphasizes the informatic character of that which corresponds to "legibility and law," remaining transparent through proximity to the value network, when she names as a requirement for reckoning with the unrecoverable pasts it produces "the imperative to respect black noise."[29]

This imperative animates Hartman's extraordinary critical fabulation of the "wayward" life of Esther Brown. Pieced together from materials collected in inmate case files at the Bedford Hills Correctional Facility for Women in Westchester County, New York, Brown's life exemplifies for Hartman the "collaboration and genius" and the revolutionary impulses that inhere beyond the value network's productive-reproductive circuits. At the same time, Hartman's method attests to the fact that Brown's life cannot be grasped as collaborative, genius, or revolutionary either from the digital-liberal perspective or from those that privilege formal relations of exchange even while calling for their abolition.[30]

Brown was arrested for vagrancy on July 17, 1917. That indictment, Hartman notes, encompasses—gives legal form to—a multitude of practices, tendencies, and desires that are only intelligible within the value-mediated imaginary as incorrigibility, recalcitrance, and formless reproduction. Deployed in the afterlife of and as a surrogate for chattel slavery, vagrancy represents a legal-imaginative technology for criminalizing what Wiener would later understand as life that "simply cannot be upgraded." Marx only half grasps this, as he is unable to consider racialization or normative sex and gender ascription as effects of value-informatic social formation. Wiener cannot even half grasp it; he figures the unupgradable population as nothing other than site of inevitable suffering, a burden to be "carried" or eliminated. The charge of vagrancy, as deployed to discipline black women like Esther Brown, seeks to encompass while remaining unable to comprehend "wild thoughts, reckless dreams, interminable protests, spontaneous strikes, nonparticipation, willfulness, and boldfaced refusal." It seeks to contain the redistribution of needs and wants and the lines of escape from debt and duty, any of which might constitute "a path elsewhere."[31] Defined against value-informatic imperatives of transparency, accumulation, and reproductive respectability, the activities collected and rendered both formless and opaque by the legal charge of vagrancy entail "not doing, withholding, non-participation, the refusal to be settled or bound by contract to husband or employer."[32] Such activities entail the refusal of valorizable form *and* the refusal of the specific kinds of ascribed formlessness that are determined by and in opposition to that form.

Hartman describes Brown's relationship to directly and indirectly value-mediated work in the following terms: "Esther Brown hated to work, the conditions of work as much as the very idea of work. Her reasons for quitting said as much. Housework: *Wages too small.* Laundry work: *Too hard.* Ran away. General Housework: *Tired of work.* Laundress: *Too hard.* Sewing buttons on shirts: *Tired of work.* Dishwasher: *Tired of work.* Housework: *Man too cross.* Live-in-service: I might as well be a slave."[33] It is this hatred, arising not from some essential property that precedes dispossession, pauperization, and differential valuation but from a clear understanding of how those processes make life unbearable, that registers upon senses that have been conditioned by the informatics of value as atonal and disordered sound. Newspaper reports of a December 1919 rebellion in Lowell Cottage—one of the five buildings reserved for black inmates at Bedford Hills—describe the prisoners' activities as a "noise strike," a "sonic revolt," an "uproarious din" that "smote the ears of the investigators before they got within sight of the building."[34]

11   ANATOMIZING "FREEDOM"

Carceral Digitality

IN 1932, THE NEW YORK TRAINING SCHOOL FOR GIRLS at Hudson, New York—a reformatory that held Esther Brown some years before her arrest and incarceration at Bedford Hills—was used by the social scientists J. L. Moreno and Helen H. Jennings as a laboratory for their pursuit of the reticular "*law of social gravity.*"[1] The work Moreno and Jennings conducted at Hudson was central to the development of sociometry, the method for mapping and optimizing social interactions that informs today's digital-nomadic ideals of productively "spontaneous" organization.[2] Ben Waber, president and CEO of Humanyze (formerly Sociometric Solutions), a behavioral analytics company that uses interaction tracking via sociometric badges to "uncover and improve how work gets done," places the method at the heart of the postindustrial economy, positing workers whose interactions are volitional and spontaneous as "happier," "more loyal," and "more productive."[3] In noting that "Google has really been out front" in understanding that "the biggest driver of performance ... is serendipitous interaction," Waber reproduces the image of inhuman use that anchors Wiener's 1950 book; for him, Google is "the antithesis of the old factory model, where people were just cogs in a machine."[4] Sociometry, then, might be understood as a technology for planning spontaneous interconnection, or anatomizing and optimizing the post-Fordist social body. In this respect, the name "Humanyze" is quite literal: it develops technologies for the human use of human beings. Moreno and Jennings's work at Hudson discloses the carceral violence upon which this explicitly reticular elaboration of social relations is premised.

In this chapter, I argue that Moreno and Jennings's work at Hudson belongs to a history of procedures through which those criminalized for trying to live beyond the value network are deployed as raw material for experiments directed at improving the health and productivity of "free" persons. These procedures entail a complex series of mediations; those for whom connection to the value network is impeded or attenuated are simultaneously marked as incorrigibly formless and regarded as sufficiently similar to those who connect more fully to avail insights about how the latter's productive and reproductive activities might be optimized. Responding to the crowds that would frequently confront surgeons and their advocates and suppliers in order to prevent them from taking bodies from the gallows to the anatomy theater, Bernard Mandeville wrote in 1725 that "the superstitious Reverence of the vulgar for a corpse, even of a Malefactor, and the strong aversion they have against dissecting them, are prejudicial to the publick."[5] Prejudicial, he continued, because "Health and sound Limbs are the most considerable of all Temporal Blessings, so we ought to encourage the improvement of Physick and Surgery." And improvement in those fields requires a ready supply of bodies because knowledge of anatomy is "inseparable from Studies of either," it being "most impossible for a Man to understand the Inside of our Bodies without having seen several of them skillfully dissected."[6]

Reading *An Enquiry into the Causes of the Frequent Executions at Tyburn* with Federici's account of the role of anatomy in the conceptual and practical transformation of proletarianized bodies into productive machines, it becomes clear that Mandeville is arguing that malefactors— "persons of no possessions of their own" who try to live beyond the value network—could be made productive by yielding knowledge pertaining to the synthesis of reliable circuits from the unreliable "free."[7] The practices of knowledge extraction derived from this principle have taken many forms. As Spillers and C. Riley Snorton have shown, by the mid-nineteenth century, the intimate medical observation of living slaves—most notably in gynecology—represented a practice of experimentation on captive, ungendered "objects" understood to share sexed physical characteristics with "free," gendered subjects.[8] Mandeville's *Enquiry* and the histories discussed by Spillers and Snorton disclose a general principle undergirding practices of experimentation on those marked with abject formlessness and devalued social form: that the knowledge derived from those practices will be used not to improve the circumstances of those experimented upon or the conditions of the communities from which they are taken, but instead to intensify the efficiency and precision with which "free" persons could be integrated into value-mediated circuits of production and reproduction.[9] Moreno and Jennings's study at Hudson should be understood as a manifestation of the same tendency, overtly directed toward the production and optimization of "flexible," "creative," or "upgradable" labor and, as I will show, covertly grounded in the problem of how to improve the efficiency and reliability with which feminized and racialized people can be deployed to perform underwaged service work.

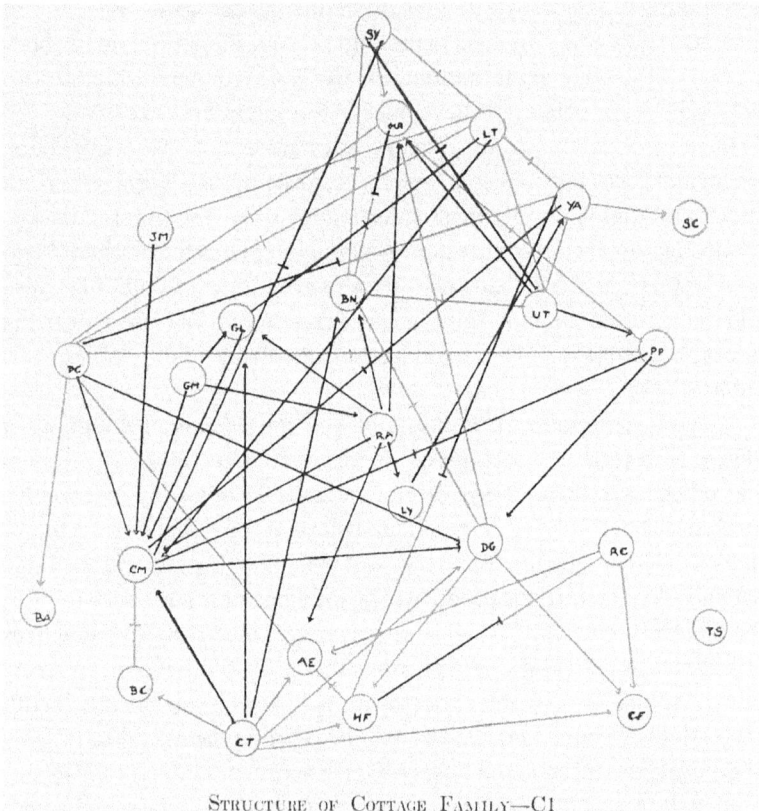

STRUCTURE OF COTTAGE FAMILY—C1

24 girls. *Isolated,* 5; *Pairs,* 5; *Mutual Rejections,* 3; *Chains,* 1; *Triangles,* 3; *Squares,* 1; *Circles,* 1; *Stars* (of *Attraction*), 1; *Centers of Rejections,* 1. *Distribution,* 58% *Attractions;* 42% *Rejections.*

Sociogram on p. 88 is here in an advanced stage of study. To the choices the responses are plotted.

Type of organization: extroverted.

Figure 11. Sociometric diagram of cottage group at Hudson. Source: J. L. Moreno, *Who Shall Survive?* (1934).

In *Who Shall Survive?*, his 1934 account of the Hudson study, Moreno writes that sociometric principles structure every kind of social group, "irrespective of its membership."[10] In the expanded 1953 edition of *Who Shall Survive?*, he attempts to thicken this claim by positing four "sociometric universalia."[11] In both editions, the diagram of interactions that sociometric analysis produces is posited as the naturally occurring shape of the social as such. Acquaintance groups and "social atoms"—"special" groups, exemplified by the "nuclear part of a family"—connect to form a larger network in which "cultural atoms" distribute "universal roles." The larger network is held together by communications networks, but those networks are formed in the image of the underlying sociometric network, not vice versa. For Moreno and Jennings, as for value, *the real is reticular.*

Indeed, Moreno explicitly defines sociometry against Freudian psychoanalysis and Marxism, writing that he and Jennings were seeking "a therapeutic procedure that does not center primarily in the idea of sublimation but which leaves man in the state in which he is spontaneously inclined to be and to join the groups he is spontaneously inclined to join." Whereas other methods "forcibly transgress the development of individuals and groups" in order to identify some psychic or economic determinant, sociometry posits social structure as an outcome of "spontaneous strivings" that occur naturally and are blocked only when the network of emotional currents and the dominant form of social interaction become accidentally misaligned.[12] The repetition of *spontaneous* across early and more recent celebrations of sociometry only emphasizes the continuity between that method and the ideal form of value-mediated social synthesis that is implied in the shape of the sociometric diagram. Moreno and Jennings understand optimal social structure as arising not from some artificial system of organization and representation—the value network, the law, power, the sociometric method—but from the uncoerced activities of free individuals. Accordingly, the sociometric concept of social change comprises four elements, all of which emphasize the untrammeled agency of self-possessed subjects: the "spontaneity-creativity potential of the group"; "the parts of the universal sociometric matrix relevant to its dynamics"; the "values it seeks to overcome"; and the values it aspires to fulfill.[13] Yet the socially synthetic effects of the spontaneity, creativity, universality, and intentionality that inhere in the sociometric image of the human could only be studied under laboratory conditions at Hudson, a site at which young women were confined when their social practices and modes of life-making were judged by police and courts to not correspond to value-informatic norms of reproductive respectability.[14] And they were only studied there because those charged with running the school sought to make it even more difficult for inmates to run away.

Following preliminary investigations at an "Italian colony" near Vienna between 1915 and 1918, Moreno and Jennings began their sociometric studies at public and private schools in New York. In the course of these studies they found that the impossibility of tracking connections beyond the school walls led to problems of "artificiality." For a fuller inquiry, Moreno writes, they would have to follow the subjects to their neighborhoods and families, and that lay "beyond the present possibility of scientific integration." The "complex loomed too large and too intricate."[15] Moreno and Jennings were invited to Hudson in 1932 after Fannie French Morse, the school's director, attended a talk by Moreno in which he detailed work on a system of prisoner classification at Sing Sing.[16] Morse, an exemplary liberal-humanist pedagogue who sought to develop through education and training "a humanized and socialized community where the ways of freedom guided [the child] through the day in every detail of life," hoped sociometry would curtail a spate of runaways.[17] Moreno and Jennings saw in the school an opportunity to develop the sociometric method in a community of five hundred to six hundred persons, a site in which, according to their understanding, "all collectives flourish—home, school, work, cultural—interlocked one with another, and at the same time which as a whole is cut off to a great extent from the population at large so that currents which might flow from without into it could be discounted without too great an error."[18] Inspired by the foundation of biogenetics in "a few carefully thought-out breeding experiments," Moreno and Jennings worked on the principle that "however unique a certain concrete sample of population may be, the methods and techniques gained in the course of investigation will be universal."[19]

In other words, Moreno and Jennings saw Hudson as a closed system that would allow them to observe formal dynamics "valid for every kind of grouping irrespective of the membership."[20] In that system, the bulk of their work consisted of conducting sociometric tests in which each inmate was asked to rank a set number of others she was attracted to and repelled by in her cottage and work groups; producing network diagrams for the cottages and work groups based on the data from the sociometric tests; ascertaining from each individual the "motivations" behind her attractions and repulsions; conducting a spontaneity test in which each

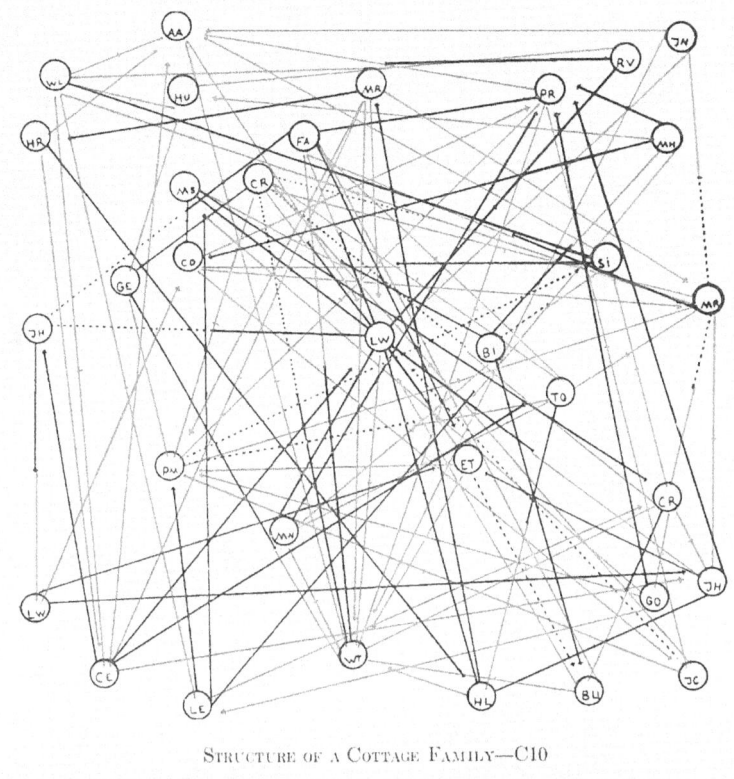

STRUCTURE OF A COTTAGE FAMILY—C10

33 individuals; isolated 4; mutual pairs 31; mutual rejections 8; incompatible 12; chains 2; triangles 2; stars 7.

Distribution, 66% Attractions, 34% Rejections.

Type of organization: introverted and inward aggressive.

Figure 12. Sociometric diagram of cottage group. Source: Moreno, *Who Shall Survive?*.

person is placed in front of each of her choices and asked to "throw yourself into a state of emotion towards X" and to "maintain that emotion throughout" while her partner receives "no instruction except to react as [she] would in real life to the attitude expressed towards [her] by the subject"; and producing diagrams and lexical analyses of the spontaneity tests.[21] Based on these tests and visualizations, they proposed changes to the inmates' distribution across the cottages and work groups designed to maximize each individual's connectivity, spontaneity, and work efficiency. In Moreno's narrative, the histories of pauperization, differential valuation,

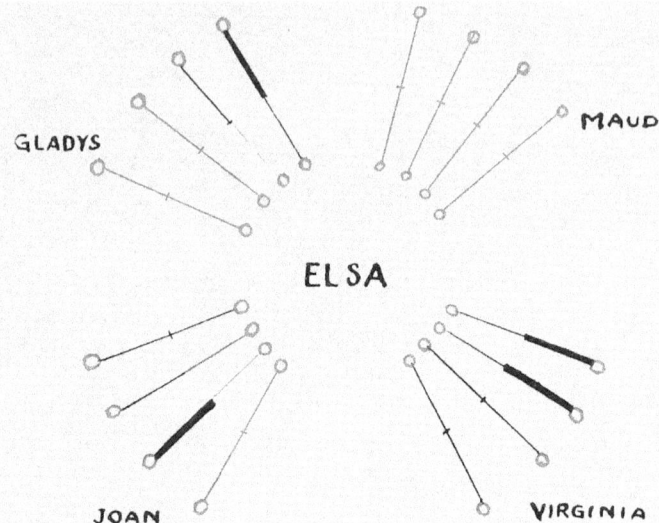

Fig. 3. Spontaneity Test. Elsa, the subject. The chart visualizes the findings of the Spontaneity Test comprising 32 situations in 16 of which Elsa took the lead four times each towards Maud, towards Virginia, towards Joan, and towards Gladys, and in the other 16 of which each of the four girls, Maud, Virginia, Joan, Gladys, each separately took the lead towards Elsa in four different situations. For description of eight of the different situations of the present Spontaneity Test see pp. 178–82. On the chart a red line indicates that *sympathy* was produced towards the opposite partner by the individual taking the lead; a green line, that *fear* was produced; a thin black line, that *anger* was produced; a heavy black line, that *dominance* was produced. Each situation is separately plotted.

The sociometric test had revealed all four individuals to be chosen by Elsa but to be rejecting her. See Fig. 2. Spontaneity Tests of Elsa in respect to these individuals and of these individuals in respect to Elsa further clarify and differentiate the relation existing between them, as plotted in the chart above. We recognize that the rejection of Elsa by Maud, Gladys, Joan, and Virginia has a different weight in each case and that her choosing of them has also a different weight in each case. Spontaneity Tests of Elsa and Maud show each of the two girls producing sympathy towards the other, although Maud had rejected Elsa in the sociometric test on the criterion of living in proximity. Elsa persistently demonstrates displeasure towards Virginia although she had chosen her and Virginia rejects Elsa both in the sociometric test and the Spontaneity Tests. The relations existing between Elsa and Joan and between Elsa and Gladys are shown to be more complex, none of the three demonstrating unmixed feelings. The states produced by Elsa towards Gladys and by Gladys towards Elsa are shown to be split, Gladys producing sympathy in half her tests towards Elsa and displeasure in the other half, Elsa reacting similarly. Lastly, in one Spontaneity Test out of four, Joan demonstrates sympathy towards Elsa and in two out of four Elsa demonstrates displeasure towards Joan.

Figure 13. Spontaneity test diagram. Source: Moreno, *Who Shall Survive?*.

and criminalization that led to the existence of the school and the inmates' presence in it appear only faintly, as if irrelevant to the immediate project of diagnosing the causes of the runaways and the longer-term project of identifying and learning how to optimize the productive dynamics of an emergent social structure. On one occasion he makes passing reference to the fact that the inmates were "sent from every part of New York by the courts" to "remain in Hudson for several years until their training has been completed."[22] Later he itemizes the reasons why it is difficult for the "girls who come to a community like Hudson" to "feel at home": the absence of "the natural bond" characteristic of a "successful family group," the absence of a "feeling of individual liberty and possession," and the absence of a "feeling of permanent arrangements and objectives."[23]

Absence of the "natural bond" of the "successful family," or reproductive respectability. Absence of "the feeling of individual liberty and possession," or the value-mediated sensibility of the possessive individual. Absence of "permanent arrangements and objectives," or homeostatic reproduction and work discipline. These absences, which Moreno offers as *explanations* for the breakdown of social connections *at* Hudson, might instead be understood as *reasons why inmates were sent there in the first place*. Each speaks of "not doing, withholding, non-participation, the refusal to be settled or bound by contract to husband or employer"—the justifications for the charge of vagrancy that Hartman identifies. Each speaks of the refusal of form and of the form-determined attribution of abject formlessness. Traces of this refusal are visible throughout *Who Shall Survive?*—for example, in the 249 choices (9.5 percent of the total) that remained unused on the test slips—but Moreno treats them in a distinctly ahistorical manner, as faults whose causes are less important than their effects on the network. This inability to see refusal, recalcitrance, and isolation as outlawed forms of social reproduction whose practitioners are fully cognizant of the reticular social ideal is visible throughout Moreno's account of the school.

The clearest evidence of this inability comes when Moreno posits the "epidemic of runaways" that started in the autumn of 1932 as *proof* of the existence of "sociometric universalia." First, he establishes the difference between those who are predisposed to running away and those who are not based on a sociometric classification: potential runaways are those who lack attachments within their cottage group, are "cut off and blocked from" connections to the larger community, and who may

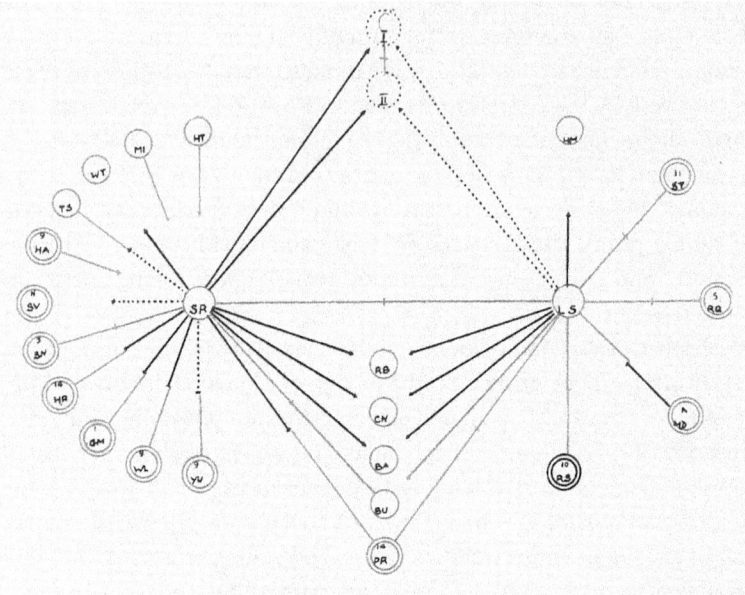

A Runaway Pair, SR and LS

The sociogram indicates mutual attraction between SR and LS. Except for the relation of SR to BU, they form an *isolated* pair in their cottage. Both reject RB, CN, and BA, girls in the same cottage. BU, whom SR likes, is also liked by LS. SR rejects I (the housemother) and II (the kitchen supervisor) and LS is indifferent to them. LS forms mutual pairs with individuals in other cottages, RQ in C5, ST in C11, and RS, a colored girl, in C10. SR is indifferent to or rejects attractions coming from outside the home group, YU of C9, WL of C9, GM of C1, HR of C14, but is attracted to SN of C5, of whom she makes an exception. Towards members of her own group (aside from LS) she is indifferent (HT, MI, WT, and TS). Both girls, SR and LS, appear cut off from the main currents and blocked, isolated and limited to each other. SR is attracted to a man outside in the community who in turn is attracted to her (not plotted on this chart) and this persisting attraction finally precipitated the running away of both girls. It can be seen that their position within the community of Hudson predisposed to this action as they had no resistance to overcome, being not a part of the community.

Figure 14. Runaway pair. Source: Moreno, *Who Shall Survive?*.

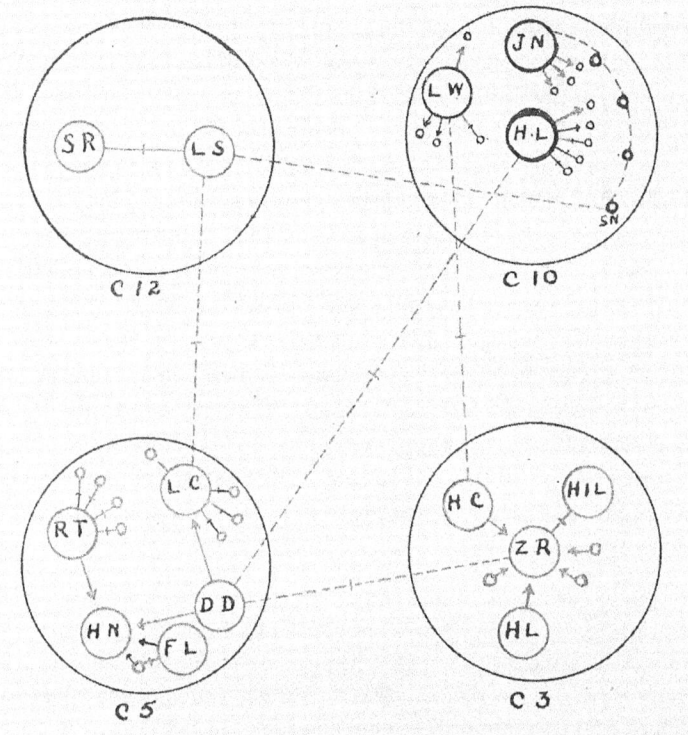

A RUNAWAY CHAIN

14 individuals comprise four sets of runaways. The positions of the sets are seen to be as follows: Set in C12, SR and LS are an isolated pair; set in C5 are interrelated and all except RT show unadjusted positions; set in C3, ZR, center of attractions of 7 individuals, a mutual pair with HIL, and attractive to HC and HL; set in C10, LW, HL, and JN, each isolated but interrelated by indirection. The interrelations between the sets are seen to be as follows: LS in C12 forms a mutual pair with LC from C5; DD in C5 is interrelated to ZR in C3; HC in C3 is interrelated to LW in C10; further, LS in C12 is interrelated with SN in C10, who, while not a participant with the set, is in a chain relation to JN in C10; also DD from C5 forms a pair with HL of C10.

Figure 15. Runaway chain. Source: Moreno, *Who Shall Survive?*.

run away "on sudden impulse."[24] The potential runaway is in every case a discrete type, defined by limited or nonexistent connection. And the solution is thus to "tune" the sociometric arrangement, developing "motivations for attachment" as "preventive measures."[25]

After identifiying through the sociometric method "far more individuals" predisposed to running away than the number that actually did run away, Moreno hypothesizes that the difference between those who ran away and those who did not can be attributed to hidden or overlooked networks "of which these 14 [runaway] girls were a part and from which the rest who were equally predisposed were left out."[26] For Moreno, the runaways prove that even when an individual appears unconnected to the larger social group, there is always an underlying sociometric network. Drawing explicitly on the language of electrical engineering, Moreno then attributes the switch from potential to actual runaway to the movement of a "current."[27] Having established these linked notions of the hidden network and the current running between the individuals it comprises, Moreno sets out an extraordinary theorization of the "runaway chain" and its conclusion. In so doing, he details a series of measures that limit instances of escape—but only to show why potential runaways don't always run away:

> The described runaway chain broke off on November 14th after 14 girls had run away. As the networks to which they belonged consisted of 94 members, 80 more girls were touched by the current and 13 of them were considered potential runaway cases if the intensity of the current had continued with equal strength and if no resistance had developed. But three instances can be considered to have contributed to stop it. One is the added watchfulness of the officers the larger the number of escapes became. Another is that the last set of runaways in the chain came from [cottage] C10, which is a colored group, and it is just there where the network is thinnest. The chances that from there new impetus would come was poor, as few contacts went from C10 to other parts of the community. Just as an electric current has differences in density within a circuit, also a psychological current has differences in a network. Finally, the two girls who started the chain had been returned to the school from their cottage, C12, on November 4th, five days after their escape. Their failure and disappointment associated with it ran now rapidly through the same network and caught the same individuals who had received an impetus before. It produced, thus, an anti-climax. It would not stop the running away of the set in C3, who escaped the next day, but it may have contained and delayed the set in C10 and stopped many potential developments.[28]

Moreno mentions three concrete measures that impede runaways: the presence and watchfulness of the officers; the segregation of the school, which the sociometric tests showed produced the "thinnest" network around the "colored" cottage C10; and the practices for capturing and returning runaways to the school, which, like the activities of the officers, are never detailed. But in Moreno's account, both the categorical distinction between potential runaway and "content" inmate and the naturalized logic of the attachments and connections that comprise social life at Hudson and everywhere else—remember that these are supposed to result from *universal laws*—remain unquestioned. The potential runaway remains a discrete outcome of an imperfectly understood and thus suboptimally managed social graph. Indeed, instances of escape are presented as the result of the universal sociometric laws reasserting themselves between suboptimally connected inmates at a level that was not yet legible to Moreno and Jennings's analysis, and thus as events that provide valuable insights into hitherto undetected aspects of those laws. What remains unthinkable within this framework is the possibility that the desire to run away is shared by the whole population of Hudson—that the sociometrically detectable mechanisms of placement in and attachment to the "community" are maintained by police, law, and officers, and that the networks of escape are in fact planned or spontaneous responses to the violently imposed artificiality of sociometric attachments.

At the root of the social graph and the notion of "formless democracy," then, lies the enclosure of lives that by accident, indifference, or design do not correspond to value-informatic protocols. In the sociometric imaginary, the enclosed population can be modeled and made productive according to the same universal laws that produce normative forms of spontaneous organization among the non-surplus.[29] The difference is only manifested concretely, in the likelihood of meeting basic needs without being incarcerated or killed. The technologies that bring these differentiated social forms into relations of commensurability make it possible to valorize the surplus population at a remove, by deploying it as raw material through which principles for the optimization of the "free" can be experimentally verified. The logic that subtends this sociometric imaginary while masking its basic relations of unfreedom becomes strikingly apparent when, reflecting on the universality of sociometric networks toward the end of his discussion of the "runaway chain," Moreno notes that those networks and the currents that flow through them are what make possible "the condition of free and independent life" that is the "privilege" of "such communities as have reached the heights of complexity and differentiation."³⁰ According to this logic, because hidden networks can be identified among the potential and actual runaways in a carceral site, the members of those groups must be understood as having been produced by the same conditions that make possible "free and independent life." It is here worth recalling that the mechanism that comprises dispossession and market dependence is precisely a means of both "freeing" people and stopping them from running away. Yet the only cause of unfreedom, according to the sociometric optic, is a lack of "constancy and differentiation." Incarceration, the logics of form and abjection that lead to incarceration, and the myriad causes of the desire to run away that are essential to those logics are thus formulated as *not impeding freedom and independent life*. Wanting (or needing) to run away is reformulated not as an attempt to "live free" (as Hartman puts it) but as evidence that the reticular ideal of freedom—that barely mediated version of the value-informatic logic of spontaneous interconnection and its permitted modes of formless democracy—persists in every situation as the true form of human sociality.³¹

In the 1953 edition of *Who Shall Survive?*, Moreno further clarifies the relationship between the use of Hudson as a laboratory for developing techniques of social optimization and the longer history of value-informatic sociality that grounds the sociometric imaginary. After reiterating the idea of Hudson as a small, self-contained model of community in general, Moreno notes that although rearranging the cottages based on evidence of mutual attraction reduced the number of runaways, it was also necessary to develop methods to ensure "adjustment later in the community at large."³² To this end, he identifies a set of techniques for "training social spontaneity."³³ It is here that the studies at Hudson most clearly connect the mechanics of value-mediated freedom to the fantasies of flexible, upgradable labor and post-Fordist accumulation in which social spontaneity—the capacity to take on, dissolve, and remake form— represents the most elevated virtue. And, just as in Wiener's account of colonial dispossession as formless possibility, the ideal of spontaneous emergence is shown to rest upon a settler imaginary. "The early American frontier," Moreno writes, "was a spontaneous movement of people" made possible by "the availability of vast unsettled territory." The movement of those people was initially constrained only by "the barriers of nature," but "industrial and cultural patterns" have come to impose additional limits.

In the earlier period of spontaneous movement "there was either rough equality or the inequalities which develop as natural expressions of individual and group differences."[34] Moreno's wish is for spontaneity training to facilitate a return to the psychic state that arises in the course of settler-colonial expansion. This return will serve as a protection against the "enfeebling" of "instinctual spontaneity" by a "crystallized social or economic structure"—a structure in which inequalities "cease to be a natural expression of the organic individual differences, physical or mental," and in which "the superior individual may find himself, due to circumstances which are beyond his control, in a social situation which is in total discord with his capabilities."[35]

As these remarks on "natural" or "organic individual differences" and "the superior individual" predict, Moreno's communication-theoretical formulation of reticular sociality ends in a Darwinian–Malthusian opposition between "creative" and superfluous persons that is strikingly similar to Wiener's formulation of upgradable labor and "that which simply cannot be upgraded." In book 6 of the 1953 edition of *Who Shall Survive?*, the answer to the question posed in the book's title is the "creative" human who will survive the automation-driven superfluization of manual labor—or "competition with the robot."[36] And then the Darwinian-Malthusian distinction appears: "The solution to the conflict of human superfluity," Moreno writes,

> lies in a heroic measure, not to surrender to the machine, not to halt its development, but to meet it on even terms and to resort in this battle to resources which are inherent within [the human] organism. Beyond the controversy, destruction of the unfit or survival of the fit, is a new goal, the survival of a flexible, spontaneous personality make-up, the survival of the creator.[37]

Moreno's response to the question "Who shall survive?" is that "*everyone should survive.*"[38] Who composes the "everyone" in this formulation? His earlier celebration of the "vast unsettled territory" that made possible the unconstrained realization of spontaneous personhood provides part of the answer: those who lived on and pursued social relations with and through that "empty" land before colonization do not exist, or do not exist as persons within the category "everyone," and thus would not survive. The gradated conditions of survival within the class "everyone" are equally revealing. Survival means adopting the "flexible, spontaneous personality make-up" that crystallizes around the form of value-informatic personhood. In other words, the route to inclusion in the "everyone" that shall survive is quite simple: *be more like us*.[39] The implications of this are starkly drawn when Moreno engages with the eugenicist Francis Galton's "idea to improve man," adding only the proviso that "eugenic measures" should seek to "improve what is worth improving" rather than "what just happens to survive in the battle of existence."[40] Refusing or failing to attain a form of personhood that contains "what is worth improving" leads to the abject formlessness of the surplus population, which arises through processes that cannot be visualized by the sociometric optic. The spontaneous-creative capacity that is fostered and optimized through sociometry—and by the informatics of value that precede it and the

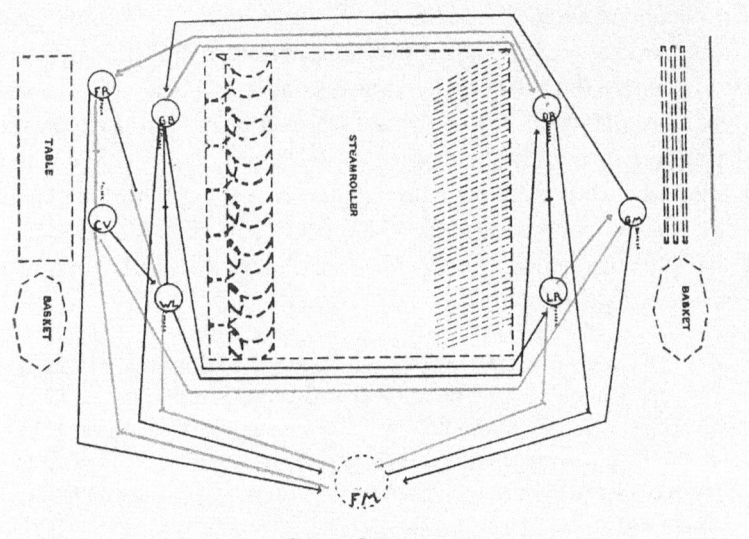

STEAM LAUNDRY

Fig. 1. 7 workers and 1 forewoman. Stella DR and Philamina LR, the feeders, reject each other. Hilda GR and Myrtle WL, the catchers, reject each other. Myrtle rejects the feeder opposite her, Philamina. Lillian FR and Rosalie CV, the two folders, attract each other. Lillian and Rosalie reject Myrtle. Esther GM, the shaker, is attracted to Lillian and rejects Hilda. Esther, Stella, Hilda, and Rosalie reject the forewoman but only Stella is rejected by her. Philamina, Myrtle, and Lillian are attracted to the forewoman. The seven workers live in C10, but all of them are not plotted on the particular sociogram of C10, p. 125, because many of them came to the community at a later date.

Figure 16. Steam laundry. Source: Moreno, *Who Shall Survive?*.

modes of digitality that succeed it—both requires and disavows its reliance on conditions that make settler-colonial occupation and sites like Hudson appear necessary. Its putative universality rests on and reproduces the assumption that populations confined in such sites are always already shaped by—and will always be better off within—the same informatic structure whose differential allocation of social form led to their incarceration.

The structural reality of the bifurcations sociometry obscures can be glimpsed when Moreno qualifies the universal attainability of survival through a distinction between the "*zootechnical animal*" and the "*creator*." Whereas creators will produce "a new race of men" who "triumph over the robot," zootechnical animals will be unable to transcend the "conserved and conserving environment" of industrial technologies and will become like "insects." Both can survive, Moreno insists, but "races of men fit for the one may be unfit for the other."[41] Reading these formulations alongside Wiener and Babbage, it is clear that the zootechnical animal—the entity that lacks the flexibility and creativity required to transcend the role of component or energy source within a larger technological system—is precisely the unupgradable laborer whose survival under deindustrialization can only be imagined as an increase in social waste. The workroom studies Moreno and Jennings conducted at Hudson point toward how the gradations within and limits of Moreno's "everyone" and Wiener's human will develop toward the uberization of production and service labor. Because although Moreno posits Hudson as nothing other than a closed system within which the "sociometric universalia" can be identified and optimized, the workroom studies model an application of rationalizing technologies to feminized and racialized labor that belies the ostensible universality of reticular personhood.

In Moreno's description of the workrooms at Hudson, it becomes clear that the amplification of the "universal" social capacity—a capacity he consistently associates with spontaneous-creative personhood—takes place through an optimization of social dynamics that is partly directed at eliminating recalcitrance in the coerced and unwaged performance of service labor. At the school, each inmate was assigned housework within her cottage and a work assignment outside it. According to Moreno and Jennings's analysis, when the majority of a group "attach their emotional interest mainly to individuals outside their group," the result "is a potential condition which may easily release disturbances of this function through lack of precision in work, superficiality of performance, tardiness, etc."⁴² Relatedly, Moreno suggests that an organization in which too many members reject the housemother or foreman would evidence "regression in the work executed accompanied by open rebellion."⁴³ The sociometric studies of the workrooms aimed to reduce imprecision, superficiality, tardiness, regression, and rebellion—or what Babbage called "the inattention, the idleness, or the knavery of human agents"—by tracking and rearranging the social currents.

In the steam laundry, Moreno recalls, workers were divided into those who fed items into the roller, those who caught the items as they exited the roller, and those who folded the items after receiving them from the catchers. Moreno writes that "mutually attracted pairs . . . are the most efficient of the workers," while antagonism between specific pairs "had the most upsetting effect upon the work process and the cooperation of the group" because, by quarreling with each other, they "failed to feed the [steam roller] evenly, delayed the feeding, or fell out of sync, leading to the machine becoming clogged."⁴⁴ The sociometric imaginary that today measures, reproduces, and elevates the flexibility and creative capacities of the upgradable laborer doesn't only emerge from experimental studies in a carceral site, then. It emerges through studies of the relationship between "spontaneous" group dynamics and the precision, efficiency, and dutifulness with which inmates performed compulsory, unwaged domestic labor within such a site.

And both the diagnosis of the causes of "lack of precision in work, superficiality of performance, [and] tardiness" and the sociometric methods that would remedy them are premised on the same logic of differentiation that informs Moreno's subsequent definition of the "zootechnical animal." In their studies, Moreno and Jennings identified "predisposing grounds for serious disturbance" among the "colored work groups" on the basis of a high level of antagonism among the feeders, catchers, and folders and between all of them and the forewoman.⁴⁵

How does Moreno explain this predisposition to disturbance? Throughout *Who Shall Survive?*, he naturalizes racialized differences by positing sociometric optimization as the solution to differentials that are only ever articulated as the raw material for the development of universal laws—for example, when he proffers a hypothetical scenario in which "a group of negroes migrates into a white community" whose members have been desiring cheap labor and more leisure time, leading to a "warm social current."⁴⁶ But his description of the steam laundry "disturbances"

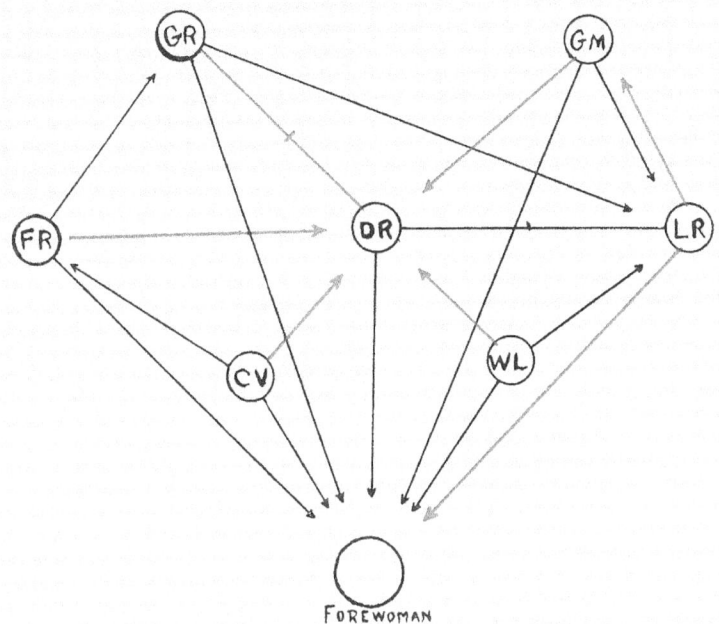

Fig. 2. Stella DR has gained a position of greater influence. In Fig. 1 she is the object of one attraction, Hilda GR; now she is the center of five attractions: Hilda GR, Myrtle WL, Lilliam FR, Rosalie CV, Esther GM, and forms with Hilda a pair. She is rejected by Philamina LR whom she rejects in return. In Fig. 1 the forewoman is rejected by four workers, now she is rejected by all but Philamina LR. The influence of Stella DR is apparent in the concentrated opposition against the forewoman. (See Chapter on Race.)

Figure 17. Steam laundry. Source: Moreno, *Who Shall Survive?*.

is a checklist of willfulness, recalcitrance, affectability, incapacity, and incorrigibility:

> Stella persisted in working as her mood dictated,—often too rapidly or too slowly for Philamina to cooperate with her. Then, on the other side of the machine, Hilda and Myrtle, the catchers, were rushed and confused or simply idle. Sometimes after quarrels with Philamina she stopped working altogether. At other times she fed the machine too many articles at once, ran around it, and grabbed them before they could become caught and tie up the machine. But in doing this she made such a game of the process by tossing her hands into the rolling hot machine that she endangered herself.

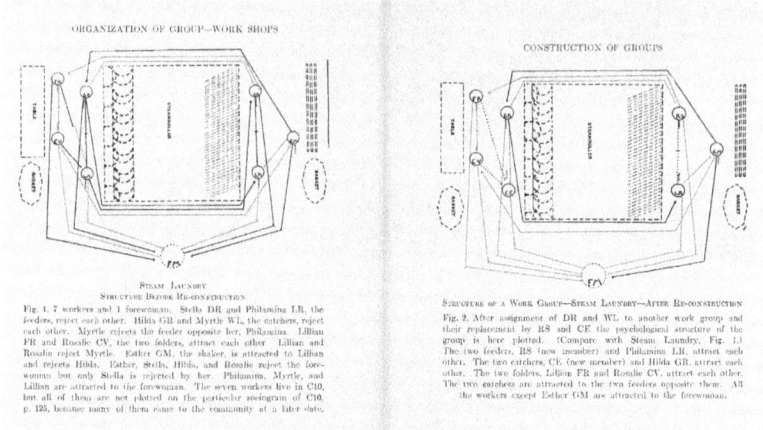

Figure 18. Steam laundry reconfiguration. Source: Moreno, *Who Shall Survive?*.

The solution Moreno and Jennings implemented consisted not of some subtle reorientation of currents, as mandated in the principles of sociometric optimization they elaborate elsewhere, but of "the removal of Stella DR, who had become the leader of a gang among the workers in the steam laundry, and of her collaborator, Myrtle WL, from the laundry to another work group where a better adjustment for them was expected."[47] To value-informatic senses, the racialization and feminization of labor precedes and cannot be modified by reticular optimization strategies. For all of Moreno's insistence on the universality of creative capacity, the steam laundry studies show how sociometry is used to optimize the activity of what he would later name zootechnical animals by removing overly affectable or unreliable "components."

As an alternative explanation for the disinterest and open rebellion that can only appear to the sociometrically trained eye as a failure of spontaneous interconnection, recall Hartman's summary of Esther Brown's responses to the kinds of work that were accessible to her, and which exemplified the illusory promise of freedom and protection: "Housework: *Wages too small.* Laundry work: *Too hard.* Ran away. General Housework: *Tired of work.* Laundress: *Too hard.* Sewing buttons on shirts: *Tired of work.* Dishwasher: *Tired of work.* Housework: *Man too cross.* Live-in-service: I might as well be a slave."[48] Yet service labor—particularly in fragmented or "flexible" forms—becomes one of the dominant media of waged life in the age of so-called post-Fordism, especially for those marked as unupgradable. The form of this labor, "detailed piece-service work, assigned to people at particular, instantly scheduled (just-in-time or 'on demand') times," requires "serendipitous interaction" just as the Googleplex does.[49] The difference lies in whether the motor of that interaction is primarily intelligible as creative capacity or as the imperative to scratch together the means of subsistence from multiple, insufficiently waged tasks.

12 THE CYBERNETICS OF CAPACITY

R. S. Hunt's "Two Kinds of Work"

IN HIS MEDIA HISTORY OF THE DIGITAL SERVER, Markus Krajewski compellingly traces "the structural terrain of informatics" to the "absolute metaphor" of the domestic servant.[1] In Krajewski's argument, the most significant of the conceptual and terminological continuities between human and computing machine are to be found in the expectations directed at those who appear dedicated to serving another.[2] Unlike a "stock metaphor" like the virtual desktop, examination of which might involve a history of files and folders and their integration into graphical user interfaces, the absolute metaphor of the server comprises processes that remain practically and logically stable when transferred from humans to machines: waiting, attending, granting access, delivering or withholding messages, and, most importantly, operating out of sight, so that users and masters need encounter nothing of the lower-level processes that their servants perform.[3]

The transfer of these functions from humans to machines is a principal concern of Krajewski's *The Server*, whose cast of proto-computational actors encompasses dumbwaiters, lazy Susans, and railways for conveying food from kitchen to dining room as well as maids, butlers, valets, and cooks. For the most part, Krajewski directs his focus at the practices, techniques, and expectations that represent "key media practices of subalternality."[4] The value relation and the forms it imprints on and through social life remain mostly absent from this inquiry save for a passing, tantalizing reference to wages as the "software" of the employer-employee system.[5] But Krajewski's analysis nonetheless reveals a great deal about the relations among labor, reproduction, and digitality whose effects I have been tracking across this book. And it is because of this proximity that I find a methodological note toward the start of the book quite intriguing. At the level of abstraction at which the continuities between (human) servant and (machine) server become apparent, Krajewski writes, "particular kind[s] of difference are cancelled out, and others are foregrounded." Because of this, he continues, his "media archaeology of the contemporary service society" must move "entirely away" from "questions of gender difference and any historical lines that follow from that fundamental distinction," the "current phenomena of global migration of service employees," and "the illegal exploitation of work relations."[6]

This methodological indifference to the production and operationalization of difference explains a glaring omission in Krajewski's depiction of Thomas Jefferson's Monticello residence as a "network" comprising "circulating doors, dumbwaiters, moveable tables as well as human beings such as cooks, maids, and footmen."[7] Krajewski suggests that Jefferson's mistrust of "silent domestics" hastened the construction of that network. But absent from his litany of domestic technologies are the enslaved people whose deployment as commodities and sources of labor made networks of commodities, "free" laborers, and property-owning statesmen possible, and whose legal classification amplified the property-bound notion of personhood through which the master's distrust of his "servants" takes shape.[8] In some contrast to Krajewski's account, Reinhold Martin itemizes the ways that Monticello's architecture was shaped not around the relationship of employer to waged domestic servant but by that of owner to slave: the widths of the corridors from parlor to bedroom and from kitchen to dining room index the differentiation of "Jeffersonian bodies carrying nothing heavier than a book" from slaves transporting food between kitchen and dining room; the "noise-canceling device of the dumbwaiter" functioned to "minimize the disorder that would have reigned had slaves from below mingled too regularly with dinner guests above"; and a system of boxes, pulleys, and shelves allowed dinner guests to "serve themselves in the knowledge that their conversation was not being overheard" while "slaves in the wine cellar below could provide the French wine necessary for American enlightenment without interrupting the meal with their bodily, aural presence."[9] As Martin points out, the sociotechnical infrastructure at Monticello rests on and reproduces a "partition of the human species."[10] And this partition reveals the historical knot of racialized differentiation, biopolitical violence, and service labor whose full implications are rendered opaque when Krajewski substitutes unnamed and implicitly waged servants for Sally Hemings in a chilling (and chillingly passing) acknowledgment that Jefferson sought to get rid of male domestics but "not the women, whom he seeks out for other purposes."[11]

I am less interested in the existence of the elisions media archaeology sanctions than I am in their methodological justification. Are the production, differential integration, and global distribution of gendered and racialized social forms truly illegible at the level of abstraction required to find conceptual and practical continuities between service labor performed by humans and the operations of computing machinery? In the following pages I want to thicken an analysis that has run throughout this book by considering more closely the ways in which the processes that shape ascriptive differentiation can be located *within* (rather than across the threshold of) the value network. In order to do this, I examine an unpublished manuscript from 1947 in which what I have been theorizing as the informatics of value are treated quite literally, posited as natural phenomena that, once identified, make it possible to quantify and optimize certain relationships among actions, objects, ideas, affects, emotions, value, and money. At the heart of this manuscript is a definition of labor as informatic transmission that eliminates distinctions between different types of concrete activity and facilitates the quasi-automatic sorting of individual producers into particular roles on the basis of their imputed capacity. Consequently, it models how racialized and feminized differentiation appear from the value-informatic perspective: not as a qualitative difference between bodies or activities, but as a constituted association between those bodies and activities and an unreliable form—weak, intermittent, or temporary—of the "signal" borne by laborers to whom higher capacity has been imputed. Through a close reading of this text, I hope to sketch the unreliable component that emerges through value-informatic processes, grounds multiple ascriptive processes, and anchors the "contemporary service society."

The manuscript is titled "Two Kinds of Work." Its author, R. S. Hunt, a British technical editor who worked on "handbooks for fire-control computers," sent it to the Marxist biologist J. B. S. Haldane in January 1951 with an accompanying letter asking him to pass it to Wiener, who was visiting London at that time.[12] In that letter, Hunt describes the manuscript as a "screed, typical of many that I have written, which no one has ever read and probably no one ever will, but which at least maybe admitted as evidence of cybernetic enthusiasm."[13] Although he writes that "on paper [he had] nothing much to recommend [him]," he hoped that his elaboration of a "generalized theory of automatic devices" might lead either to an opportunity to study with Wiener at MIT or to paid employment "of a cybernetic nature."[14] Haldane did pass on the manuscript, but a return letter from Wiener's secretary, G. B. Baldwin, shows Hunt's prediction about its impact to have been accurate. Thirteen months after receiving it, Wiener had not yet looked at the manuscript, and he would "not have time in the near future to study it."[15] Furthermore, he was unable to offer any opportunities for employment or study. Baldwin suggests Hunt direct his inquiries about the latter to the dean of the graduate school at MIT.

After describing it as a "screed," Hunt goes on to claim that "Two Kinds of Work" elaborates nothing less than a technique for finding "the work (in the sense of mental energy) required to solve any task."[16] He writes:

> My aim has always been to put metaphysics within the scope of physics—it now is to physics as alchemy was to chemistry. I think I have succeeded, and that I could measure ethical quantities by the method of physical laboratories. Aesthetic qualities like violin tone have been so measured (Helmholtz did it) but not such quantities as beauty, virtue, and happiness. Will-power is another quantity I think I could measure, and by quite a simple servo arrangement.[17]

This passage suggests that the manuscript's principal import will be at the level of methodology—that it will show how cybernetic technologies make it possible to overcome the artificial division between physical, ethical, aesthetic, and affective phenomena. However, Hunt's suggestion that mental energy is the true content of every task, along with the telling implication that this form of "energy" can be *found* (rather than serving as a representational schema for something that has no properly material existence separate from the bodies and social arrangements that produce it), hint at a different aim. The similarities between these prescriptions and the concept of value as transhistorical substance that Marx identifies in bourgeois political economy point toward the true focus of Hunt's project.[18]

Although the letter to Haldane suggests that Hunt's manuscript was primarily intended to demonstrate its author's knowledge of and facility with the methods and terminology of information theory, it is neither a straightforward essay on the history and significance of that field nor a survey of specific techniques or technologies. It is a wide-ranging treatise that deploys cybernetic concepts, supported by references to the natural sciences, materialist philosophy, and computing, in order to quantify the value "content" conveyed by a range of qualitatively different activities.[19]

It might be best described as an information theory of value. Given the pivotal but invisibilized role of value mediation in his discussions of automation, labor, the human, and communicational freedom, Wiener might have gained something by reading it. Hunt's bibliography includes many of the foundational texts of information theory, from James Clerk Maxwell's Rede Lecture "The Telephone" (1878), to Herbert Nyquist's "Certain Factors Affecting Telegraph Speed" of 1924, to Shannon's "A Mathematical Theory of Communication." Although not a single work of economic theory appears among those texts, it is clear from the manuscript's opening sentences that the technological and philosophical matters Hunt raises in his letter to Haldane are for him inseparable from economic concerns. These sentences introduce concepts of "G-energy" and "G-work" as the cornerstones of a value-informatic economic theory. Hunt writes:

> The words "work", "energy", and "power" are defined in dictionaries. Though the definitions do not explicitly state it, there are two entirely different kinds of work, or energy. Energy definable in units such as the erg or foot-ton is here defined as A-energy. Energy not so definable, but verbally defined in a dictionary, will be defined as G-energy.
>
> Absence of any absolute units in which to measure G-energy is the most remarkable hiatus in human knowledge at the present time.
>
> By far the greater part of human activity consists in increasing the G-energy of material systems. Monetary conventions are an attempt to provide symbols representing the G-energy of the material systems for which they may be exchanged. All academic studies outside the pure and applied sciences are concerned with assessment of the G-energy of material systems, such as objects of art, or the merit of those who exert power which is not A-power, such as public speakers, military leaders, actors and musical virtuosi. . . .
>
> The industrial wage-bill is almost wholly in respect of G-work performed by employees. It is a rule of industrial management that a workman shall do a minimum of A-work, for that is more cheaply and readily done by a machine. . . . Having so little occasion to perform A-work, and not being paid for nothing, the workman is evidently paid for G-work done. He does in fact transform material systems from a more to a less probable, and from a less to a more costly condition. This is as true of mathematical symbols as of a piece of metal.[20]

In Hunt's system, "G" designates a type of energy that is distinct from that which is measurable in terms of force over distance, light, or heat. When transmitted into "material systems," this energy increases those systems' value. In addition to the metal and mathematical symbols Hunt mentions here, these "systems" include those in which the beauty, virtue, happiness, and willpower he mentions in the letter to Haldane circulate— or the substrates of so-called intellectual, creative, and aesthetic activities and, more significantly, service labor. In contrast to what Hunt defines as A-energy, or that which takes the form of heat, light, motion, and so on, and which is subject to the laws of thermodynamics, the principal effect of this transmission is to move the destination system "from a more to a less probable condition" (iv). The implications of this definition are clear, even if Hunt doesn't state them outright: to transmit G-energy is to impart form, and to impart form is to increase value. In Hunt's account, this takes place in a realm that is separate from but of equal historical and political-economic importance to that of A-energy.[21]

Hunt's theorization of G-energy as the transmission of form marks the point at which his "screed" departs from the nineteenth-century fantasy of labor without exhaustion whose emergence, Anson Rabinbach notes, was coeval with that of the modern concept of energy and constrained by the second law of thermodynamics.[22] By inventing the concept of G-energy in order to theorize work as the transfer of an abstract, form-bearing substance, Hunt seeks to reverse the nineteenth-century transformations through which dominant ideas of labor came to emphasize "the expenditure and deployment of energy as opposed to human will, moral purpose, or even technical skill."[23] And it is in trying to effect this reversal that he explicitly posits what is intuited and implied in Marx and explicated by Elson: that value, as an objectification of abstract labor that shapes social relations without direct coercion, appears informatic in character.

Recall that in the introduction to "Two Kinds of Work" Hunt states that he is pursuing his investigation into G-energy in order to determine the quality of—and thus to better quantify— labor's "content." In his system, money is a representation of computed G-energy, "an attempt to provide symbols representing the G-energy of the material systems for which they may be exchanged." But if this definition seems to align with classical labor theories of value, the subsequent suggestion that a commodity's value corresponds to the "accuracy with which it conforms to some ideal configuration" (7) reveals a desire to synthesize that species of theory with marginalist explanations of price. In his system, the price of a commodity arises from both the labor-derived abstraction encoded in it *and* the satisfaction it affords its purchaser, and this dual determination of price is made possible by the connection G-energy effects between labor and perception. This aspect of his definition of labor appears aligned with Marx's account of the simple form of the latter as "living, form-giving fire."[24] However, Hunt's informatic concept of value does away with some of the complications that are underscored in Marx's definition. In Marx, the notion of living, form-giving fire comprises abstract and concrete registers and implies that having a form is not a prerequisite for giving form. The latter may encompass the "asocial" entities that are frequently marked as formless through operations extending from the value network. By contrast, Hunt deploys the technical and terminological developments of computation and information theory to cement the exact ontological equivalence between the value extracted from labor (the process of giving form) and naturalized energetic phenomena (such as fire) that Marx subverts. The concept of G-energy thus allows Hunt to synthesize two of the major currents of liberal economics: classical labor theories of value, and the marginalist and neoclassical traditions. Or, his use of the G-energy concept to synthesize those currents shows that both were already shaped by the informatic logic through which value appears to naturally—spontaneously—operate.

Hunt goes on to argue that it only became possible to "discover" G-energy after the development of computing machines and information theory provided the conceptual frame required to distinguish it from (A-)energy and matter. In his elaboration, these epistemic conditions are bound to the practical possibility of automating processes that can be imagined as "thinking." Such "early devices as the 'spinning jenny' displaced men in alarming numbers," he writes, "but only, it seemed, in respect of mechanical abilities." Consequently, in the eighteenth century it proved impossible to understand weaving in informatic terms, as the transmission of G-energy. But when computing devices "invaded the domain of higher intelligence," making thought "definable in terms of an electronic circuit," it became possible to recognize and quantify all activity in G-energetic terms (4–5). Indeed, one of the most striking aspects of Hunt's manuscript is that it does not limit the informatic definition of labor to so-called intellectual or creative tasks. Hunt defines labor in general as the transfer of an informatic substance (G-energy) that sometimes requires "higher intelligence" and at other times manual operations. Labor becomes subject to a kind of retrospective continuity; it is rendered always already informatic. Living, form-giving fire is reconceived as the movement of electrons through relays and logic gates, encoders, channels, and receivers. And, for the first time, the informatics of value become visible in an information theory of labor.

The conceptual schema through which Hunt formulates labor as informatic transmission is centered on the *bedator*, which he defines as "any device able to perform G-work" (iv). The bedator, he writes, is the "G-physical analogue of the prime mover of A-physics" (7). According to this definition, a bedator is a source whose output moves a material system from a more to a less probable state, increasing its value. Immediately after advancing this definition, Hunt reiterates his claim that "the money changing hands in any transaction tends to be a measure of the G-energy in the systems involved" (7). From this perspective, it seems clear that G-work is simply labor, and the bedator is simply a laborer. And, by presenting the bedator as a source, he effectively posits G-energy transmission as a process dependent on that source's capacity rather than the system of relations between G-energy and the "material systems" in which it circulates. He goes on to state that a bedator can be "natural" or "artificial." And, in the introduction to "Two Kinds of Work," he states that the G-worker's (or bedator's) transformation of "material systems" from a "more to a less probable, and from a less to a more costly condition" is "as true of mathematical systems as of a piece of metal" (2). When these definitions and qualifications are put together, it appears that, by establishing a system of equivalences across manual, cognitive, affective, and intellectual labor performed by living things and machines, Hunt aims to specify the quantitative gradations necessary to optimize the purchase and allocation of G-energy.

After defining the bedator as the source of G-energy, Hunt makes a distinction between *cleverness* and *drive* that partially—but not exhaustively—maps onto variable and fixed capital. Whereas *drive* describes transmission without transformation, *cleverness* "implies a transformation in the mathematical form of the data handled" (8). A "sound-reproducer . . . may displace a hundred orchestral performers," Hunt writes, but because its "original input was obtained from a living orchestra" and because the "output" has the same form as the input (changes resulting from the production process notwithstanding), this piece of equipment "is credited with *drive*, ability to transmit data, but has zero cleverness" (8).[25] However, although "the living bedator falls short of the artificial in point of drive, and far surpasses it in cleverness," the distinction does not absolutely cleave to that between organic and artificial (8). In Hunt's schema, a mechanical telephone system exhibits both characteristics: "Its channel-selecting mechanism exhibits cleverness," while "its ability to transmit data through a selected channel is mere drive" (8). G-work, then, can involve cleverness and drive in different quantities. The former describes the degree of *selection* and *transformation* involved in a procedure, while the latter describes the degree of *projection*. Or, where a drive-bedator can transmit a fixed quantity of G-energy but does not increase it, a cleverness-bedator increases the magnitude of G-energy in the process of transmission.

As Hunt's analysis develops, it becomes clear that the commingling of fixed and variable capital in the bedator concept is designed to isolate and quantify not the "essence" of value-productive activity so much as the capacity of its bearer. This becomes apparent when he establishes a common medium for the transmission of "intellectual" and "manual" labor performed by humans, nonhuman animals, and machines. This medium is the bedator's "*internal communication system,* ICS" (7). Hunt admits that for a living bedator the ICS can be defined as "CNS (central nervous system)," but he is quick to state that in practice "ICS will serve for both" (7). The "basis for absolute measurement" of the G-energy a given bedator is able to transmit, then, rests upon the aggregate capacity of its ICS. Since "all non-random behaviour of bedators is due to a flow of data in some channel or channels of the ICS," the "performance of bedators may therefore be assessed in terms of channel-parameters." Each bedator is "limited" not by the protocols of exclusion and integration that place it within the circuits of G-energy circulation but "by a constant available G-power, expressible by speed (e.g. operations per second) times a function of accuracy or quality" (10). Capacity—that unmarked repository of differential valuation and the uneven distribution of survival chances—is coded as *bandwidth*.

From this point onward, Hunt formulates a series of tasks from the perspective of the demands they place on a bedator's ICS capacity, speed, accuracy, and quality. He first considers behaviors "interpretable as TS" (telegraph signal), or as a stream of discrete symbols. This category includes typing, various forms of marksmanship, radar operation, and the aggregate activities of mail delivery. Next, he considers behaviors interpretable as a CS (continuous signal): handwriting, speech, and servo behavior (26–28). But his figuration of productive activity as information processing is not limited to ballistics and communication. The most revealing of his formulations come in a passage from the TS section titled "G-power of Some Homely Tasks":

> The man-made bedator excels in such academic exercises as the evaluation of functions, but boggles at more homely tasks. No really satisfactory ~~hop~~ potato-harvester has been devised, and no hop-picker seems to have been contemplated.
> The hop-picker's q [ratio of unsuccessful to successful actions] is the number of volume elements within reach of his hand such as might contain a hop, divided by the number that (on the average) do contain a hop. The number of unsuccessful attempts to pick a hop is a measure of p [PFO—probability of false operation], and θ [PRF—pulse recurrence frequency] is to be measured in hop/sec. . . .
> The same considerations apply to potato-harvesting.
> The humble task of threading a needle puts the bedator on something like full load. . . . PFO is high, about 2/3 (needle threaded at third attempt). q is very high: the number of volume elements in which the thread may lie of which only one is the needle. The trembling of the fingers mainly responsible for PFO is easily identified with r(t) [noise]. (23–24)

Agriculture and textiles—two of the earliest sites of formal subsumption—are here formatted in terms of the more or less precise specification of a message within a field of potential error. The PRF and PFO are measures of a given bedator's speed and accuracy. The computation of PRF and PFO in the transmission of G-energy takes place against a field of potential error whose incursion into the channel serves as a mark of the bedator's lack of "quality." This computation provides an abstract, value-informatic measure of what appeared to Babbage in 1832 as inattention, idleness, and knavery. PRF and PFO, which are in every case located within the bedator rather than in its environment, make legible the value-informatic processes through which labor is marked with a degree of capacity after being sorted according to imputed levels of reliability and cost.

The "trembling fingers" that are mainly responsible for the PFO in the needle-threading example index the ways that the informatics of value externalize the incapacity they impose as an internal feature of differentiated laboring bodies. Hunt writes that when a task is performed at constant speed, as all socially average labor is imagined to be, "G-power loss can only be exhibited as increased PFO" (21). Fatigue appears in this equation not as the wearing down of life, a bodily expression of the contradiction between abstract and concrete labor, or between conditions of computation and congelation, but as a decrease in the precision with which selections are made and transmitted. Which is to say, it appears only as a decrease in the quantity of G-energy transmitted through the bedator's ICS. To "prove" this claim, Hunt calculates the G-power loss exhibited by a computer whose PFO rises from 10^{-6} to 10^{-3} over six hours of work as a result of accumulated latency and insists that the same calculation is "applicable to any task" (20). The conceptualization of labor as G-energy transmission requires incapacity—including that resulting from fatigue—to be defined as compromised mechanical-intellectual efficiency that allows noise to enter the "channel." And this definition allows the attribution of more and less "skillful" labor to be posited in terms that conflate decreased capacity with impurity. Trembling "is easily identified with noise."

On first glance, Hunt appears to want to quantify fatigue in terms of G-power loss in order to facilitate the more efficient allocation of tasks. "When a bedator is unfitted by fatigue for an exacting task," he states, "it will continue to do G-work under slightly less exacting conditions" (20). He appears to be proposing information theory as a means of mitigating "the inevitability of decline, dissolution, and exhaustion" that was made visible by nineteenth-century physics.[26] But recall that at the start of "Two Kinds of Work" he establishes as the major significance of his intervention its implications for the allocation of wages: "not being paid for nothing, the workman is evidently paid for G-work done." I want to argue that, read alongside the definitions of G-energy and G-work that precede it, Hunt's measurement of bedators in terms of PRF and PFO mediates capital's need to more precisely enact differential valuation and flexibilization in pursuit of its basic, impossible goal—the perfect continuity of production and circulation, or the elimination of the temporal gap between abstract and concrete. Hunt's conceptualization of bedators as G-energy sources of variable capacity, the link he makes between capacity and cost, his definition of fatigue as compromised capacity, his theorization of imprecise work as the incursion of noise, and the distinction he makes between cleverness and drive all point toward the ways people are formatted by the informatics of value as components with higher or lower levels of reliability, quality, flexibility, and cost. And his desire to calculate those levels by using G-energy as a proxy for value shows how the latter informs the cybernetic formulation of cognition and social interaction long before the age of so-called platform capitalism.

I have already argued that the informatics of value should be understood in terms of *the synthesis of reliable circuits using less reliable components*. Hunt's method seeks to quantify the "quality" of spontaneous interconnection in order to optimize the use of less reliable components in service of this synthesis. "Where performance of an assembly depends on quality of many components," he writes, "the mean performance obtained will always be higher than the worst acceptable performance," while "the extent by which performance exceeds the worst acceptable is broadly proportional to the G-energy of components" (36). More than the intensified rationalization of individual production processes, the value-informatic determination and integration of "less reliable" components that Hunt diagrams evokes the processes through which residual value is scraped from bodies whose ascribed reliability and quality may not afford a livable wage—processes that allow the informatics of value to accommodate shifting structural conditions. Hunt's stated aim is to increase the control with which social synthesis can be effected by making it possible to more precisely measure the shifting capacity and cost of a given "component" and to integrate that component accordingly.

According to the ontology given theoretical form in "Two Kinds of Work," all bedators are marked as more or less "reliable," but the depth and ascriptive power of that marking varies according to how closely a given bedator approaches maximal channel capacity. At the "more reliable" end one might find those whose individual intentions are not explicitly aligned with the workings of the informatics of value and their tendential movement toward the extraction of surplus value, but who nonetheless maintain regular connection, a high channel capacity and PRF, and a low PFO. At the "less reliable" end are those who connect intermittently, whether as "redundant" bodies available to join and knit together parts of the value network or as uberized workers who must labor excessively—or return a high PRF—in order to approximate a survivable production-reproduction loop. It is in these abstract formulations of connection and capacity that the feminization and racialization of labor become legible as informatic processes. Let me conclude by recounting four ways that a symptomatic reading of "Two Kinds of Work" makes legible the multitude of social forms this "spontaneous" allocation produces within and across the threshold of the value network.

First, Hunt's location of a given bedator's G-energy capacity and the cause of any decline in that capacity not in the system of relations that constitutes it as a bedator but in its ICS diagrams the centrality of the value network to the structural formation of the possessive individual—and vice versa. As an explication of value-informatic logic—as much an unveiling as it is a mediation—Hunt's theorization of the bedator as a variable component in a naturally occurring communication system shows how the wage-mediated promises of self-possession, autonomy, and expectation are conditional on regular, high-"quality" connection. By equalizing qualitatively different activities as information flows, differentiating labor via the measurement of those flows, and allocating tasks accordingly, Hunt formalizes the mechanism through which the distinction between skilled and unskilled labor is value-informatically produced and then mapped onto living bodies. "The whole of human experience," he insists, "can go without loss through a communication channel of a scalar time function" (5). This possibility of transmission without loss, which subtends the G-energetic definition of fatigue, exemplifies the processes through which the informatics of value individualize capacity and mark bodies, so that the "quality" of a given person's labor, the frequency with which it is employed, the types of task associated with it, and the wages it warrants all appear to arise from that person's essential capacity.

Recall that, as Marx shows, value is computed not from the concrete particulars of a given laborer but from socially average abstract labor—the "data" to value's "information."[27] Recall, too, that wages are determined not by a person's capacities but by the cost of their reproduction, which is modulated by availability and the projection of "natural needs" that vary according to "the conditions in which, and consequently on the habits and expectations with which, the class of free workers have been formed." Hunt models in informatic terms how these linked mechanisms of socially average labor and the attribution of "habits and expectations" to particular bodies appear in the value network as a distribution of capacity. Concrete conditions of freedom, bondage, necessity, and precarity are compressed into a single metric. The implicit and explicit distinctions Hunt makes between different bedators based on the dimensions of their ICS and the speed with which they can process selections without introducing noise thus models the gradated access to homeostatic personhood that the informatics of value limn. Those distinctions also reveal how market dependence becomes naturalized through value-informatic processes as an automatic tendency toward connection—one of the principal ways that digitality remediates value's socially synthetic function. This naturalization leads to digital connectivity becoming a proxy for "free" personhood, especially in the absence of its directly value-mediated form. Although digital connection is not directly necessitated by dispossession and market dependence, it draws meaning and utility from the conditions those mechanisms produce, linking new expressions of agency—such as the user and the partner—to value relations that include but are not limited to new kinds of piecework.

Second, in addition to manifesting a postindustrial fantasy of surplus extraction without human labor, Hunt's insistence that the bedator can be a human, a nonhuman animal, or a machine symptomatically visualizes the disavowal of the racialized and feminized dynamics through which different ratios of wages, social security, consumer debt, and waged and unwaged reproductive labor make up the "input" required to maintain a bedator in a functional state. By positing the bedator as the "prime mover" of G-energy systems, Hunt offers it as a given, a source without a source. In this respect, his conceptualization of the bedator can be revealingly posited in the terms in which Federici critiques theorizations of *the body*: "The Power by which [it] is produced appears as a self-subsistent, metaphysical entity, ubiquitous, disconnected from social and economic relations, and as mysterious in its permutations as a godly Prime Mover."[28] Each bedator appears "free" from its own history and thus individually responsible for its own capacities.

But, as Hartman notes, the "free(d) individual" is "nothing if not burdened, responsible, and obligated."[29] Overlapping with the disavowal of the concrete conditions of reproduction, the commingling of human, nonhuman animal, and machine in the bedator concept tropes the generalization of the "free," self-possessed laborer and the obfuscation of conditions in which living labor is deployed as fixed capital, whose exemplar is in chattel slavery.[30] In Hunt's system, the concrete conditions in which the bedator lives and labors have no effect on the quality of the "signal." Nor do the ascriptive processes that shape and are shaped in the yawning gap between putatively self-reproducing subjects and those for whom "the price that is paid" represents "no more than the anticipated and capitalized surplus-value or profit that is to be extracted."[31] In other words, Hunt does not diagram bedator reproduction. And because of this, the bedator renders as information flow the variegated conditions of reproduction that span: living "bedators" that are purchased as commodities, provided with subsistence "inputs," and worked until "failure" before being replaced with another; "bedators" that appear to steadily maintain their own ICS on the basis of the wages they receive in exchange for G-energy transmission; and a distribution of regularly and irregularly deployed "bedators" whose degree of connection is determined by the value-informatic allocation of capacity.[32]

Third, Hunt's distinction between activities characterized by "cleverness" and "drive" maps onto Wiener's upgradable and unupgradable labor, Babbage's intellectual workers and street nuisances, and Moreno's creative and zootechnical life. Each is grounded in what Wynter calls the dynamics of selection and dysselection, and each foreshadows what Tadiar identifies as the postindustrial bifurcation of capitalizable and commodifiable life.³³ Since "the living bedator falls short of the artificial in point of drive, and far surpasses it in cleverness," association with "drive" work represents a principal marker of dysselection and consignment to the category of unupgradable, zootechnical, nuisance, or commodifiable life. This is clearly evident in the kinds of work activities Moreno and Jennings observed at Hudson—the prior refusal of which in all likelihood both led to the inmates' confinement at the school and intensified their desire to run away. "Drive" here functions as a synonym for the "manual" classification, that, as Hartman shows, both distinguishes those associated with it from intellectual activity and marks them with a status closer to machinery than to the human.³⁴

Put another way, the distinction between cleverness and drive abstracts a distinction between "*life worth living*" and "*life worth expending*" under which those allocated to the latter category function (or are imagined to function) as, in Tadiar's words, "vital *media* of other lives," as "technologies of reproduction rather than full-fledged sovereign (self-determining, self-owning) individual subjects."³⁵ Contrary to Krajewski's insistence that such operations are illegible at the level of abstraction at which continuities between electronic and human servers become apparent, Hunt's cybernetic methods reveal the value-informatic specification of what Tadiar identifies as the "worldwide service/servant stratum," those whose allocated function is to relieve higher-quality "components" of the need to spend time that might otherwise be used to more valuable ends on "mere" reproduction.³⁶

But in asserting this distinction between cleverness and drive, Hunt inadvertently reveals the value network's reliance on practices and needs it can neither sustain nor represent. To the value-informatic optic, indirectly value-mediated activities contain no data and thus produce no surplus, while value-mediated reproductive labor transmits low levels of G-energy to the material systems of higher-capacity bedators. The conceptual dyad of G-energy and A-energy upon which "Two Kinds of Work" is premised—and through which it models the internal world of the value network—collapses here. If the bedator is the "prime mover" of G-energy systems, how can its content be a form of A-energy transmitted in the form of waged or unwaged activity? Does reproductive labor transmit G-energy to the "material system" of the bedator in its waged form but not in its unwaged form? Is the wage form the cause (rather than the content) of a given activity's status as G-energy-bearing? The distinction between cleverness and drive appears designed to resolve this contradiction. Through it, service labor can appear the "drive" to so-called productive labor's "cleverness," facilitating the latter's capacity to give form to objects and social systems. Consequently, and as the association between "drive" activities and "artificial" bedators implies, the labor of transmitting such energy is "spontaneously" allocated either no price or a very low price and allocated to persons marked with low ICS capacity. The racialized and feminized condition of facilitating the reproduction of a higher-valued other is thus explicitly equated with machinery. Hunt here foreshadows Tadiar's observation that the labor of vital energy transmission, exemplified in the activities of migrant domestic workers, formats its bearers as "*machines*," appliances whose "design or designated purpose is to 'save' their employers' valuable life-times."[37] Kalindi Vora identifies the same logic in terms that overtly align with Hunt's when she writes of the "*transmission*" of vital energy "from areas of life depletion to areas of life enrichment" through a global distribution of "life support" labor.[38] To provide such labor, Vora continues, is to function as a "*channel* for the investment of one's own vital energy into others."[39]

Fourth: immediately before he defines the "accuracy or quality" of bedators as a function of their ICS, Hunt briefly introduces a collective form of life that does not channel G-energy but instead serves as a "material system" to which G-energy is transmitted by another. "In a field of indefinite size," he writes,

> sheep are distributed at unit density. They move at random. In the field is a pen in which the sheep-density has some higher value. In the absence of G-work the sheep would stray from pen to field till the sheep-density in both was equal. The system would lose G-energy. If a dog constrains sheep to go from field to pen, the system gains G-energy. . . . The dog does G-work. (9)

The sheep become a repository of G-energy not as commodity food but as a corralled mass. If the dog is understood as a bedator, the sheep must be the "material system" upon which that bedator operates. Does this example model care, or coercion? Like many of the ostensibly unupgradable, zootechnical, nuisance, or commodifiable lives to which the labor of waiting on and transmitting vital energy to higher-valued others is allocated, the sheep are a form of life marked as raw material for another's activity. And their straying from the pen implies the existence of activity that cannot be understood as the transmission of either value or vital energy. If Hunt's elaborations of channel capacity, speed, quality, accuracy, fatigue, cleverness, and drive model the ways in which social forms produced through gradated access to the value network appear within that network, perhaps the example of the sheep and the sheepdog abstracts the relationship between the desire to run away and the means of curtailing that desire.[40] And those means of curtailment can take the form of care *or* incarceration; in addition to the value-informatic relations of dispossession, connection, and survival that prevent those for whom the possibility of connection remains open from running away, they range from the relations of obligation and dependency that structure the reproductively responsible family to the warehousing of populations in prisons and other sites of confinement.

Finally, the example of the sheepdog and the sheep implies that the possibility of being corralled by another only appears as such in the absence of "free" connection to the value network.[41] And in so doing, it reveals that the desire to run away without already being fully disconnected is both ubiquitous and unthinkable within the value-mediated social imaginary. This desire inheres in the gap between the higher- or lower-capacity component and the living person that houses it, that is worn down by its computation, and that introduces noise and impedance to the circuits of accumulation. And it signals other ways of being free, those which are everywhere outlawed or located beyond the value-mediated horizon of expectation, but which persist in forging connections that are not mediated by value or its digital-mediatic proxies.

CODA

The Human Surge

OVER THE COURSE OF THIS BOOK I have argued that the reticular form, the ideals of homoeostatic agency, and the principles of social interaction at the center of so-called digital culture have their roots in the core dynamics of racial capitalism: dispossession, market dependence, differential valuation, attenuated reproduction, and ascriptive marking. I hope to have shown that the imaginative and practical integration of digitality and capital, which is clearly visible in the HSBC and Google campaigns I discussed in the Introduction, arose not through some process of allegorical figuration or mirroring but from a reticular impulse that emerges through the informatics of value to animate the valorization of the informatic: the drive to synthesize reliable circuits from unreliable components. In this Coda I consider the ways Eduardo Williams's 2016 film *El auge del humano* (*The Human Surge*) maps labor and digitality across three postcolonial spaces: Buenos Aires, Argentina; Maputo, Mozambique; and Bohol, Philippines. Williams's film shows how the production and distribution of unreliable components, the "spontaneous" synthesis of those components into productive networks, and the resultant generation and platform-mediated integration of superfluous populations function and fail to produce the structural and imaginative forms of the digital-liberal person. In depicting the social-reproductive activities of those who have been constituted as unreliable components *and know it*, the film shows how the promises of value and digitality can appear less tenable the more closely they become intertwined.

In Buenos Aires, a man, Exe, wakes up, gets dressed, and opens a door to torrential rainfall. Later, he wades through floodwater while talking on the phone, trying to explain why he is late for his job in a supermarket

Figure 19. Buenos Aires. Source: *El auge del humano* (Dir. Eduardo Williams, 2016).

stockroom. After work, he visits family, takes a carrot to eat, reveals that he has been fired, and tries to get online. The next day, he meets some friends at a park. When one asks why he "abandoned" them, he explains that he got the supermarket job a week ago, so "at least [he was] working." After again trying and failing to get online, he visits a house where four men unenthusiastically participate in a pornographic webcam show. Later, he is shown working the cash register at a convenience store. The

camera follows a customer as she leaves, meets a friend, talks about his job, and walks with him to a house. Exe enters the same house and sits at a computer on which a Chaturbate cam show from Maputo is streaming in one of several windows. He follows a link in a Facebook post to an article likening vibrating proteins to violin strings. As the men performing on the stream perfunctorily simulate intercourse with a banana and discuss the number of viewers, the camera tracks in until the Chaturbate window fills the frame. The stream buffers.

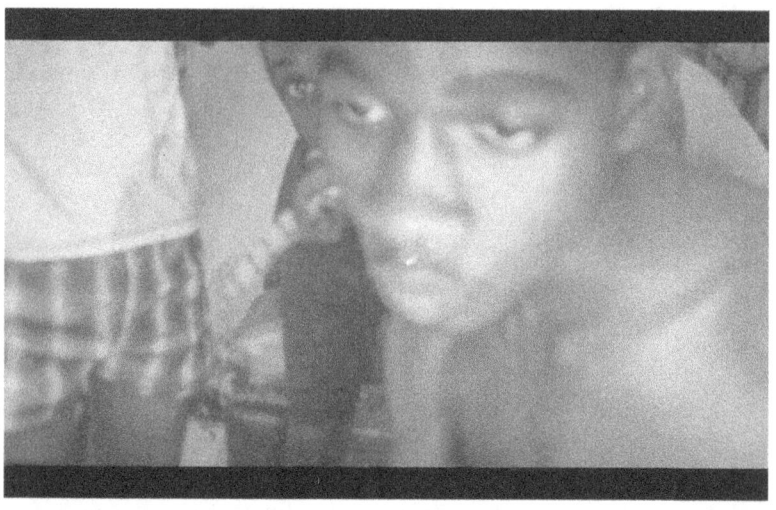
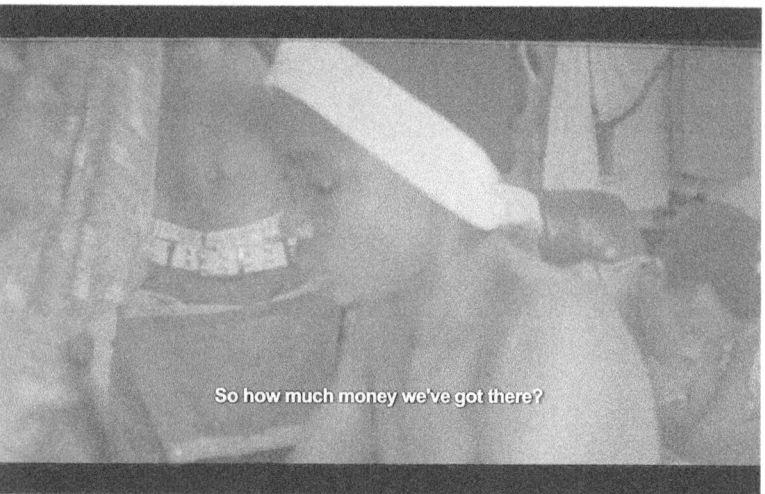

Figure 20. Maputo. Source: *El auge del humano.*

The film cuts from the Chaturbate window in Buenos Aires to the men performing in Maputo. They joke about the requests they receive, talk about their preference for PVT (private) over public cam sessions, and calculate the amount of money they have raised. After the show ends, the men discuss hanging out until sunrise. One says that the sun will not come up tomorrow. The next day, one of the men, Marcio, wakes up, checks his cell phone, and goes to work in an office.[1] At his desk, he takes

a conical device from a drawer and alternates between looking into it and entering data on a desktop computer. Later, Marcio walks with a co-worker who tells him about a "fucked up scene" that he wants to show him. Marcio visits his co-worker's house but becomes uncomfortable and leaves. After a short scene in which another of the men from the Chaturbate show talks on his cell phone while at work in an arcade, Marcio is shown calling in sick to work. Later, he tells a group of women he wants

Figure 21. Bohol. Source: *El auge del humano.*

to quit his job because he doesn't like it and only does it for money. They mock him. Later, Marcio walks with his cousin down a cliffside path while discussing the possibility of using a jersey as a technology of flight. Marcio talks about how difficult his life has been since his phone was stolen using "black magic." At dusk, he walks out into a savanna with Milyx, another of the men from the Chaturbate show. They complain about being called lazy. They camp overnight. In the morning, Milyx urinates onto an anthill. The camera tracks into the anthill. Six minutes later, it follows some ants as they emerge in Chocolate Hills, Bohol.

In Bohol, a woman flicks the ants away while typing messages on a damaged smartphone. The woman, Chai, is disturbed by a security guard who tells her she shouldn't be there. She runs into a wooded area. A group of children tell stories in a hole in the ground. Chai meets Kuya, who says he is leaving for work but becomes evasive when she asks him where. When she tries to kiss him, he says he is nervous about being seen. They encounter a man carrying a heavy bundle, and she offers to help him. Kuya's cell phone rings and he wanders off. He helps the caller with a math problem, then says he is exhausted. He meets with a woman, Ate. Kuya and Ate collect a child, Rixel, who is reticent to leave his friends. Ate walks to a water hole where a number of children and young people are swimming and telling stories. Chai and Rixel are there. Chai and Ate talk about a job to which they don't want to return. Chai asks if anyone knows the location of a nearby internet café and then leaves to find it. At dusk, she walks along a path and arrives at a shop. The shopkeeper points her in the direction of an internet café, but isn't sure if it is open. Chai asks for water. The shopkeeper tells her it costs ten pesos. Chai asks a man about the location of the internet café. He invites her to get online at his house, but the connection is faulty. She asks a passerby for the location of the café and he tells her about a place up ahead that should be open because the shopkeeper stays late playing cards. She walks into the distance and asks, "Is this supposed to be an internet café?"

The film cuts to a heavily automated factory in which women solder components onto circuit boards. Here, the roving handheld camerawork of the preceding sequences is replaced with a series of static shots. A recorded voice repeats "OK." One of the workers sings a wordless song. Over a close-up of women's hands soldering, an unseen speaker whispers, "You came back! No."

The continuities and disparities across these spaces are marked by the use of distinct photographic technologies. The Buenos Aires scenes are photographed on a 16 mm ARRI S2; the footage for the Maputo scenes was shot on a Blackmagic pocket digital camera and recaptured onto Super 16 mm from a computer monitor; and the Bohol sequence was filmed on a RED Scarlet camera. There is no discernible valorization of the photochemical over the digital, no implied equation between analogicity and authenticity. None of the formats is correlated more closely than any

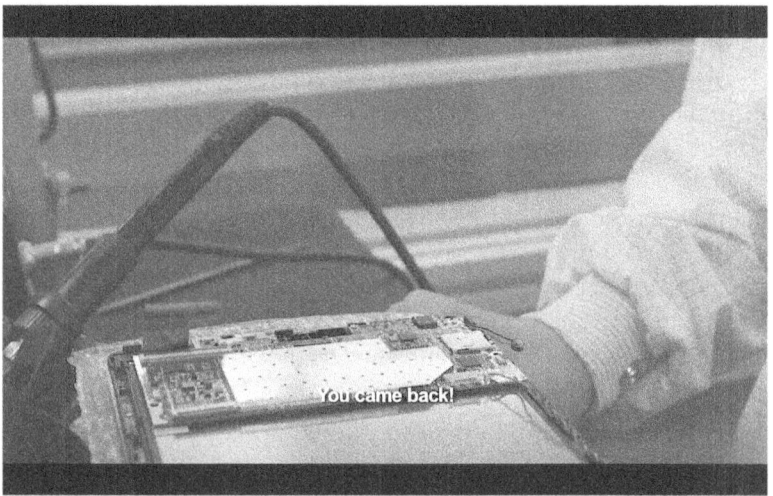

Figure 22. Electronics factory. Source: *El auge del humano*.

other to a specific social position or dynamic. Nor does their deployment follow a narrative of development or progress. The highest-resolution image is closest to the electronics factory, but it is not clear that the photochemically recaptured, lower-resolution digital images of the Maputo scenes represent an intermediary between a "photochemical" Argentina and a "digital" Philippines. In the absence of any clear correlation between format and content, the film's depiction of unreliable components through the nonhierarchical juxtaposition of image formats evokes the accrual of mediations across capitalism's *longue durée*, the impossibility of depicting the production and distribution of social forms across the contemporary world system using any single mode of representation.

The transitions through the computer screen and the anthill evoke "formless democracy," the digital-liberal imaginary of untrammeled communication and spontaneous interconnection that, as I have argued throughout this book, derives its spatial and temporal logics from linked idealizations of the value network and digital technologies. In contrast, the depictions of attenuated reproduction that these transitions connect are rife with instances of media-technological failure. In Chocolate Hills, Chai's interminable search for an internet café directly follows a conversation about a "tiring" job to which she doesn't want to return. In Maputo, scenes of Marcio working are interspersed with his protracted attempts to locate friends who may be uncontactable either because they have to work or because their phones are broken. Connection to the value network and nonconnection to the cell-phone network equally impinge upon the pursuit of "unproductive" sociality—a suggestion that is reinforced when a conversation between Marcio and his cousin quickly shifts from the possibility of human flight to the stress of phonelessness. In Buenos Aires, Exe's acknowledgment that he lost his warehouse job and may have to return to an "awful" job at the bus company, Rutamar, takes place alongside a series of failed attempts to get online: the wired connection doesn't work; the Wi-Fi is down; his phone won't charge. The close relationship between precarious labor, compromised reproduction, and media-technological failure is clearest in the transition to Maputo through the buffering Chaturbate stream, which comes at the end of a sequence in which a man weighs the relief of "finally" drawing a wage against the long hours and arduous conditions of his warehouse job. If a buffering web page is experienced by users "as temporary emotional distress, as a disruption that triggers various bodily reactions, and as an enduring and unrecognized affective response of anxiety," as Neta Alexander argues, then the enforced gaps between periods of employment might be understood as value-informatic buffering.[2] Perhaps it is the latter, appearing in mediated form, that animates the anxieties provoked by the former. In both cases, the shift from buffering to "ordinary" operation may be experienced as a palliative even when "ordinary" conditions are palpably wearing.

What, if anything, do those faulty or inaccessible technologies analogize? They might trope those who have been rendered unreliable, low-capacity "components" through the devaluation and flexibilization of their labor power. Or they might stand in for the failures internal to the informatics of value: their disabling of "unproductive" social practices; their waning capacity to maintain people in stable conditions of wage-mediated reproduction; and their production and differential integration of growing numbers of unreliable components, to which they can guarantee nothing other than the opportunity to piece together means of reproduction through a distributed network of casualized work, indirectly value-mediated social relationships (family, friends, partners), and debt.

In truth, the two cannot be separated; capital's structural incapacity is externalized as labor's personal incapacity as an essential function of the former's homeostatic mechanisms. In this respect, the technologies depicted in *El auge del humano* are neither analogy nor allegory. Insofar as the characters have been constituted as unreliable components, there is a structural identity between their appearance to the value network and the telecommunications network's "view" of a broken or intermittent device.

For these unreliable components, the imbrication of digitality and value-mediated reproduction is closest in the webcam shows, participation in which supplements or replaces wages that are too irregular or too meager to meet basic needs. To those who labor in them, these shows represent a means of synthesizing a livable income in the absence of a sufficient wage elsewhere. To those who own the services and the infrastructure on which they run, they function as a means of extracting surplus value from redundant components without the concomitant need to ensure those components' reproduction through the guarantee of regular, sufficiently waged connection. The cam shows exemplify the uberization of reproduction, connecting the current form of the global service sector to the histories of devaluation, ascription, and sorting through which those who do not connect get marked as lacking connective capacity and are thus made available for cheap, irregular connection. And, as the final shots in the electronics factory underscore, the conditions that make productive connection to the value network a prerequisite for survival structure digital culture in multiple ways. On the one hand, the factory sequence underscores the importance of electronic devices not only to the upgradable laborers of the so-called creative, digital, or postindustrial economy but also to the putatively unupgradable lives consigned to the global service stratum, for whom mobile telephones and internet access are increasingly necessary both for survival (finding ways to earn money) and for pursuing social practices not entirely subordinated to the informatics of value.[3] On the other hand, the whispered "You came back" that haunts the workers as they solder gestures to the system-level automation that dispossession and market dependence effect, constraining social-reproductive possibilities just as automatic machinery minimizes deviations from the production process.

Yet even the highest technologies of automation cannot curtail the unseen worker's song. Throughout *El auge del humano,* characters steal time back from their employers. They do their jobs with the minimum of effort. They call in sick so that they can spend more time wandering around with their friends. When not working, they sit around in parks, wade into the ocean, walk out into the savanna, and swim at water holes, their conversations alternating between complaints about work and plans to run away. In the cam shows, the participants spend as much time joking among themselves as they do performing. Still: none of this can be fully disentangled from the labor through which the characters sustain their lives. Exe's wanderings pass through different supermarket jobs and the cam show, with the possibility of the "awful" job at the bus company a constant backdrop. The participants' desultory engagement with user requests in both cam shows is interspersed with their close attention to viewer numbers and money raised. As Milyx and Marcio walk out into the savanna, they talk about needing to sleep because they have to return to work the next day. As they hang out at the water hole and talk about never returning to work, Chai and her friends look after multiple children, freeing up the value-productive time of parents or employers.

By depicting a global distribution of unreliable components from the side of their reproduction, *El auge del humano* shows the equation between connection and freedom to be grounded not in the universal capacities of the possessive individual but in the practical reality that survival remains a material precondition for all other social practices. If the superimposition of digital and value-mediated connection hints at the abstract social matrix that grounds both, the narrative dilation that results from the characters' recalcitrance, the drudgery of their jobs, their failures of connection, and their "unproductive" sociality attest to the impedance they present to the value network's optimal form and operation. The informatics of value and the digital imaginary extend the same promise, but the fact of this extension does not automatically reproduce the fantasy of upgradable or creative life, nor does it obviate the desire for escape, refusal, or "unproductive" sociality. At times this promise appears in its barest form, not a promise at all but a series of commands and threats. *The work is too hard—but you'll still come back. Connect or disappear. Connect or you'll never get free. Connect or you'll be all alone. Connect or die.*

While dispossession, market dependence, and differential valuation continue to structure social reproduction, the pursuit of connection already constitutes a slow death—slower for those who successfully connect to the value network than for those who search for connection with limited or no success. All are marked as unreliable components, although the degrees of capacity and reliability they are allocated vary, and those variations are indexed to ascriptive processes that naturalize the placement of certain bodies closer to the status of life-to-be-computed while positioning others as life-to-be-congealed. Recognizing the informatics of value in their mediated forms of appearance, many of which constitute the foundational concepts and social norms of digital culture, reveals the latter's connection to the historical and present violence of racial capitalism. This recognition might then entail the realization that there is no spontaneous interconnection, no homeostatic reproduction; that computation cannot be separated from congelation; that the synthesis of reliable circuits requires the distribution of incapacity; and that it is necessary to find ways of living otherwise, modes of connection and relation not subordinated to the demand for accumulation. That path is already mapped out in the histories of life lived below, beyond, against, or in a relationship of indifference to value-informatic demands, the existence of which stands testament to the immutable fact that connections severed from the circulation of value are the foundations of the fullest collectivity.

ACKNOWLEDGMENTS

I owe a huge debt of gratitude to the many people whose insights, critiques, support, and friendship allowed me to complete this book.

Arabella Stanger encouraged me to intensify, sharpen, and justify more or less every aspect of the project. Jon Beller, Amy De'Ath, and Jane Elliott generously read and commented on multiple chapter drafts. Alex Galloway read the entire manuscript and made a number of useful suggestions during the final stretch. Thanks to all of you for your exacting comments and rigorous critiques, each of which helped me to improve the book.

Every stage of the research and writing process was shaped by conversations with friends, comrades, and collaborators. Thanks to Mal Ahern, Sita Balani, Erika Balsom, Clare Birchall, Zach Blas, Adelene Buckland, Natalia Cecire, Fabienne Collignon, Andrew Culp, Martin Dines, Alex Dubilet, Beatrice Fazi, Anna Watkins Fisher, Jacob Gaboury, Bernard Dionysius Geoghegan, Paul Gilroy, Jette Gindner, Elena Gorfinkel, Johanna Gosse, Orit Halpern, Leigh Claire La Berge, Michael Lawrence, Mara Mills, Julie Napolin, Penny Newell, Sean O'Brien, Christine Okoth, Ella Parry-Davies, Jasbir Puar, Rita Raley, John David Rhodes, Luke Roberts, Jordy Rosenberg, Joshua Scannell, Anna Snaith, Sam Solomon, Neferti Tadiar, Antoine Traisnel, Myka Tucker-Abramson, Mark Turner, Marina Vishmidt, Leif Weatherby, and Damon Young. I am also grateful to have worked with such inspiring students at King's College London, especially those in the MA in Contemporary Literature, Culture, and Theory. Thanks to all of you for being such insightful and committed interlocutors.

Several of the ideas I explore here started to take shape during a conversation with Jasbir Puar and Patricia Clough at the CUNY Center for the Humanities in February 2016. I thank Jasbir, Patricia, and the other participants for their brilliant contributions, as well as the organizers at the James Gallery for making the event happen. Invitations to present work at the Pratt Institute, the University of Michigan, University of California Berkeley, and Vanderbilt University gave me opportunities to test early versions of some of the ideas and analyses contained in the book. Thanks to Jon Beller, Anna Watkins Fisher, Damon Young, and Alex Dubilet, Jessie Hock, Haerin Shin, and Ben Tran for organizing these events. The participants in a summer 2019 writing workshop in Brighton let me read their amazing work and provided invaluable commentary on what ended up becoming chapter 11. In addition to those named above, I thank Molly Geidel, Sophie Jones, Rachel O'Connell, Nisha Ramayya, Patricia Stuelke, and David Wylot. While working on the final draft, I had the opportunity to present parts of the manuscript at the University of Washington, University of California, Santa Barbara, and Berkeley. I am grateful to Mal Ahern, Rita Raley, and Jacob Gaboury for organizing these visits, and to the audience members whose questions and provocations helped me to improve the final version of the book.

The archivists at the Library of Congress, the Department of Distinctive Collections at MIT, and the Wellcome Collection provided invaluable research support. Special thanks to Myles Crowley at MIT for assistance with finding materials related to R. S. Hunt's "Two Kinds of Work."

Work toward this project was generously supported by two Faculty of Arts and Humanities small grants. Thanks to my heads of department at King's, Richard Kirkland and Janet Floyd, for supporting my applications.

Rita Raley supported this project from its early stages as editor of the Electronic Mediations series; Danielle Kasprzak, Leah Pennywark, and Jason Weidemann at the University of Minnesota Press steered the book through the acquisition, writing, and production processes; Anne Carter provided invaluable editorial support throughout; and Rachel Moeller and Mike Stoffel were hugely helpful and patient during the production stages. I thank you all. Thanks, too, to Neferti Tadiar and one anonymous reviewer for encouraging me to develop the project from proposal to book, and for providing such detailed and exacting suggestions about how I might do so.

Finally, I am grateful to Sondra Perry for allowing me to use the image that appears on the cover, which is from her extraordinary video installation *Typhoon coming on*.

NOTES

Introduction

1. https://www.hsbc.com/who-we-are/our-brand.
2. On the colonial prehistory of subsea internet cables see Nicole Starosielski, *The Undersea Network* (Durham: Duke University Press, 2015), 31–37, 99–111.
3. Michael D. Francois, Chris George, and Jane Stowell, "Introducing Equiano, a Subsea Cable from Portugal to South Africa" (2019), https://cloud.google.com/blog/products/infrastructure/introducing-equiano-a-subsea-cable-from-portugal-to-south-africa.
4. On these longer and more diffuse histories see, for example, Alexander R. Galloway, *Laruelle: Against the Digital* (Minneapolis: University of Minnesota Press, 2014).
5. Sean Cubitt, *Finite Media: Environmental Implications of Digital Technologies* (Durham: Duke University Press, 2017), 13.
6. *The Interesting Narrative of the Life of Olaudah Equiano, or Gustavus Vassa, the African, Written by Himself*, in Olaudah Equiano, *The Interesting Narrative and Other Writings* (London: Penguin, 2003), 58.
7. Equiano, 60–61.
8. Karl Marx, *Capital: A Critique of Political Economy*, vol. 1, translated by Ben Fowkes (London: Penguin, 1976), 349. Unless otherwise noted, all subsequent quotations are from this edition.
9. Saidiya V. Hartman, *Scenes of Subjection: Terror, Slavery, and Self-Making in Nineteenth-Century America* (Oxford: Oxford University Press, 1997), 21.
10. Equiano, *Interesting Narrative*, 51; D. W. Davies, "Proposal for a Digital Communication Network" (London: National Physical Laboratory, 1966), 9.
11. In 1776, Adam Smith wrote: "As it is the power of exchanging that gives occasion to the division of labour, so the extent of this division must always be limited by the extent of that power, or, in other words, by the extent of the market." His first example of an industry that can only flourish in a market of

a certain size is that of domestic service—"A porter." Smith, *An Inquiry into the Nature and Causes of the Wealth of Nations* (London: W. Strahan and T. Cadell, 1776), 1:21. Smith's pronouncement usefully connects the expansion and granularization of the world market and the division of labor attested to in the HSBC and Google campaigns to the proliferation of app-mediated service work. The principal technologies of market expansion and division of labor in the centuries surrounding Smith's theorization of capital, which, as Peter Linebaugh and Marcus Rediker show, include the commons, the plantation, the ship, and the factory, provide a useful blueprint for understanding the histories of violence that precede and inform the so-called digital economy. See Linebaugh and Rediker, *The Many-Headed Hydra: Sailors, Slaves, Commoners, and the Hidden History of the Revolutionary Atlantic* (Boston: Beacon Press, 2000), 327–29.

12. Gayatri Chakravorty Spivak, "Can the Subaltern Speak?," in *Marxism and the Interpretation of Culture,* edited by Cary Nelson and Lawrence Grossberg (Urbana: University of Illinois Press, 1988), 279. Emphases added.

13. Marx, *Capital,* 1:128. Emphasis added. In Samuel Moore and Edward Aveling's earlier translation, Marx's *Gallerte*—the noun translated by Fowkes as "congealed quantity"—is translated as "congelation." See Karl Marx, *Capital: A Critique of Political Economy,* vol. 1, translated by Samuel Moore and Edward Aveling, in *Karl Marx and Frederick Engels: Collected Works* [hereafter *MECW*], vol. 35 (London: Lawrence and Wishart, 1996), 48. For a rich critical account of this translation, see Keston Sutherland, "Marx in Jargon," *World Picture* 1 (Spring 2008), http://www.worldpicturejournal.com/WP_1.1/KSutherland.html. For a notable exception, see Marx's description of value's transformation of "every product of labor into a social hieroglyphic." *Capital,* 1:167.

14. Marx, *Capital,* 1:128. On value as an empty form that takes hold of material relations, see Christopher J. Arthur, "The Spectral Ontology of Value," *Radical Philosophy* 107 (2001).

15. The implications of Marx's use of *Gallerte* have been discussed widely. See Jacques Derrida, *Specters of Marx: The State of the Debt, the Work of Mourning, and the New International,* translated by Peggy Kamuf (New York: Routledge, 1994), 243n35; and Nicole Shukin, *Animal Capital: Rendering Life in Biopolitical Times* (Minneapolis: University of Minnesota Press, 2009), 75. Sutherland writes in "Marx in Jargon" that *Gallerte* refers not to a generic "congealed quantity" but more specifically to "animal products industrially boiled down into condiments." The concrete violence this term locates in the material expressions of the value relation is emphasized in Sutherland's observation that, through the mediations of capital, "The worker who starts out a real body and brain is reduced to *Gallerte* through submission to capitalist wage labor." But also present in this passage are the relationships between the value relation and the protocols of exploitation, dispossession, humanization, and dehumanization with which Spivak is more broadly concerned; "the

capitalist who is in essence nothing but capital itself," Sutherland observes, "nonetheless assumes in his interactions with human beings the local habitation of a body and the name of an individual." Sianne Ngai argues that Marx's superimposition of the abstract and the grossly visceral is central to his specification of the "*socially binding or plasticizing action of capitalist abstractions.*" Ngai, "Visceral Abstractions," *GLQ* 21, no. 1 (2015): 41–45, 50.

16. Shukin evokes this relationship between computation and congelation through "the double entendre of rendering." Noting that the term signifies both representation—most overtly in the production of computer graphics—and the industrial extraction of matter from animal remains, Shukin posits rendering as a "provocation to analyse the discomfiting complicity of symbolic and carnal technologies of reproduction." *Animal Capital,* 20–21.

17. Jacques Lacan, *The Seminar of Jacques Lacan, Book II: The Ego in Freud's Theory and in the Technique of Psychoanalysis, 1954–1955,* translated by Sylvana Tomaselli, edited by Jacques-Alain Miller (New York: Norton, 1991), 75. Second and third emphases added.

18. "Meant not to support health but rather simply to ensure subsistence," Smallwood continues, "the diet on which captives tried to survive provided, at best, a consistent intake of nutritionally empty calories." Stephanie E. Smallwood, *Saltwater Slavery: A Middle Passage from Africa to American Diaspora* (Cambridge: Harvard University Press, 2007), 43–44.

19. Marx, *Capital,* 1:873.

20. "With the discovery of the New World and its vast exploitable lands that process which has been termed the 'reduction of Man to Labour and of Nature to Land' had its large scale beginning. From this moment on Western Man saw himself as 'the lord and possessor of Nature.' The one way transformation of Nature began. Since man is a part of Nature, a process of dehumanization and alienation was set in train. In old societies with traditional values based on the old relation, resistance could be put up to the dominance of the new dehumanizing system. In new societies like ours, created for the market, there seemed at first to be no possibility of such a tradition. . . . But from early, the planters gave the slaves plots of land on which to grow food to feed themselves in order to maximize profits. We suggest that this plot system, was . . . the focus of resistance to the market system and market values." Sylvia Wynter, "Novel and History, Plot and Plantation," *Savacou* 5 (1971): 99.

21. See Orlando Patterson, *Slavery and Social Death: A Comparative Study* (Cambridge: Harvard University Press, 1982).

22. Lacan, *Seminar II,* 89.

23. Lacan, 54.

24. Spivak, "Can the Subaltern Speak?," 272.

25. On debilitation and slow death as outcomes of capitalist social organization, see Jasbir K. Puar, *The Right to Maim: Debility, Capacity, Disability* (Durham: Duke University Press, 2017), especially xiv–xviii.

26. As Cedric Robinson puts it, "The tendency of European civilization through capitalism was thus not to homogenize but to differentiate—to exaggerate regional, subcultural, and dialectical differences into 'racial' ones. As the Slavs became the natural slaves, the racially inferior stock for domination and exploitation during the early Middle Ages, as the Tartars came to occupy a similar position in the Italian cities of the late Middle Ages, so at the systemic interlocking of capitalism in the sixteenth century, the peoples of the Third World began to fill this expanding category of a civilization reproduced by capitalism." Robinson, *Black Marxism: The Making of the Black Radical Tradition* (Chapel Hill: University of North Carolina Press, 2000), 26. Adding expropriation to the fundamental capitalist dynamics of exchange and exploitation, Nancy Fraser clarifies the relationship between this logic of differentiation and the basal mechanisms of capital accumulation. In addition to "territorial conquest, land annexation, enslavement, coerced labor, child labor, child abduction, and rape . . . prison labor, transnational sex trafficking, corporate land grabs, and foreclosures on predatory debt," Fraser writes, "expropriation plays a role in the construction of distinctive, explicitly racialized forms of exploitation—as, for example, when a prior history of enslavement casts its shadow on the wage contract, segmenting labor markets and levying a confiscatory premium on exploited proletarians who carry the mark of 'race' long after their 'emancipation.'" These differentiating mechanisms are structural conditions for accumulation, she continues, because "a system devoted to the limitless expansion and private appropriation of surplus value gives the owners of capital a deep-seated interest in acquiring labor and means of production below cost, if not wholly gratis—and not simply by virtue of greed. Expropriation lowers capitalists' costs of production, supplying inputs for whose reproduction they do not fully pay." Fraser, "Exploitation and Expropriation in Racialized Capitalism: A Reply to Michael Dawson," *Critical Historical Studies* 3, no. 1 (2016): 166–67.
27. Robinson, *Black Marxism*, xxviii–xxix.
28. On the complex dynamics of racial ascription in software and algorithms, see Lisa Nakamura, *Cybertypes: Race, Ethnicity, and Identity on the Internet* (New York: Routledge, 2002); Safiya Umoja Noble, *Algorithms of Oppression: How Search Engines Reinforce Racism* (New York: New York University Press, 2018).
29. Gayatri Chakravorty Spivak, "Scattered Speculations on the Question of Value," *Diacritics* 15, no. 4 (1985): 90.
30. Marx, *Capital*, 1:138, 274–75.
31. Marx, *Capital*, 1:255. "Whereas [Lehman] Brothers, thanks to computers, 'earned about $2 million for . . . 15 minutes of work,'" Spivak writes, "the entire economic text would not be what it is if it could not write itself as a palimpsest upon another text where a woman in Sri Lanka has to work 2,287 minutes to buy a t-shirt." "Scattered Speculations," 88. Spivak quotes Desmond Smith, "The Wiring of Wall Street," *New York Times*, October 23, 1983.

32. This process comprises the reduction of "(phonic) materiality" that Fred Moten identifies as "modern thought's most fundamental protocol." Moten, "Knowledge of Freedom," *CR: The Centennial Review* 4, no. 2 (2004): 272.
33. John von Neumann, response to Ralph W. Gerard, "Some of the Problems concerning Digital Notions in the Central Nervous System," *Cybernetics: Circular Causal and Feedback Mechanisms in Biological and Social Systems* (Transactions of the Seventh Conference, March 23–24, 1950, New York), edited by Heinz von Foerster, Margaret Mead, and Hans Lukas Teuber (New York: Josiah Macy, Jr. Foundation, 1950), 19–20.
34. Von Neumann, 27.
35. Jason W. Moore, *Capitalism in the Web of Life: Ecology and the Accumulation of Capital* (London: Verso, 2015), 2–3. Moore distinguishes Nature—the "external, controllable, reducible" form made by "manifold projects of capital, empire, and science"—from "nature as a whole: *nature* with an emphatically lowercase *n* . . . nature as us, as inside us, as around us."
36. Moore, 2.
37. See Iyko Day, *Alien Capital: Asian Racialization and the Logic of Settler Colonial Capitalism* (Durham: Duke University Press, 2016), 10–16. Also see Neil Levi, "See That Straw? That's a Straw: Anti-Semitism and Narrative Form in *Ulysses*," *Modernism/Modernity* 9, no. 3 (2002): 375–88.
38. Nicholas Negroponte, *Being Digital* (London: Hodder and Stoughton, 1995), 4.
39. The signal text is, of course, N. Katherine Hayles, *How We Became Posthuman: Virtual Bodies in Cybernetics, Literature, and Informatics* (Chicago: University of Chicago Press, 1999). Also see Friedrich Kittler, "There Is No Software," *Stanford Literary Review* 9, no. 1 (1992): 81–90. For just one of the many influential claims for the reality and importance of digital immateriality, see John Perry Barlow's insistence that "Cyberspace consists of transactions, relationships, and thought itself, arrayed like a standing wave in the web of our communications . . . there is no matter here." Barlow, "A Declaration of the Independence of Cyberspace," February 8, 1996, https://www.eff.org/cyberspace-independence.
40. John von Neumann, "Probabilistic Logics and the Synthesis of Reliable Organisms from Unreliable Components," transcript by R. S. Pierce, in *Automata Studies*, edited by Claude E. Shannon (Princeton: Princeton University Press, 1956), 44. This series of five lectures was delivered at the California Institute of Technology, January 4–15, 1952. Also see John von Neumann, "Reliable Organization of Unreliable Elements," lecture delivered the University of Maryland, November 17, 1952, box 20, folder 9, John von Neumann and Klara Dan von Neumann Papers, Library of Congress, Washington, D.C.
41. Von Neumann, "Probabilistic Logics," 44. Emphasis added.
42. Karl Marx, *Grundrisse: Foundations of the Critique of Political Economy*, translated by Martin Nicolaus (London: Penguin, 1993), 548–49.

43. See Walter Johnson, "The Pedestal and the Veil: Rethinking the Capitalism/Slavery Question," *Journal of the Early Republic* 24, no. 2 (2004): 299–308. Johnson's argument develops a historical claim that remains latent in Marx's insistence that "the veiled slavery of the wage labourers in Europe needed the unqualified slavery of the New World as its pedestal" (*Capital*, 1:925).
44. For Johnson, Marx's claim that "Whilst the cotton industry introduced child-slavery in England, it gave in the United States a stimulus to the transformation of the earlier, more or less patriarchal slavery, into a system of commercial exploitation," places capitalism and slavery "in terms of dynamic simultaneity rather than simple supercession, though it does so with careful attention to the historically different relations of production—slavery and wage labor—which characterized the two poles of this single Atlantic economy" ("The Pedestal and the Veil," 305).
45. On expressive causality—the treatment of social forms as more or less mediated expressions of a common substrate—see Fredric Jameson, *The Political Unconscious: Narrative as Socially Symbolic Act* (London: Routledge, 2002), 13–19.
46. Alfred Sohn-Rethel, *Intellectual and Manual Labour: A Critique of Epistemology*, translated by Martin Sohn-Rethel (Atlantic Highlands, N.J.: Humanities Press, 1978), 34, 78.
47. "While the concepts of natural science are thought abstractions, the economic concept of value is a real one. It exists nowhere other than in the human mind but it does not spring from it. Rather it is purely social in character, arising in the spatio-temporal sphere of human interrelations. It is not people who originate these abstractions but their actions." Sohn-Rethel, 20. Emphasis in original. On the elaboration of the concept of real abstraction after Marx, see Alberto Toscano, "The Open Secret of Real Abstraction," *Rethinking Marxism* 20, no. 2 (2008): 273–87.
48. Marx, *Capital*, 1:135.
49. On the "long downturn"—the "extraordinarily extended" period of declining economic growth that starts in the advanced capitalist economies (primarily, North America, Western Europe, and Japan) in the late 1960s, see Robert Brenner, *The Economics of Global Turbulence: The Advanced Capitalist Economies from Long Boom to Long Downturn, 1945–2005* (London: Verso, 2006). On the commingling of computing machinery and capital after the 1970s see Nick Dyer-Witheford, *Cyber-Proletariat: Global Labor in the Digital Vortex* (London: Pluto, 2015). Others have examined the ways that so-called digital labor represents a shift in relations of accumulation that require new kinds of Marxian analysis. Exemplary in this regard are Tiziana Terranova's "Free Labor: Producing Culture for the Digital Economy," *Social Text* 18, no. 2 (2000): 33–58; and Matteo Pasquinelli's "Google's PageRank Algorithm: A Diagram of Cognitive Capitalism and the Rentier of the Common Intellect," in *Deep*

Search, edited by Konrad Becker and Felix Stalder (London: Transaction, 2009), 134–52. Also see Christian Fuchs, *Digital Labor and Karl Marx* (New York: Routledge, 2014). Although I find the questions raised in these texts quite compelling, here I want to focus attention less on explicitly computer-augmented forms of work and more on the complex of abstraction, determination, abjection, and the differential allocation of freedom, self-possession, and self-organization that precedes and shapes those forms of work.

50. Dyer-Witheford considers such a shared history when he asks whether capitalism should be understood as a computer. In evaluating and responding to this possibility, he focuses on quantification before turning to the possibility of using computational technologies to organize noncapitalist forms of large-scale social organization. See Nick Dyer-Witheford, "Red Plenty Platforms," *Culture Machine* 14 (2013), https://culturemachine.net/wp-content/uploads/2019/05/511-1153-1-PB.pdf.
51. Cheryl I. Harris, "Whiteness as Property," *Harvard Law Review* 106, no. 8 (1993): 1735.
52. Margaret Jane Radin, "Property and Personhood," *Stanford Law Review* 34, no. 5 (1982): 968.
53. Harris, "Whiteness as Property," 1730.
54. Lacan, *Seminar II*, 54.
55. As Rosemary Hennessy writes, "the space of unmet needs" is capitalism's "outside." This space is not autonomous from but is rather produced through the linked dynamics of dispossession and partial integration into value-mediated relations of reproduction: "Because the minimum wage cannot cover even the most basic needs for living—food and clothing and housing and health care, no less education and time for intellectual and creative development—many unmet needs for living a full human life are virtually 'outlawed.'" Hennessy, *Profit and Pleasure: Sexual Identities in Late Capitalism* (New York: Routledge, 2000), 207, 216.
56. In comparison to the "selected," or what Wynter calls Man2—"a jobholding Breadwinner, and even more optimally, as a successful 'masterer of Natural Scarcity' (Investor, or capital accumulator)"—the dysselected "can no longer be defined in the terms of the interned Mad, the interned 'Indian,' the enslaved 'Negro' in which it had been earlier defined. Instead, the new descriptive statement of the human will call for its archipelago of Human Otherness to be peopled by a new category, one now comprised of the jobless, the homeless, the Poor, the systemically made jobless and criminalized—of the 'underdeveloped'—all as the category of the economically damnés, rather than, as before, of the politically condemned." Sylvia Wynter, "Unsettling the Coloniality of Being/Power/Truth/Freedom: Towards the Human, after Man, Its Overrepresentation—an Argument," *CR: The New Centennial Review* 3, no. 3 (2003): 321.

57. Sylvia Wynter, "Rethinking 'Aesthetics': Notes Toward a Deciphering Practice," in *Ex-Iles: Essays on Caribbean Cinema*, edited by Mbye B. Cham (Trenton, N.J.: Africa World Press, 1992), 245. "Each human order," Wynter writes later in the same essay, "effects its autopoeisis as a living, self-organizing (i.e. cybernetic) system" (259).
58. Lisa Nakamura, "Indigenous Circuits: Navajo Women and the Racialization of Early Electronic Manufacture," *American Quarterly* 66, no. 4 (2014): 920.
59. Although Sohn-Rethel doesn't mention the latter three phenomena, preferring a more general notion of exchange as the concrete "spatio-temporal activity" that subtends the value abstraction, thinking in terms of forms of disposal clarifies the central role that compromised conditions of reproduction play in the maintenance of that abstraction and its capacity to effect social synthesis.
60. My use of "disposal" here owes much to Neferti X. M. Tadiar's theorization of disposability under global neoliberalism, which stresses the figuration of "forms of bare life, at-risk populations, warehoused, disposable people, [and] urban excess" as the raw material of expanded reproduction and speculative finance and as a site of "struggle to make and remake social life" that people engage in "under conditions of their own [ascribed] superfluity." I aim to build on Tadiar's important work by developing a theory of value as an informatic mechanism that operates across capitalism's *longue durée*, connecting dispossession, enslavement, and conquest to the digital imaginaries that surround and reconfigure the relationship between those marked as essential and those marked as disposable. Tadiar, "Life-Times of Disposability within Global Neoliberalism," *Social Text* 115, no. 31 (2013): 23–24.
61. On capitalism's perceptual economy, the process through which "capitals confronting other capitals, simultaneously in competition and mutual dependency," generate "the surface appearances, prejudices, and representations of modern society," see Beverley Best, "Distilling a Value Theory of Ideology from Volume Three of *Capital*," *Historical Materialism* 23, no. 3 (2015): 101–41.
62. Although I focus on digitality here, the logic of value is linked to other forms of disposal. Jordy Rosenberg's critical account of recent philosophical and theoretical appeals to the molecular is a particularly rich study of one such form. Rosenberg writes: "When the social, historical contexts are elided from our understanding of what embodiment is—of what molecules 'are' or appear to be—then those molecules become the occasion for an anticipation, an affect of possession and agency that recalls the abstractions (and, indeed, the racial ontologies) at the heart of the property-form." Comparing second-order forms of disposal such as digitality and the molecular helps to show how different forms are grounded in different aspects of capital accumulation. The molecular, Rosenberg shows, reproduces the temporality of settler colonialism in a series of claims about the inherently resistant (because

aleatory) character of matter. Rosenberg, "The Molecularization of Sexuality," *Theory and Event* 17, no. 2 (2014): n.p.
63. Elena Ferrante, *Those Who Leave and Those Who Stay*, translated by Ann Goldstein (New York: Europa Editions, 2014), 113–14, 106–9. Hereafter cited parenthetically as *TWL*.
64. Silvia Federici, *Caliban and the Witch* (New York: Autonomedia, 2004), 12.
65. As Heather Merrill summarizes, "Italian colonial expansion in Libya, Somalia, Eritrea and Ethiopia and the production of southern Italy as a source of surplus labor in the nineteenth century provided a foundation for the racialization of labor today." This does not mean that southern Italians and Africans occupy a homogeneous space of abjection across shifting modes of production. Merrill writes: "Racial logic began to circumscribe social relationships when southern Italian and African populations were socially and scientifically classified with atavistic traits linked with criminal behavior. In Italy, where regional identity is intertwined with racialized thinking and structural racism, southern Italians have been categorized in distinction from lighter skinned northern Italians and discriminated against in northern cities. But in the contemporary context of neoliberal globalization and the influx of immigrants beginning in the late 1980s, southern Italians are now in a position of greater privilege as citizen insiders *vis-à-vis* 'blacks.'" Merrill, "Migration and Surplus Populations: Race and Deindustrialization in Northern Italy," *Antipode* 43, no. 5 (2003): 1550, 1543. On the marking of southern Italians as "biologically inferior beings, semi-barbarians or total barbarians" made by nature to be "lazy, incapable, criminal, and barbaric," see Antonio Gramsci, "Some Aspects of the Southern Question," in *Selections from Political Writings, 1921–1926*, translated by Quintin Hoare (London: Lawrence and Wishart, 1978), 444. On the relationship between the "southern question," colonialism, and the (biopolitical) valuation of populations, see Rhiannon Noel Welch, *Vital Subjects: Race and Biopolitics in Italy, 1860–1920* (Liverpool: Liverpool University Press, 2016).
66. Grace Kyungwon Hong, *The Ruptures of American Capital: Women of Color Feminism and the Culture of Immigrant Labor* (Minneapolis: University of Minnesota Press, 2006), 76–78.
67. Hartman, *Scenes of Subjection,* 141. In theorizing this relationship between self-possession and violence, Hartman writes specifically of racial slavery and post-emancipation racialized subjection in the United States, but this differential mechanism—abstraction energized by real conditions of dispossession and differential inclusion, directed at accumulation, and determining the distribution of survival, freedom, and agency—produces a wide range of social forms.
68. W. Ross Ashby, "Can a Mechanical Chess-Player Outplay Its Designer?" *British Journal for the Philosophy of Science* 3, no. 9 (1952): 44–57. Also see Norbert

Wiener, *Cybernetics, or Control and Communication in the Animal and the Machine* (1948; New York: Wiley, 1949), 193–94; and Claude Shannon, "Programming a Computer for Playing Chess," *Philosophical Magazine*, series 7, 41, no. 314 (1950): 256–75. Shannon's article was first presented at the National Institute of Radio Engineers convention, March 9, 1949.

69. Ashby, "Can a Mechanical Chess-Player Outplay Its Designer?," 51.

70. Ashby elaborated on this principle of responsiveness to external information in a presentation on mechanical chess players at the ninth Macy conference. There he proposed the use of a "suitably worked up" Geiger counter or "Brownian movements" as the "random source of moves." W. Ross Ashby, "Mechanical Chess Players," in von Foerster, Mead, and Teuber, *Cybernetics*, 152.

71. John A. V. Bates to W. Ross Ashby, May 6, 1953, GC/179/B.29, John Bates and the Ratio Club, Wellcome Collection, London. Bigelow raises a similar objection after Ashby's presentation at the ninth Macy conference, stating, "It is not at all clear that the addition of Brownian movement adds one iota of information to the system." Von Foerster, Mead, and Teuber, *Cybernetics*, 153.

72. Bates to Ashby, May 6, 1953.

73. W. Ross Ashby to John A. V. Bates, May 14, 1953, GC/179/B.29, John Bates and the Ratio Club, Wellcome Collection, London.

74. Ashby to Bates, May 14, 1953.

75. W. Ross Ashby, "Requisite Variety and Its Implications for the Control of Complex Systems," *Cybernetica* 1, no. 2 (1958): 87.

76. This distinction resonates with Kyla Schuller's account of the "biophilanthropic" migration of impoverished immigrant children from New York City carried out by Charles Loring Brace's Children's Aid Society. "Targeting bodies deemed undesirable, yet potentially redeemable, on account of their youthful impressibility," Schuller writes, biophilanthropy "works via the steady accumulation of impressions that will redirect a class or race from foreordained death and force it to persist, as a newly proletarianized group, for the economic and moral health of the settler colonial project." Brace's conviction was that this could be achieved "through the large-scale migration of children away from their families and out of the tenements, whereby 'the change of circumstance, the improved food, the daily moral and mental influences, the effect of regular labor and discipline, and, above all, the power of Religion awaken the[ir] hidden tendencies to do good . . . while they control and weaken and cause to be forgotten those diseased appetites or extreme passions which these unfortunate creatures inherit directly,' effectively rewriting their hereditary material. Reformers set about eradicating family connections. Yet despite these goals, youth and families drew on the services of CAS and similar organizations as part of a centuries-old strategy of labor in which indigent boys and girls contracted with rural families for several-year stints, earning room and board and relieving their poverty-stricken families of the same."

Schuller, *The Biopolitics of Feeling: Race, Sex, and Science in the Nineteenth Century* (Durham: Duke University Press, 2018), 136. Schuller quotes Charles Loring Brace, *The Dangerous Classes of New York, and Twenty Years' Work among Them,* 3rd ed. (New York: Wynkoop, 1880), 45–46.

77. As Macarena Gómez-Barris argues in her theorization of the "extractive zone," the "violence that capitalism does to reduce, constrain, and convert life into commodities" informs and is modulated by "the epistemological violence of training our academic vision to reduce life to systems." Gómez-Barris, *The Extractive Zone: Social Ecologies and Decolonial Perspectives* (Durham: Duke University Press, 2017), xix.

1. Things Communicated

1. Friedrich A. Kittler, "The History of Communication Media," in *On Line: Kunst Im Netz,* edited by Helga Konrad (Graz: Steirische Kultur Initiative, 1992), 66.
2. Kittler, 67.
3. Kittler, 67. In the second of these formulations Kittler quotes Niklas Luhmann, "Wie ist Bewusstsein an Kommunikation beteiligt?," in *Materialität der Kommunikation,* edited by Hans Ulrich Gumbrecht and K. Ludwig Pfeiffer (Frankfurt a.M.: Suhrkamp, 1988), 901.
4. As Philip Mirowksi and Edward Nik-Kah note, OR was "promoted as a Theory of Everything, which evinced a distinct interest in blurring most conventional ontological boundaries between the Natural and the Social, between agency and structure." Its projection of "physical models onto agglomerations of men and machines" became "the source and inspiration of many of the academic postwar social sciences, from decision theory to artificial intelligence, from management science to computational theory, from logical positivism to American neoclassical economics." Mirowski and Nik-Kah, "Markets Made Flesh: Performativity, and a Problem in Science Studies, Augmented with Consideration of the FCC Auctions," in *Do Economists Make Markets? On the Performativity of Economics,* edited by Donald McKenzie, Fabian Muniesa, and Lucia Siu (Princeton: Princeton University Press, 2007), 195. While acknowledging its longer histories, Deborah Cowen argues that the specific collection of techniques, technologies, and imaginaries that constitute logistics (as distinct from other disciplines for organizing production and circulation) can be traced to Bernard J. LaLonde, John R. Grabener, and James F. Robeson's article "Integrated Distribution Systems: A Management Perspective," published in 1970 in the inaugural issue of the *International Journal of Physical Distribution* (now the *International Journal of Physical Distribution and Logistics Management*). See Cowen, *The Deadly Life of Logistics: Mapping Violence in Global Trade* (Minneapolis: University of Minnesota Press, 2014), 23–24. Cowen's periodization is important because it makes it possible to track

against shifting structural conditions the mediated forms of appearance and the emerging technological substrates with which I am here concerned.
5. Cowen, *Deadly Life of Logistics*, 1. Also see Charmaine Chua, Martin Danyluk, Deborah Cowen, and Laleh Khalili, "Turbulent Circulation: Building a Critical Engagement with Logistics," *Environment and Planning D: Society and Space* 36, no. 4 (2018): 617–29. Logistics, they write, "seeks to effect the spatial disposition of bodies, information, and infrastructures in ways that promote the construction and operation of global supply networks" (622).
6. In Jasper Bernes's words, "a chain of transmitted symbolic representations that flows opposite to the physical movement of commodities." Bernes, "Logistics, Counterlogistics, and the Communist Prospect," *Endnotes* 3 (2013): 183.
7. Philip E. Agre, "Surveillance and Capture: Two Models of Privacy," *Information Society* 10, no. 2 (1994): 101–4, 107–10. Logistics, Agre argues, entails not only techniques and technologies for tracking persons and things, but also the work of organizing activities "even in the tricky and exceptional cases, so that they can be parsed within such-and-such a vocabulary of discrete units" (110).
8. See Philip E. Agre, "Beyond the Mirror World: Privacy and the Representational Practices of Computing," in *Technology and Privacy: The New Landscape*, edited by Agre and Marc Rotenberg (Cambridge: MIT Press, 1998), 29–61.
9. Friedrich A. Kittler, *Gramophone Film Typewriter*, translated by Geoffrey Winthrop-Young and Michael Wutz (Stanford: Stanford University Press, 1999), 1–2.
10. Lev Manovich, *The Language of New Media* (Cambridge: MIT Press, 2001), 36. Manovich goes on to define the new media object as "*mutable* and *liquid*." Both Kittler's and Manovich's definitions of digital fungibility clearly prefigure Bernes's description of logistics as "the active power to conjoin and split flows; to speed up and slow down; to change the type of commodity produced and its origin and destination point; and, finally, to collect and distribute knowledge about the production and circulation of commodities as they stream across the grid."
11. Bernes, "Logistics," 181; Hayles, *How We Became Posthuman*, xi.
12. Alberto Toscano has argued that, far from being "a view from nowhere of Capital-as-subject," logistics "is a deeply incoherent, contradictory, conflicted, and competitive domain; a strategic field of fierce competition sitting uneasily with state and security coordination, as well as inevitable processes of standardization. Process mappings, while striving towards homogeneity of spaces and codes, remain strategic weapons in the hands of capitalist agents, not overviews by 'capital.' Ideas of full visibility as integral flexibility are part of the ideology (and fantasy) of logistics, which in many ways is just a later iteration of other ideologies of capitalist efficacy: Taylorism, Toyotism, etc." As I argue throughout this book, the overcoding of incoherent, contradictory,

and violent processes by the fantasy of "full visibility" and the "homogeneity of spaces and flows" is determined by the basal logic of capital accumulation and marks the primary point of continuity between that logic and digitality. Toscano, "Lineaments of the Logistical State," *Viewpoint* 4, https://www.viewpointmag.com/2014/09/28/lineaments-of-the-logistical-state.

13. See Cowen, *Deadly Life of Logistics*, 2.
14. "In 1975, forty Malay operators were seized by spirits in a large American electronics plant based in Sungai Way. A second large-scale incident in 1978 involved some 120 operators in the microscope sections. The factory had to be shut down for three days and a spirit-healer (*bomoh*) was hired to slaughter a goat on the premises. The American owner wondered how he was to explain to corporate headquarters that '8,000 hours of production were lost because someone saw a ghost.' In late 1978, a Penang-based American microelectronics factory was disrupted for three consecutive days when fifteen women became afflicted by spirit possession." Aihwa Ong, *Spirits of Resistance and Capitalist Discipline: Factory Women in Malaysia* (New York: SUNY Press, 1987), 204.
15. For a detailed recent account of computational modes of labor control in warehouses, agriculture, platform-mediated "gig work," and elsewhere, see the *AI Now 2019 Report* (New York: AI Now Institute, 2019), https://ainowinstitute.org/AI_Now_2019_Report.html. As is documented by Cowen, the threat of disruption "has prompted the creation of an entire architecture of security that aims to govern global spaces of flow. This new framework of security—supply chain security—relies on a range of new forms of transnational regulation, border management, data collection, surveillance, and labor discipline, as well as naval missions and aerial bombing" (*Deadly Life of Logistics*, 2).
16. Although Kittler's writing can be generative when extended in this way, value understood as a mode of mediation is a consistent (perhaps structuring) absence. In the afterword to the 1987 second edition of *Discourse Networks 1800/1900*, for example, he distinguishes his approach, which treats literature as an information system, from the "sociology of literature" which "reads texts as reflections of relations of production." Kittler, *Discourse Networks 1800/1900*, translated by Michael Metteer, with Chris Cullens (Stanford: Stanford University Press, 1990), 370.
17. Kittler, "History of Communication Media," 68.
18. Sohn-Rethel, *Intellectual and Manual Labour*, 60.
19. In Stefano Harney and Fred Moten's words, modern logistics with its "ambition to connect bodies, objects, affects, information, without subjects," is "founded with the first great movement of commodities, the ones that could speak. It was founded in the Atlantic slave trade, founded against the Atlantic slave." Harney and Moten, *The Undercommons: Fugitive Planning and Black Study* (Wivenhoe: Minor Compositions, 2013), 92.

20. See, for example, Kenneth E. Boulding and W. Allen Spivey, *Linear Programming and the Theory of the Firm* (New York: Macmillan, 1960), 1–16. On the historical proximity between cybernetics, computer metaphors, and linear programming see Philip Mirowski, *Machine Dreams: Economics Becomes a Cyborg Science* (Cambridge: Cambridge University Press, 2002), 256–62.
21. Geert Reuten and Michael Williams, *Value-Form and the State: The Tendencies of Accumulation and the Determination of Economic Policy in Capitalist Society* (London: Routledge, 1989) 60.
22. A limited version of this argument is central to *Control: Digitality as Cultural Logic* (Cambridge: MIT Press, 2015), in which I focus on the ways that cybernetic modes of seeing, knowing, and organizing encrypt and modulate the logic of the commodity and its foundational exclusions, so that they appear in distorted forms in the kinds of late twentieth- and early twenty-first-century economic imaginaries that tend to jettison labor, production, and dispossession in favor of creative, immaterial, or cognitive forms of accumulation. I hope to expand here on the informatic logic of value that makes that encryption and modulation possible and to show how that logic produces (and thus encodes in digitality) social differentiation.
23. See Alexander R. Galloway, *Protocol: How Control Exists after Decentralization* (Cambridge: MIT Press, 2004); Wendy Hui Kyong Chun, *Control and Freedom: Power and Paranoia in the Age of Fiber Optics* (Cambridge: MIT Press, 2005).
24. Moishe Postone, *Time, Labor, and Social Domination: A Reinterpretation of Marx's Critical Theory* (Cambridge: Cambridge University Press, 1993), 125.
25. Diane Elson, "The Value Theory of Labour," in *Value: The Representation of Labour in Capitalism*, edited by Elson (London: Verso, 2015), 174. The concept of form-determination is derived from Marx's use of the noun *Formbestimmung* to describe the abstract social form conferred by value. This appears as "formal determination" in some English translations. See, for example, Victor Schnittke's rendering of Marx's argument that circulating and fixed capital should be understood "not as two particular types of capital, capital of two particular types, but as different *formal determinations of the same capital.*" Karl Marx, *Outlines of the Critique of Political Economy*, translated by Victor Schnittke, *MECW*, vol. 29 (London: Lawrence and Wishart, 1987), 10 (emphasis in original). Others eliminate "determination"; see, for example, Martin Nicolaus's translations of *Formbestimmung* as "specific form," "economic form," and "economic form-character." Marx, *Grundrisse*, 203, 267, 311 (for the original German see *Karl Marx Friedrich Engels Gesamtausgabe* [*MEGA*], Band II/1.1 [Berlin: Dietz Verlag, 1976], 132, 190, 229). Isaak Rubin emphasizes the "large role" that *Formbestimmung* plays in Marx's system, where it accounts for the "social *function* which is realized through a thing." In order to emphasize this social functionality, Rubin argues, "determination of form" or "definition of form" should be used instead of "formal determination."

I. I. Rubin, *Essays on Marx's Theory of Value*, translated by Miloš Samardžija and Fredy Perlman (Montreal: Black Rose, 1973). Subsequently, theorists have used form-determination to emphasize the logic of abstract domination over forms of appearance such as specific instances of concrete labor. On form-determination as capitalism's distinctive mode of domination see, for example, Christopher J. Arthur, *The New Dialectic and Marx's "Capital"* (Leiden: Brill, 2004), 81 ("In the value form there is not only a split between form and content, but the former becomes autonomous and the dialectical development of the structure is indeed form-determined"); and "Communisation and Value-Form Theory," *Endnotes* 2 (April 2010): 93 (value-form theory "demonstrates how the social life process is subsumed under—or 'form-determined' by—the value-form. What characterises such 'form-determination' is a perverse priority of the form over its content").

26. Hortense Spillers, "Mama's Baby, Papa's Maybe: An American Grammar Book," *Diacritics* 17, no. 2 (1987): 67.
27. Sohn-Rethel, *Intellectual and Manual Labour*, 5. Luc Boltanski and Ève Chiapello present an inverted form of Sohn-Rethel's argument (albeit in relation to dominant modes of representation and the direct application of concepts in management theory, rather than to imagination, desire, and fantasy and the underlying continuities between ostensibly separate realms such as capital and digitality) when they claim that "the forms of capitalist production accede to representation in each epoch" by "mobilizing concepts and tools that were initially developed largely autonomously in the theoretical sphere or the domain of basic scientific research. This is the case with neurology and computer science today." Boltanski and Chiapello, *The New Spirit of Capitalism*, translated by Gregory Elliott (London: Verso, 2005), 104.
28. Which is not to say that the transformation of quality into quantity and the relationship of this conversion to value and violence aren't important or revealing. See Jonathan Beller, *The Message Is Murder: Substrates of Computational Capital* (London: Pluto, 2017), especially 76–96.

2. Reliable Circuits, Unreliable Components

1. The "hard core of information theory," Shannon writes, "is, essentially, a branch of mathematics, a strictly deductive system. A thorough understanding of the mathematical foundation and its communication application is surely a prerequisite to other applications." Shannon, "The Bandwagon," *IRE Transactions on Information Theory* 2, no. 3 (1956): 3.
2. "If, for example, the human being acts in some situations like an ideal decoder, this is an experimental and not a mathematical fact, and as such must be tested under a wide variety of experimental situations" (Shannon, 3). For a similar argument in the form of satire, see Peter Elias, "Two Famous Papers,"

IRE Transactions: Information Theory 4 (1958): 99. Here Elias discusses two invented papers, each of which satirizes a major tendency in the application of information theory: "Information Theory, Photosynthesis, and Religion" spears the application of information-theoretical terminology across natural and social sciences; and "The Optimum Linear Square Wave Filter for Separating Sinusoidally Modulated Triangular Signals from Randomly Sampled Stationary Gaussian Noise, with Applications to a Problem in Radar" takes aim at the use of the mathematical techniques of information theory to solve physical problems that have "obvious nonlinearity," generally through the substitution of an "unrelated linear problem which is more amenable to analysis."
3. Claude Shannon, response to Donald M. Mackay, "In Search of Basic Symbols," in *Cybernetics: Circular Causal and Feedback Systems in Biological and Social Systems* (Transactions of the Eighth Conference, March 15–16, 1951, New York), edited by Heinz von Foerster, Margaret Mead, and Hans Lukas Teuber (New York: Josiah Macy, Jr. Foundation, 1951), 207–8.
4. Ronald R. Kline suggests as much in a discussion of the popularization and generalization of cybernetics and information theory (and of what he regards as Shannon's and Norbert Wiener's differing appetites for such generalization and popularization). Kline, *The Cybernetics Moment, or Why We Call Our Age the Information Age* (Baltimore: Johns Hopkins University Press, 2015), 125–26.
5. Claude Shannon, "Information Theory," in *Claude Elwood Shannon: Collected Papers*, edited by N. J. A. Sloane and Aaron D. Wyner (New York: Institute of Electrical and Electronics Engineers 1993), 212.
6. Shannon, 212.
7. See Claude E. Shannon, "Recent Developments in Communication Theory," *Electronics,* April 1950, 80–83.
8. Shannon, "Information Theory," 213.
9. Although media technologies and those of production cannot be easily separated, note that servomechanisms "and other data-processing devices," those foundational technologies of industrial automation, are among the uses of information Shannon lists in the *Encyclopædia* entry. Shannon's work was positioned as central to the development of those technologies. In a letter confirming acceptance of Shannon's 1936 master's thesis for publication in the *Transactions* of the American Institute of Electrical Engineers, Charles S. Rich, the president of that institute, writes: "While this paper deals specifically only with switching and relaying of electrical circuits, the fundamental analysis has much wider application. Mechanical linkages, hydraulic or pneumatic arrangements, or even optical systems could be analyzed and synthesized by the methods Mr. Shannon employs." Charles S. Rich to Vannevar Bush, May 8, 1938, box 1, folder 1, Claude Elwood Shannon Papers, Manuscript Division, Library of Congress, Washington, D.C.

10. Marx, *Capital*, 1:163–64.
11. Karl Marx, "Results of the Immediate Process of Production," *Capital*, 1:1020–21.
12. Amanda Armstrong has observed that Marx intended something similar with his choice of wood. Because of the specific demands of working with wood, which pose challenges to the outright dominance of the concrete by the abstract, "Marx's play with metaphor . . . suggests that, as much as he is interested in tracking the force of abstraction in an era dominated by capital, he also inclines to show how the bodies and materials upon which capital accumulation depends set limits to capitalization and its attendant abstraction of labor. Marx cannot but register in his work the recalcitrance of the concrete, the injury of abstraction." Armstrong, "The Wooden Brain: Organizing Untimeliness in Marx's *Capital*," *Mediations* 31, no. 1 (2017), http://www.mediationsjournal.org/articles/wooden-brain.
13. Evelyn Nakano Glenn, *Unequal Freedom: How Race and Gender Shaped American Citizenship and Labor* (Cambridge: Harvard University Press, 2002), 105.
14. John Perlin, *A Forest Journey: The Role of Wood in the Development of Civilization* (Cambridge: Harvard University Press, 1989), 266.
15. Claude Shannon, "A Mathematical Theory of Communication," *Bell Systems Technical Journal* 27, no. 3 (1948): 379.
16. See, for example, Hayles, *How We Became Posthuman*, 53–54; Mark B. N. Hansen, *New Philosophy for New Media* (Cambridge: MIT Press, 2004), 76–78; Alexander R. Galloway and Eugene Thacker, *The Exploit: A Theory of Networks* (Minneapolis: University of Minnesota Press, 2007), 55–57.
17. Claude Elwood Shannon, "A Symbolic Analysis of Relay and Switching Circuits" (master's thesis, Massachusetts Institute of Technology, 1936), 1–3.
18. Shannon, "Recent Developments," 81.
19. Warren Weaver, "Some Recent Contributions to the Mathematical Theory of Communication," in Claude E. Shannon and Warren Weaver, *The Mathematical Theory of Communication* (Urbana: University of Illinois Press, 1964), 4.
20. Indeed, Shannon locates both meaning and the effects of a given transmission outside the purview of communication theory in the discussion at the eighth Macy conference cited above. "In the communication problem," he states, "the particular problem you are interested in is 'How much channel do I need to transmit this information?' and entropy is a quantity which measures or determines the amount of channel required. So long as you ask that question, that is the answer. If you are asking what does information mean to the user of it and how is it going to affect him, then perhaps [a different system] might be appropriate" (von Foerster, Mead, and Teuber, *Cybernetics*, 208).
21. Wiener, *Cybernetics*, 155. Of these shifts and mutations (albeit without acknowledging their proximity to dynamics of accumulation and dispossession) Hayles writes that "Shannon and Wiener defined information so that it

would be calculated as the same value regardless of the contexts in which it was embedded, which is to say, they divorced it from meaning. *In context,* this was an appropriate and sensible decision. *Taken out of context,* the definition allowed information to be conceptualized as if it were an entity that can flow unchanged between different material substrates" (*How We Became Posthuman,* 53–54).

22. J. D. Bernal, *Science in History,* vol. 3 (London: Watts and Co., 1954), 544.
23. Karl W. Deutsch, *The Nerves of Government: Models of Political Communication and Control* (New York: The Free Press, 1966), 82.
24. Gregory Bateson, "Form, Substance, and Difference," *General Semantics Bulletin* 37 (1970): 6–7. Bateson first delivered this paper as the Korzybski Memorial Lecture at the Harvard Club, New York, January 9, 1970. It is reprinted in Bateson, *Steps to an Ecology of Mind* (San Francisco: Chandler, 1972), 454–71.
25. Sohn-Rethel, *Intellectual and Manual Labour,* 7.
26. Marx, *Grundrisse,* 161.
27. "The private character of the production of the exchange-value-producing individual itself appears as an historical product—his isolation, his self-establishment as an independent point within the production is determined by a division of labour which, for its part, rests on a whole range of economic conditions through which the individual is conditioned on every side in his connections with other individuals and in his own mode of existence." Marx, *Second Draft of Critique of Political Economy,* translated by Yuri Sdobnikov, *MECW,* 29:465.
28. Karl Marx to Ludwig Kugelmann, July 11, 1868, translated by John Peet, Michael Slattery, and Sergei Syrovatkin, *MECW,* vol. 43 (London: Lawrence and Wishart, 1988), 68.
29. Ernest Mandel, introduction to Marx, *Capital,* 1:51.
30. As Marx puts it, under capitalism the "proportional distribution" of labor operates through the form of value. Marx to Kugelmann, 68.
31. Robert Brenner, "The Origins of Capitalist Development: A Critique of Neo-Smithian Marxism," *New Left Review* 104 (1977): 32.
32. Étienne Balibar, "The Basic Concepts of Historical Materialism," in Louis Althusser, Étienne Balibar, Roger Establet, Pierre Macherey, and Jacques Ranciére, *Reading Capital: The Complete Edition,* translated by Ben Brewster and David Fernbach (London: Verso, 2015), 418.
33. Michael Heinrich, *An Introduction to the Three Volumes of Karl Marx's "Capital,"* translated by Alex Locasio (New York: Monthly Review Press, 2012), 50–51.
34. Heinrich, 50–51. Emphasis added.
35. Marx, *Capital,* 1:129.
36. Karl Marx, *Theories of Surplus Value, Part Three,* translated by Jack Cohen (London: Lawrence and Wishart, 1972), 135. Also see Elson, "The Value Theory of

Labour," 132, where she notes that "value is not the *same* as a quantity of socially necessary labour-time: it is an objectification or materialisation of a certain aspect of that labour-time, its aspect of being simply an expenditure of human labour power in general, i.e. abstract labour."

37. Marx identifies the abstract form of value-mediated labor as an effect of the system in which it functions when he writes: "Indifference towards specific labours corresponds to a form of society in which individuals can with ease transfer from one labour to another, and where the specific kind is a matter of chance for them, hence of indifference. Not only the category, labour, but labour in reality has here become the means of creating wealth in general, and has ceased to be organically linked with particular individuals in any specific form" (*Grundrisse*, 104).

38. See Raya Dunayevskaya, *Marxism and Freedom from 1776 to Today* (New York: Bookman Associates, 1958), 138. In Elson's argument, the object of Marx's theory of value is labor, and its aim is not to explain how value constitutes the substance of price but rather to "seek an understanding of why labor takes the form it does, and what the political consequences are" ("The Value Theory of Labour," 123).

39. Elson, "The Value Theory of Labour," 123.

40. Arthur, *The New Dialectic*, 105.

41. Roberto Finelli, "Abstraction versus Contradiction: Observations on Chris Arthur's *The New Dialectic and Marx's 'Capital*,'" translated by Peter Thomas, *Historical Materialism* 15 (2007): 63.

42. Marx, *Grundrisse*, 241.

43. Heinrich, *Introduction*, 53.

44. Marx, *Capital*, 1:142.

45. Rubin, *Essays on Marx's Theory of Value*, 97.

46. Rubin, 120.

47. Heinrich, *Introduction*, 46.

48. Heinrich, 51.

49. As Marx writes, "If the same amount of the means of subsistence can be produced in a shorter working period owing to an increase in the productivity of real labour, the value of labour capacity will fall, and along with that the labour time required for its reproduction. . . . If we take the total capital of society, hence the whole capitalist class vis-à-vis the working class, it is clear that the capitalist class can only increase surplus value without extending the overall working day and without lessening the normal wage in so far as a greater productivity of labour, a higher development of the productive power of labour, makes it possible to maintain the working class as a whole with less labour, to produce the total amount of its means of subsistence more cheaply, and therefore to reduce the amount of labour time in total that the working class requires for the reproduction of its own wages. But this total amount

consists simply of the total amount of individual means of subsistence and the total amount of the specific branches of labour; hence of the total amount of the individual branches of labour which produce these means of subsistence; hence of the total amount of the reductions in labour time on account of the increased productive power of labour in each of these individual branches." Karl Marx, "Economic Manuscript of 1861–1863," translated by Ben Fowkes, *MECW,* vol. 30 (London: Lawrence and Wishart, 1988), 235–37.
50. Marx, *Capital,* 1:275–76.
51. Diane Elson and Ruth Pearson, "'Nimble Fingers Make Cheap Workers': An Analysis of Women's Employment in Third World Export Manufacturing," *Feminist Review* 7 (1981): 93–94.
52. "If the owner of labor-power works today, tomorrow he must again be able to repeat the same process in the same conditions as regards health and strength." Marx, *Capital,* 1:275.
53. Bernard Mandeville, *The Fable of the Bees* (1714; London: Penguin, 1970), 209. Marx quotes this passage in the chapter of *Capital* on the process of accumulation, along with a comparable passage from Mandeville's *An Essay on Trade and Commerce*: "'Temperate living and constant employment the direct road, for the poor, to rational happiness' (by which the author means the longest possible working days and the smallest possible amount of the means of subsistence), 'and to riches and strength for the state' (namely for the landowners, capitalists, and their political dignitaries and agents)." Marx, *Capital,* 1:765n3. Parenthetical comments Marx's.
54. The defining characteristic of capitalist production, Marx writes, is that "labour-power is not purchased under this system for the purpose of satisfying the personal needs of the buyer, either by its service or through its product. The aim of the buyer is the valorization of his capital, the production of commodities which contain more labour than he paid for, and therefore contain a portion of value which costs him nothing and is nevertheless realized [*realisiert*] through the sale of those commodities. The production of surplus-value, or the making of profits, is the absolute law of this mode of production. Labour-power can be sold only to the extent that it preserves and maintains the means of production as capital, reproduces its own value as capital, and provides a source of additional capital in the shape of unpaid labour. The conditions of its sale, whether more or less favourable to the worker, include therefore the necessity of its constant re-sale, and the constantly extended reproduction of wealth as capital" (*Capital,* 1:769).
55. For an extensive cybernetic treatment of Marxian reproduction schemata, see Oskar Lange, *Introduction to Economic Cybernetics,* translated by Józef Stadler (Oxford: Pergamon Press, 1970), 49–62.
56. Finelli, "Abstraction versus Contradiction," 66.

57. Finelli, 66; Marx, *Capital*, 1:873.
58. Marx, *Capital*, 1:271–72.
59. Marx, 280.
60. See C. B. Macpherson, *The Political Theory of Possessive Individualism: Hobbes to Locke* (Oxford: Oxford University Press, 1964), 263–64. On these pages Macpherson itemizes the assumptions that comprise possessive individualism. His summary includes the following propositions: "(i) What makes a man human is freedom from dependence on the wills of others"; "(ii) Freedom from dependence on others means freedom from any relations with others except those relations which the individual enters voluntarily with a view to his own interest"; "(iii) The individual is essentially the proprietor of his own person and capacities, for which he owes nothing to society"; "(iv) Although the individual cannot alienate the whole of his property in his own person, he may alienate his capacity to labour"; "(v) Human society consists of a series of market relations"; "(vi) Since freedom from the wills of others is what makes a man human, each individual's freedom can rightfully be limited only by such obligations and rules as are necessary to secure the same freedom for others"; "(vii) Political society is a human contrivance for the protection of the individual's property in his person and goods, and (therefore) for the maintenance of orderly relations of exchange between individuals regarded as proprietors of themselves."
61. Theodor Adorno, *Negative Dialectics,* translated by E. B. Ashton (London: Routledge, 2004), 178.
62. Individuals "*seem* independent," Marx writes, but "this is an independence which is at bottom merely an illusion, and it is more correctly called indifference" (*Grundrisse,* 163).
63. Bruno Latour, *Reassembling the Social: An Introduction to Actor-Network Theory* (Oxford: Oxford University Press, 2005), 218.
64. Hayles foregrounds four characteristics the posthuman: the privileging of "informatic pattern" over material instantiation; the epiphenomenal status of consciousness; an understanding of the body as the original prosthesis, so that "extending or replacing the body with other prostheses becomes a continuation of a process that began before we were born"; and the absence of any "essential differences or absolute demarcations between bodily existence and computer simulation, cybernetic mechanism and biological organism, robot teleology and human goals" (*How We Became Posthuman,* 3).
65. Hayles, 4–5.
66. Gunther Teubner, "Enterprise Corporatism: New Industrial Policy and the 'Essence' of the Legal Person," *American Journal of Comparative Law* 36, no. 1 (1988): 134–36.
67. Teubner, 136.
68. Teubner, 139.

69. For a sustained theorization of legal form as a matrix for facilitating value-mediated relations rather than a stable set of claims or principles, see Evgeny Bronislavovich Pashukanis's *The General Theory of Law and Marxism* of 1924: "Only by starting from [the exchange of commodity values] can one understand why a whole series of other social relations assume legal form." Pashukanis, *The General Theory of Law and Marxism*, translated by Barbara Einhorn (New Brunswick, N.J.: Transaction, 2003), 64.
70. Drawing on the Japanese Marxists Uno Kōzō and Karatani Kōjin, Gavin Walker evocatively describes this synthesis of unreliable components as capital's "sublime perversion." This "thing that should be impossible," Walker writes, "manages to work quite well." And this is "because capitalist society is so exquisitely perverse, and thereby perfectly sublime, not in spite of its 'defects' but because of them." Walker, *The Sublime Perversion of Capital* (Durham: Duke University Press, 2016), 12–13.
71. Charles Babbage, *On the Economy of Machinery and Manufactures* (London: Charles Knight, 1832), 39.
72. E. F. Moore and Claude Shannon, "Reliable Circuits Using Less Reliable Relays," *Journal of the Franklin Institute* 262, no. 3 (1956): 191.
73. See, for example, the discussion of redundancy in Paul Baran's *On Distributed Communications: I. Introduction to Distributed Communications Networks*, RAND memorandum RM-3420-PR (1964). Also notable is Robert T. Braden's "Requirements for Internet Hosts—Communication Layers" (RFC 1122, 1989), 8: "A basic objective of the Internet design is to tolerate a wide range of network characteristics—e.g., bandwidth, delay, packet loss, packet reordering, and maximum packet size. Another objective is robustness against failure of individual networks, gateways, and hosts, using whatever bandwidth is still available. Finally, the goal is full 'open system interconnection': an Internet host must be able to interoperate robustly and effectively with any other Internet host, across diverse Internet paths."
74. Stuart Hall, "Marx's Notes on Method: A Reading of the '1857 Introduction,'" *Cultural Studies* 17, no. 2 (2003): 125. Emphasis added.
75. Hall quotes the sentences on the "beauty and greatness" of capital's "material and mental metabolism."
76. Federici, *Caliban and the Witch*, 140. Emphasis in original.

3. The Informatics of Dispossession

1. Michael Denning, "Wageless Life," *New Left Review* 66 (2010): 80.
2. Marx, *Capital*, 1:874.
3. See part 8 of Marx, *Capital*, vol. 1.
4. Marx, 1:899. In analyzing the role of primitive accumulation vis-à-vis the network of exchange that appears the primary means of social management (or

domination) under capitalism, Marx focuses on procedures such as the enclosure of common land; the concomitant expropriation of rural populations; "bloody legislation" intended to implement the discipline required for wage labor—including contract laws, the regulation of "combinations of workers," and prohibitions on begging and "vagabondage"; colonial expansion; slavery; and public debt (902, 896, 919).

5. Werner Bonefeld, "Primitive Accumulation and Capitalist Accumulation: Notes on Social Constitution and Expropriation," *Science & Society* 75, no. 3 (2011): 396. Bonefeld contrasts this definition to those elaborated in Massimo de Angelis, "Marx and Primitive Accumulation: The Continuous Character of Marx's Enclosures," *The Commoner* 2 (2001): 1–22; and David Harvey, *The New Imperialism* (Oxford: Oxford University Press, 2003).

6. Rosa Luxemburg, *The Accumulation of Capital*, translated by Agnes Schwarzschild (London: Routledge, 2003), 345. The ongoing imposition of market dependence onto conditions of social reproduction is visible in Ribeirinho Raimundo Braga Gomes's account of his forced movement from the forest alongside the Xingu River as a result of the construction of the Belo Monte dam. Before this displacement, Braga says, "I didn't need money to live happy. My whole house was nature. The lumber, straw, didn't need any nails. I had my patch of land where I planted a bit of everything, all sorts of fruit trees. I'd catch my fish, make manioc flour. If I wanted something else to eat, I'd grab a hen I'd raised. If I wanted meat, I'd hunt in the forest. And to make money, I'd fish some more and sell it in town. I raised my three daughters, proud of what I was. I was rich. Now . . . I have to buy everything I need. . . . Since I don't have money to buy what I want, I buy what I can. I like manioc flour, but I can only afford rice. I used to harvest 400 good watermelons, but today I can't buy even a bad one. I used to pick the hen I wanted to eat, but today I can't buy one. I used to have a living river, today I have a dead lake—and to get there I have to pay for transportation." Eliane Brum, "They Owned an Island, Now They Are Urban Poor: The Tragedy of Altemira," *The Guardian*, February 6, 2018, https://www.theguardian.com/cities/2018/feb/06/urban-poor-tragedy-altamira-belo-monte-brazil.

7. Processes of social reproduction, Federici argues, represent "a set of phenomena that are absent in Marx, but which remain extremely important for capitalist accumulation" (*Caliban and the Witch*, 12). The archive of classic literature here is vast and heterogeneous. In addition to Federici, see, for example, Mariarosa Dalla Costa and Selma James, *The Power of Women and the Subversion of the Community* (Bristol: Falling Wall Press, 1972); Gayle Rubin, "The Traffic in Women: Notes on the 'Political Economy' of Sex," in *Toward an Anthropology of Women*, edited by Rayna Reiter (New York: Monthly Review Press, 1975), 157–210; Maria Mies, *Patriarchy and Accumulation on a World Scale: Women in the International Division of Labour* (London: Zed Books,

1980); Angela Y. Davis, "The Coming Obsolescence of Housework: A Working-Class Perspective," in *Women, Race, and Class* (1981; New York: Vintage Books, 1983), 222–44; Leopoldina Fortunati, *The Arcane of Reproduction: Housework, Prostitution, Labor, and Capital*, translated by Hillary Creek (1981; New York: Autonomedia, 1995); Evelyn Nakano Glenn, "From Servitude to Service Work: Historical Continuities in the Racial Division of Paid Reproductive Labor," *Signs* 18, no. 1 (1992): 1–43. The concept of unwaged feminized labor as indirectly market-mediated is from Endnotes, "The Logic of Gender," *Endnotes* 3 (2013): 56–90.

8. On the relationship of capitalism to slavery see Marx, *Capital*, 1:925; Eric Williams, *Capitalism and Slavery* (1944; Chapel Hill: University of North Carolina Press, 1994); Robinson, *Black Marxism*; Johnson, "The Pedestal and the Veil" and *River of Dark Dreams: Slavery and Empire in the Cotton Kingdom* (Cambridge: Harvard University Press, 2013); John J. Clegg, "Capitalism and Slavery," *Critical Historical Studies* 2, no. 2 (2015): 281–304. On its structural relationship to "free" labor see Hartman, *Scenes of Subjection*; and Nikhil Pal Singh, *Race and America's Long War* (Oakland: University of California Press, 2017), 74-97. On slavery's carceral afterlives, see Ruth Wilson Gilmore, *Golden Gulag: Prisons, Surplus Crisis, and Opposition in Globalizing California* (Berkeley: University of California Press, 2007). On settler-colonial occupation and primitive accumulation, see Glen Sean Coulthard, *Red Skin, White Masks: Rejecting the Colonial Politics of Recognition* (Minneapolis.: University of Minnesota Press, 2014). Coulthard stresses that "Increased European settlement combined with an imported, hyperexploited non-European workforce meant that, in the post-fur trade period, Canadian state formation and colonial-capitalist development required first and foremost *land*, and only secondarily the surplus value afforded by cheap, Indigenous labor." Which isn't to suggest that "the long-term goal of indoctrinating the Indigenous population to the principles of private property, possessive individualism, and menial wage work did not constitute an important feature of Canadian Indian policy" (12–13).

9. Robert Nichols, *Theft Is Property! Dispossession and Critical Theory* (Durham: Duke University Press, 2020), 70.

10. One important difference, Nichols notes, is that "primitive accumulation in Western Europe took place in a global context in which no other capitalist societies already existed." While Marx's original framework "attempts to explain the strange alchemy of capital's emergence out of *noncapital*, subsequent focus shifts to the subsumption of noncapital by *already existing* capital" (Nichols, 69).

11. As Walker describes it, "the process of primitive accumulation and its enclosure, followed by the criminalization of vagabondage and wandering, was a process not of freeing in the strict sense, but paradoxically of freeing in order to more effectively 'capture' and control the movement and circulation

of individuals"—or the synthesis of a reliable circuit from "unreliable" components (*The Sublime Perversion of Capital*, 81).
12. As Gilles Deleuze and Félix Guattari put it, the forms of regulatory violence that shape and are shaped by these processes represent a primitive accumulation that is "not produced once at the dawn of capitalism" but is "constantly reproducing itself." Deleuze and Guattari, *Anti-Oedipus: Capitalism and Schizophrenia* (Minneapolis: University of Minnesota Press, 1983), 231.
13. Smallwood, *Saltwater Slavery*, 44.
14. See Hartman, *Scenes of Subjection*, 24: "It is a tricky matter to detail the civil existence of a subject who is socially dead and legally recognized as human only to the degree that he is criminally culpable."
15. Federici, *Caliban and the Witch*, 9.
16. "Assuring women that even a small loan could solve their economic problems, [microfinance] has subsumed their informal activities, made of exchanges with poor unemployed women like themselves, to the formal economy, forcing them to pay a weekly amount as part of their loan repayment." Silvia Federici, "From Commoning to Debt: Financialization, Microcredit, and the Changing Architecture of Capital Accumulation," *South Atlantic Quarterly* 113, no. 2 (2014): 236.
17. Paula Chakravartty and Denise Ferreira da Silva, "Accumulation, Dispossession, and Debt: The Racial Logic of Global Capitalism—an Introduction," *American Quarterly* 64, no. 3 (2012), 363–64.
18. On racialization and feminization as immanent dynamics of capital accumulation, see Robinson, *Black Marxism*; P. Valentine, "The Gender Distinction in Communization Theory," *LIES: A Journal of Materialist Feminism* 1 (2012): 191–208; Endnotes, "The Logic of Gender"; Chris Chen, "The Limit Point of Capitalist Equality," *Endnotes* 3 (2013): 202–23; FTC Manning, "Closing the Conceptual Gap: A Response to Cinzia Arruzza's 'Remarks on Gender,'" *Viewpoint*, May 24, 2015, https://www.viewpointmag.com/2015/05/04/closing-the-conceptual-gap-a-response-to-cinzia-arruzzas-remarks-on-gender/; Amy De'Ath, "Gender and Social Reproduction," in *The SAGE Handbook of Frankfurt School Critical Theory*, edited by Beverley Best, Werner Bonefeld, and Chris O'Kane (London: SAGE, 2018), 1534–50.
19. Marx, *Capital*, 1:794.
20. Marx, 796.
21. Marx, 796.
22. This is the process Marx sometimes describes as a change in the organic composition of capital. See, for example, *Capital*, 1:781.
23. Marx, 781–83.
24. Marx, 784.
25. Marx, 784.
26. Marx, 789.

27. Marx, 790–92.
28. Marx, 796.
29. And as Dalla Costa and James point out, in many cases feminized labor in the home then performs an essential homoeostatic function within the surplus population. Women, she writes, "always receive back into the home all those who are periodically expelled from their jobs by economic crisis. The family, this maternal cradle always ready to help and protect in time of need, has been in fact the best guarantee that the unemployed do not immediately become a horde of disruptive outsiders." Dalla Costa and James, *The Power of Women*, 34.
30. For a useful overview of this tendency see Aaron Benanav and John Clegg, "Misery and Debt: On the Logic and History of Surplus Populations," *Endnotes* 2 (2012): 20–51.
31. Karl Marx, *Capital: A Critique of Political Economy*, vol. 3, translated by David Fernbach (London: Penguin, 1991), 298.
32. Note that the global distribution and technological organization of production and services cannot be reduced to the displacement of productive labor from the Global North to the Global South, producing a clean division between discrete "postindustrial" and "industrial" regions. Although such displacements are central to the modulation of socially necessary labor time, and hence to the drive to maintain or grow surplus over necessary labor, they are accompanied by the expansion of service labor across "peripheral" and "core" countries, albeit at different speeds and centered on different types of service. "As capitalist deterritorialization is developing from the center to the periphery," Deleuze and Guattari write, "the decoding of flows on the periphery develops by means of a 'disarticulation' that ensures the ruin of traditional sectors, the development of extraverted economic circuits, a specific hypertrophy of the tertiary [service] sector, and an extreme inequality in the different areas of productivity and in incomes" (*Anti-Oedipus*, 231–32).
33. Marx, *Capital*, 1:686.
34. As Lisa Gitelman and Virginia Jackson remind us, following Geoffrey C. Bowker, data, like quanta of socially average abstract labor, are always cooked, never raw: "Data need to be imagined as data to exist and function as such." Gitelman and Jackson, introduction to *"Raw Data" Is an Oxymoron*, edited by Lisa Gitelman (Cambridge: MIT Press, 2013), 3.
35. For electronics-grade copper, for example, copper sulphate is extracted from mines, crushed, ground, mixed with water and chemicals, subject to thermal techniques "including several stages of heating in furnaces that melt the concentrate, catalyze chemical reactions, and break the bonds between Cu and other 'impurities,'" and then electrolytically refined to dissolve the copper atoms from slabs of "almost pure" copper, producing a material that is "99.99

percent pure." Nicole Starosielski, "Thermocultures of Geological Media," *Cultural Politics* 12, no. 3 (2016): 297.
36. Starosielski, 299.
37. As Brenna Bhandar and Davina Bhandar write, racialized and gendered formations "are not contingent but constitutive of dispossession—as it unfolds across material, social, psychic, and juridical fields." Bhandar and Bhandar, "Cultures of Dispossession: Rights, Statuses, and Identities," *Darkmatter* 14 (May 16, 2016), http://www.darkmatter101.org/site/2016/05/16/cultures-of-dispossession.

4. Differentiation as Regulation

1. Roderick Ferguson, *Aberrations in Black: Toward a Queer of Color Critique* (Minneapolis: University of Minnesota Press, 2004), ix.
2. Ferguson, 15.
3. As Bhandar and Bhandar put it, "Cultural formations of dispossession reflect the uneven impact of several hundred years of capitalist accumulation, centralised through the agency of the possessive individual and its corollary, the subject (always-already) ontologically and politically dispossessed of the capacity to appropriate and own, to be self-determining" ("Cultures of Dispossession").
4. Ruth Wilson Gilmore, "Fatal Couplings of Power and Difference: Notes on Racism and Geography," *The Professional Geographer* 54, no. 1 (2002): 21.
5. Ruth Wilson Gilmore, "Race and Globalization," in *Geographies of Global Change: Remapping the World*, edited by R. J. Johnston, Peter J. Taylor, and Michael J. Watts, 2nd ed. (Malden, Mass.: Blackwell, 2002), 261.
6. Gilmore, "Race and Globalization," 261.
7. Marx, *Capital*, 1:797.
8. Alexander G. Weheliye, *Habeas Viscus: Racializing Assemblages, Biopolitics, and Black Feminist Theories of the Human* (Durham: Duke University Press, 2014), 3. Also see Nikhil Pal Singh, *Black Is a Country: Race and the Unfinished Struggle for Democracy* (Cambridge: Harvard University Press, 2004), 223: "We need to recognize the technology of race . . . precisely as those historic repertoires and cultural, spatial and signifying systems that stigmatize and depreciate one form of humanity for the purposes of another's health, development, safety, profit or pleasure." Lindon Barrett identifies the doubling of these mechanisms in the operations of value when he writes that "at its simplest, value is a configuration of privilege, and, at its crudest, race is the same. Insofar as value, as a theoretical dynamic, promotes one form(ation) to the detriment of another (or others), race proves a dramatic instantiation of this principle." Barrett, *Blackness and Value: Seeing Double* (Cambridge: Cambridge University Press, 2001), 1–2.

9. See Lisa Lowe, *Immigrant Acts: On Asian American Cultural Politics* (Durham: Duke University Press, 1996), 28. Lowe's indispensable theorization of the race and gender formations that are shaped by the dynamics of capital accumulation, free and unfree labor, and political equality continues in her *The Intimacies of Four Continents*. Consider, for example, her account of the 1803 "Secret Memorandum from the British Colonial Office to the Chairman of the Court of Directors of the East India Company" that "laid the groundwork for the introduction of Chinese indentured laborers" into Trinidad, which emphasizes the dynamic production of racial forms in response to specific economic demands. "For two centuries," Lowe writes, "British mercantile colonialism depended on the settlement of the Americas and West Indies that displaced and dispossessed native peoples, and the command of the British Atlantic slave system that transported captured West and Central African peoples to labor on plantations in the Americas. After two centuries, this British plan to import Chinese workers appears to mark a significant, yet largely ignored shift in the management of race and labor in the West Indian colonies. The decision to experiment with a different form of labor was explicitly racialized—'a free race . . . who could be kept distinct from the Negroes'—but moreover it framed the importation of this newly, and differently, 'raced' Chinese labor as a solution to both the colonial need to suppress Black slave rebellion and the capitalist desire to expand production." Lowe, *The Intimacies of Four Continents* (Durham: Duke University Press, 2015), 22–23.
10. Day, *Alien Capital*, 9.
11. Day, 193.
12. Marx, *Capital*, 1:275.
13. Heinrich, *Introduction*, 232n24.
14. Raji C. Steineck, "Time Subsumed or Time Sublated?," *Asiatische Studien/ Études Asiatiques* 71, no. 4 (2018): 1349.
15. Marx, *Capital*, 3:345. For a more recent iteration of this process, see Anna Curcio and Gigi Roggero's account of the way that the Bossi-Fini migration law in Italy functions "first and foremost as a labor law that effectively shows border management as a mechanism to devalue the workforce by facilitating the blackmailing and exploitation of workers," producing "competition between national and foreign workers for largely underqualified jobs and for access to a largely destructured welfare system." Curcio and Roggero, "Logistics Is the Logic of Capital," translated by Tommaso Manfredini, *Viewpoint*, https://www.viewpointmag.com/2018/10/25/logistics-is-the-logic-of-capital/.
16. Sylvia Wynter, "Black Metamorphosis: New Natives in a New World" (unpublished manuscript, n.d.), 33.
17. Sylvia Wynter, "Beyond the Categories of the Master Conception: The Counterdoctrine of Jamesian Poesis," in *C. L. R. James's Caribbean*, edited by Paget

Henry and Paul Buhle (Durham: Duke University Press, 1992), 81. Also see Wynter, "Black Metamorphosis," 29 ("over 40 they were sold as 'refuse' at cut rate prices"); and Wynter, "On How We Mistook the Map for the Territory, and Re-imprisoned Ourselves in Our Unbearable Wrongness of Being, of *Désêtre*: Black Studies toward the Human Project," in *Not Only the Master's Tools: African-American Studies in Theory and Practice*, edited by Lewis R. Gordon and Jane Anna Gordon (London: Routledge, 2016), 165n7.

18. Lowe, *Intimacies*, 8.
19. See Hartman, *Scenes of Subjection*, 115–24; Lowe, *Immigrant Acts* and *Intimacies*; Day, *Alien Capital*; Kalindi Vora, *Life Support: Biocapital and the New History of Outsourced Labor* (Minneapolis: University of Minnesota Press, 2015); Neferti X. M. Tadiar, "City Everywhere," *Theory, Culture and Society* 33, nos. 7–8 (2016): 71; Lilly Irani, "The Cultural Work of Microwork," *New Media and Society* 17, no. 5 (2015): 720–39.
20. Chen, "Limit Point of Capitalist Equality," 209.
21. Elson and Pearson, "'Nimble Fingers Make Cheap Workers,'" 92. Emphasis in original
22. Elson and Pearson, 92–93.
23. Elson and Pearson, 94.
24. Endnotes, "The Logic of Gender," 76–77.
25. Starosielski, "Thermocultures of Geological Media," 299.
26. Denise Ferreira da Silva, *Toward a Global Idea of Race* (Minneapolis: University of Minnesota Press, 2007), 47.
27. Silva, xv–xvi.
28. Silva, xxxviii.
29. Silva, 47.
30. Silva, 54.
31. Silva, 53: "Though instituted laws constrain individual's actions, preventing and punishing only those that affect another's freedom, the determinants of freedom reside inside man, in the mind, which, unlike the bodies of nature—the ones without thought, will, or volition—has been endowed with self-determination. Consistently, affectability has no ontological significance, because rationality, through instituted (universal) laws, mediates the relationships among the members of the political society." As Schuller illustrates, in mid-nineteenth-century impressibility discourse this racialized threat of affectability informs feminizing protocols. Although "elasticity, springiness, responsiveness, sensibility, impressionability, and sentimentality" were posited as marks of the civilized, Schuller notes, "the latter two terms hint at a problem: one could certainly be overly sensitive, too easily moved by external objects, as well as overly guided by emotional identification rather than abstract justice. Indeed, impressibility was deemed to be heightened among

the feminine: ladies, children, artists, and homosexuals, among others" (*Biopolitics of Feeling*, 15–16).
32. Marx, *Capital*, 1:138.
33. Marx, *Grundrisse*, 164.
34. Silva, *Toward a Global Idea of Race*, xl.
35. Denise Ferreira da Silva, "1 (life) ÷ 0 (blackness) = $\infty - \infty$ or ∞ / ∞: On Matter beyond the Equation of Value," *e-flux* 79 (2019), https://www.e-flux.com/journal/79/94686/1-life-0-blackness-or-on-matter-beyond-the-equation-of-value/.
36. Silva, "1 (life) ÷ 0 (blackness)."

5. Two Models

1. Samuel R. Delany, *Neveryóna, or: The Tale of Signs and Cities* (1983; London: Grafton, 1988), 215–16. Subsequent references are abbreviated to *N*.
2. In Pryn's description of this process, which Madame Keyne notes is very close to Belham's, "The water remembers its higher position and leaps up . . . to regain the level of the source!" (*N* 217).
3. For a brilliant account of Delany's formulation of economic abstraction's grounding in racialized dispossession see Jordy Rosenberg and Brit Rusert, "Framing Finance: Rebellion, Dispossession, and the Geopolitics of Enclosure in Samuel Delany's Nevèrÿon Series." *Radical History Review* 118 (2018): 64–91.
4. This quotation is from René Thom, *Structural Stability and Morphogenesis: An Outline of a General Theory of Models*, translated by D. H. Fowler (Reading, Mass.: W.A. Benjamin, 1975), 127.
5. See Thom, 219–21.
6. The first of these epigraphs contains a methodological note on the importance of attending both to the network of market-mediated relations and to "material life, which is related to market prices but is not always affected or changed by them" (*N* 159). The second concerns what might be called the secondary abstractions of the "market economy"—those ledgers, balance sheets, and legal proceedings that fill "page after page in urban archives, private archives of merchant families, judicial and administrative archives, debates of chambers of commerce, and notarial records" (*N* 185). Both are from Fernand Braudel, *Afterthoughts on Material Civilization and Capitalism*, translated by Patricia M. Ranum (Baltimore: Johns Hopkins University Press, 1977), 42, 51–52, 41.
7. Braudel, 16–17.
8. Braudel, 28.
9. Braudel, 53.
10. Robinson, *Black Marxism*, 13–14.

11. Braudel, *Afterthoughts*, 35.
12. "In capitalism," Postone continues, "social labor is not only the object of domination and exploitation but is itself the essential ground of domination" (*Time, Labor, and Social Domination*, 125).
13. Ngai, "Visceral Abstractions," 50.
14. Samuel R. Delany, *Return to Nevèrÿon* (London: Grafton Books, 1989), 399. Subsequent references are abbreviated to *RN*. This is the final anecdote in the final appendix to the final volume of the Nevèrÿon series.
15. Samuel R. Delany, Constance Penley, and Sharon Willis, "Sword and Sorcery, S/M, and the Economics of Inadequation: The *Camera Obscura* Interview," in Samuel R. Delany, *Silent Interviews: On Language, Race, Sex, Science Fiction, and Some Comics* (Hanover, Conn.: Wesleyan University Press, 1994), 129.
16. Samuel R. Delany, *Tales of Nevèrÿon* (London: Grafton, 1988), 9. Subsequent references are abbreviated to *TN*.
17. Samuel R. Delany and Thomas Deja, "The *Black Leather in Color* Interview," in Samuel R. Delany, *Shorter Views: Queer Thoughts and the Politics of the Paraliterary* (Hanover, Conn.: Wesleyan University Press, 1999), 118.
18. In an interview with Larry McCaffery, Delany states: "In my Neveryon stories, for example, it should slowly creep up on readers that the barbarians, who have just come to the city and who are creating many social problems, are blond and blue-eyed, while the indigenous citizens are dark. The dark-skinned citizens learn to live with and/or ignore the blond barbarians in some public space that's, say, the prehistoric equivalent of a bus terminal, as if the barbarians weren't there—like middle-class New Yorkers avoiding the many people who hang out and even live in the Port Authority bus station. This kind of reversal serves to distance the contemporary situation. At the same time one recognizes it as *structure*, rather than as *content*; the reader sees a set of relationships, largely economic, a set of positions that anyone might fill, regardless of color rather than a collection of objects, dark-skinned folks and light-skinned folks, each with an assigned value." Larry McCaffery, "An Interview with Samuel R. Delany," in *Across the Wounded Galaxies: Interviews with Contemporary American Science Fiction Writers* (Urbana: University of Illinois Press, 1990), 75–76.
19. As Hartman writes, "Most often when the productive labor of the slave comes into view, it is as a category absent gender and sexual differentiation." Saidiya Hartman, "The Belly of the World: A Note on Black Women's Labors," *Souls* 18, no. 1 (2016): 166.
20. Hartman, 167.
21. Hartman, *Scenes of Subjection*, 116–17.
22. "... she cannot conceivably tolerate in her presence the represented principle of not *sympathizing*, not *associating*, not *amusing* the only child of her Awful Enemy, the rival whose real name she will never sully her lips with—

'that envious witch'—is sign sufficient—who does not rule but defiantly is the unrectored chaos." W. H. Auden, *The Sea and the Mirror: A Commentary on Shakespeare's "The Tempest"* (Princeton: Princeton University Press, 2003), 29. Emphasis in original.

23. The same phrase appears later in *Neveryóna* when Pryn becomes "overcome with the notion that if she followed the road further, it would soon give out entirely and she would have to confront the ultimate wildness, the unrectored chaos, the unthinkable space in which distinctions between earth, air, and water would soon break down" (*N* 340). And again, in the third book of the Nevèrÿon series: "You are lost on a side road that has detoured you into the unrectored chaos where anything may happen and any lie, falsehood, illusion, or reality is game, he said to himself." Samuel R. Delany, *Flight from Nevèrÿon* (London: Grafton, 1989), 87.

6. Human Use, or The Digital-Liberal Person

1. Norbert Wiener, *The Human Use of Human Beings: Cybernetics and Society* (London: Eyre and Spottiswoode, 1950), 8.
2. Norbert Wiener, *The Human Use of Human Beings: Cybernetics and Society*, 2nd ed., with a new introduction by Steve J. Heims (London: Free Association Books, 1989), xvii. Kline notes that Jason Epstein, an editor at Doubleday, urged Wiener to revise the book "in order to broaden its appeal." Like Heims, Kline observes that the revisions were directed at espousing a philosophy—a "philosophy of life based on entropy." And he concludes that Wiener's "hard work paid off," as "sales of *The Human Use of Human Beings* climbed to more than fifty thousand copies by the end of 1956, while the total sales of *Cybernetics* plateaued at thirty-three thousand at the end of 1959." Kline, *The Cybernetics Moment*, 82–83.
3. Wiener, *Human Use* (2nd ed.), 16.
4. Wiener, *Human Use* (1st ed.), 2.
5. Marx, *Grundrisse*, 692.
6. "[Wiener] was less interested in seeing humans as machines than he was in fashioning human and machine alike in the image of an autonomous, self-directed individual. In aligning cybernetics with liberal humanism, he was following a strain of thought that, since the Enlightenment, had argued that human beings could be trusted with freedom because they and the social structures they devised operated as self-regulating mechanisms." Hayles, *How We Became Posthuman*, 7.
7. Wiener, *Human Use* (1st ed.), 15.
8. Marx, *Second Draft of Critique of Political Economy*, 465.
9. Wiener, *Human Use* (1st ed.), 103.
10. Wiener, 217.

11. Wiener, 16.
12. Wiener, 15.
13. Wiener, Human Use (1st ed.), 59, Human Use (2nd ed.), 50. In a similar vein, Wiener offers a critique of settler colonialism in the United States that rests upon a teleological formulation of abstract political freedom and levels of civilizational development: "Besides this gross injustice [of unequal resources], there was a semantic injustice, which was perhaps even greater. The Indians as a hunting people had no idea of land as private property. For them there was no such ownership as ownership in fee simple, though they did have the notion of hunting rights over specific territories. In their treaties with the settlers, what they wished to convey were hunting rights, and generally only concomitant hunting rights over certain regions. On the other hand, the whites believed, if we are to give their conduct the most favorable interpretation that can be assigned to it, that the Indians were conveying to them a title to ownership in fee simple. Under these circumstances, not even a semblance of justice was possible, nor did it exist" (*Human Use* [1st ed.], 116; *Human Use* [2nd ed.], 109).
14. Kalindi Vora and Neda Atanasoski name as *technoliberalism* the "political alibi of present-day racial capitalism that posits humanity as an aspirational figuration in a relation to technological transformation, obscuring the uneven racial and gendered relations of labor, power, and social relations that underlie the contemporary conditions of capitalist production." I am here interested in tracking the reticular, value-informatic, and communicational aspects of liberal personhood that precede and inform that figuration. Vora and Atanasoski, *Surrogate Humanity: Race, Robots, and the Politics of Technological Futures* (Durham: Duke University Press, 2019), 5.
15. Norbert Wiener, "The Computing Machine and Form (Gestalt)," paper presented at the conference "Les machines à calculer et la pensée humaine," Paris, January 1951, box 29B, folder 665, Norbert Wiener Papers, Institute Archives and Special Collections, MIT Libraries, Cambridge, Massachusetts.
16. Wiener, "The Computing Machine and Form (Gestalt)."
17. Karl Marx, *Economic and Philosophical Manuscripts of 1844*, translated by Martin Milligan and Dirk J. Struik, *MECW*, vol. 3 (London: Lawrence and Wishart, 1975), 302.
18. Wiener, "The Computing Machine and Form (Gestalt)."
19. Nichols succinctly elaborates the terms of this contradiction, writing that "because workers in capitalist countries have no direct access to the means of production, they have no way of actualizing a proprietary claim in their labor power, except, that is, by alienating it to someone else . . . in those circumstance workers have a strange form of 'negative property' in their labor power, the precise character of which comes to light when we read the de jure change

against the de facto conditions of its actualization in its socioeconomic context" (*Theft Is Property!*, 134).
20. Ralph Ellison, *Invisible Man* (London: Penguin, 1965), 10.
21. See, for example, Valve Software's infamous *Handbook for New Employees* (2012), which opens by celebrating a "flat" organizational structure that allows employees to "steer" the company "toward opportunities and away from risks" before detailing the company's symbolization and materialization of that structure in the wheels attached to every desk, which serve as both "a symbolic reminder that you should always be considering where you could move yourself to be more valuable" and as "literal wheels" that allow "whole teams [to] move their desks to be closer to each other." Valve, *Handbook for New Employees* (Bellevue: Valve, 2012), 6; available at http://media.steampowered.com/apps/valve/Valve_Handbook_LowRes.pdf.
22. Alexander R. Galloway, *The Interface Effect* (Cambridge: Polity, 2012), 33.
23. Frantz Fanon, *Black Skin, White Masks*, translated by Richard Philcox (New York: Grove Press, 2008), xii.
24. Julian Bigelow, response to Gerard, in Von Foerster, Mead, and Teuber, *Cybernetics: Circular Causal and Feedback Mechanisms in Biological and Social Systems*, 27. Bernhard Siegert suggests that the disavowal that founds the digital is thus aligned with the sacred, constituting "that which lies in a forbidden zone and to which normal mortals have no access," so that certain elements of "analog" reality are maintained as "nonreality." This, for Siegert, "is perhaps the deepest level to which an archaeology of coding can take us." I want to suggest that, before it directly informs the conceptual armature of digitality, the constitutive structure of this coding is modulated by the value relation. Siegert, "Coding as Cultural Technique: On the Emergence of the Digital from Writing AC," *Grey Room* 70 (2018): 9.
25. One way of provisionally framing this dynamic relationship between form and formlessness is through Deleuze and Guattari's description of primitive accumulation as a set of processes through which land and populations are *deformed*—decoded—so that they may be *reformed* as the private property and bearers of labor power across which value flows: "Great accidents were necessary, and amazing encounters that could have happened elsewhere, or before, or might never have happened, in order for the flows to escape coding and, escaping, to nonetheless fashion a new machine bearing the determinations of the capitalist socius. Thus the encounter between private property and commodity production, which presents itself, however, as two quite distinct forms of decoding, by privatization and by abstraction. Or, from the viewpoint of private property itself, the encounter between flows of convertible wealth owned by capitalists and a flow of workers possessing nothing more than their labor capacity" (*Anti-Oedipus*, 140).

7. Elemental Space

1. Wiener, *Human Use* (1st ed.), 29–31. The italicized paragraph remains in the second edition. See *Human Use* (2nd ed.), 44.
2. Wiener, *Human Use* (1st ed.), 45.
3. Michael Hardt and Antonio Negri's influential definition of millennial capitalism's spatial character exemplifies these digital fantasies: "Empire establishes no territorial center of power and does not rely on fixed boundaries or barriers. It is a decentered and deterritorializing apparatus of rule that progressively incorporates the entire global realm within its open, expanding frontiers. Empire manages hybrid identities, flexible hierarchies, and plural exchanges through modulating networks of command." Hardt and Negri, *Empire* (Cambridge: Harvard University Press, 2000), xii–xiii.
4. Bernhard Siegert, *Passage des Digitalen: Zeichenpraktiken der neuzeitlichen Wissenschaften, 1500–1900* (Berlin: Brinkmann & Bose, 2003), 75. My translation.
5. Siegert, *Passage des Digitalen*, 19. It may be a cliché in discussions of cybernetics at this point, but it is nonetheless worth recalling that word's origin in order to foreground the conceptual associations and conflations that determine its deployment: "the art of pilot or steersman." Wiener, *Human Use* (1st ed.), 9.
6. Sylvia Wynter, "1492: A New World View," in *Race, Discourse, and the Origin of the Americas: A New World View*, edited by Vera Lawrence Hyatt and Rex Nettleford (Washington, D.C.: Smithsonian Institution Press, 1995), 10–11.
7. Frantz Fanon, *The Wretched of the Earth*, translated by Constance Farrington (New York: Grove Press, 1963), 51.
8. This double projection can be found in the language of wonder that, as Lorraine Daston and Katherine Park have noted, proliferates in fifteenth- and sixteenth-century accounts of the exploration and conquest of the Americas. See Daston and Park, *Wonders and the Order of Nature* (New York: Zone Books, 2001), 146–59. Alexander Galloway and Jason R. LaRivière associate it with a mode of "abstract compression" that synthesizes romantic ideas of nature with the logic of techno-scientific rationalization. In the resultant imaginary, "nature is an unknowable space of excess, quite literally a heart of darkness, and its energies must be released, harnessed, and developed according to the rules of the machine." In this imaginary, the specificity of concrete technologies—whether they are "more like fifteenth-century Portuguese carracks or twentieth-century Deleuzian desiring machines"—matters less than "the underlying narrative that fuels them: nature is unknowable, infinite, bottomless, and uncompressible; technology is the discoverer, developer, exploiter, and harnesser of nature. In short, *technology is nature's compressor.*" Galloway and LaRivière, "Compression in Philosophy," *boundary 2* 44, no. 1 (2017): 132. Emphasis in original.

9. Equiano, *Interesting Narrative*, 59,
10. James Wallace, *A General and Descriptive History of Ancient and Present State of the Town of Liverpool, Comprising a Review of Its Government, Police, Antiquities, and Modern Improvements; the Progressive Increase of Streets, Squares, Public Buildings, and Inhabitants, Together with a Circumstantial Account of the True Causes of Its Extensive African Trade. The Whole Carefully Compiled from Original Manuscripts, Authentic Records, and Other Warranted Authorities* (Liverpool: R. Philips, 1795), 224–25.
11. Wiener, *Human Use* (1st ed.), 29.
12. "While modern biological racism had yet to emerge, conceptions of racial difference and, crucially, European superiority were conditioned at this time by the concept of land use." Brenna Bhandar, *The Colonial Lives of Property: Law, Land, and Racial Regimes of Ownership* (Durham: Duke University Press, 2018), 44.
13. Bhandar, 37–50. Petty's plan, Bhandar elaborates, was premised on calculating the value of the Irish based on the projected productivity of their labor. "Viewing the Irish as an amalgam of economic units," she continues, "was bound to his valuation of the land, which began with the Civil Survey [of 1654]" (40).
14. Bhandar, 47.
15. Bhandar's examples include the doctrine of *terra nullius*, which encodes "the racial abstraction embodied in the figure of the Savage or Native" and was thus used to rationalize the 1858 implementation of the Torrens system of registration in South Australia; the justification of settlement in mid-nineteenth-century Canada through an ideology of improvement under which land can "only serve the public interest if they were thrown open for pre-emption," a process that relies on taking that land from Indians who have "no rights to the land because they made no use of the lands"; and Arthur Ruppin's political-anatomical distinction between "the backward styles of cultivation of the fellahin" and the "rather more elevated quality" of the settler's agricultural labor, which justifies and naturalizes the occupation of Palestine (82, 55, 123–26).
16. Bhandar, 96.
17. Katherine McKittrick, *Demonic Grounds: Black Women and the Cartographies of Struggle* (Minneapolis: University of Minnesota Press, 2006), 92.
18. Bhandar notes that "although Petty did not seem to attribute Irish laziness to the state of their bodily constitution, he did see Irish and English difference as somehow inherently biological. His solution for quelling Irish rebellion involved the intermarriage of English women and Irish men, and Irish women to English men, who would raise their children to be English speaking, and the 'whole Oeconomy of the Family' would be English. The deficiencies of the Irish could be ameliorated by mixing their blood with that of the English." Bhandar, *Colonial Lives of Property*, 43. Bhandar cites William Petty, *Political Anatomy of Ireland with the establishment for that kingdom when the late

Duke of Ormond was Lord Lieutenant: to which is added Verbum sapienti, or, An account of the wealth and expenses of England, and the method of raising taxes in the most equal manner (London: D. Brown and W. Rogers, 1691), 158. On assimilation as elimination as a fundamental settler-colonial technique see Patrick Wolfe, "Settler Colonialism and the Elimination of the Native," *Journal of Genocide Research* 8, no. 4 (2006): 387–409. Also see Coulthard, *Red Skin, White Masks*, 4 ("the reproduction of the colonial relationship between Indigenous peoples and what would eventually become Canada depended heavily on the deployment of state power geared around genocidal practices of forced *exclusion* and *assimilation*"). On indigenous endurance in the face of settler-colonial techniques of elimination see J. Kēhaulani Kauanui, "'A Structure, Not an Event': Settler Colonialism and Enduring Indigeneity," *Lateral* 5, no. 1 (2016), https://csalateral.org/issue/5-1/forum-alt-humanities-settler-colonialism-enduring-indigeneity-kauanui/.
19. Wiener, *Human Use* (1st ed.), 16.
20. Schuller, *Biopolitics of Feeling*, 218n49.
21. Barlow, "A Declaration of the Independence of Cyberspace."
22. "Wear Space: A Wearable Device That Gives the User a Personal Psychological Space," https://panasonic.net/design/flf/works/wear-space/.
23. Identifying the dialectical character and the settler-colonial history of this abstract mechanism exposes the settler logic of unmarked utopian appeals for a return to or reinstatement of *the* commons; as Coulthard writes, "what must be recognized by those inclined to advocate a blanket 'return to the commons' as a redistributive counterstrategy to the neoliberal state's new round of enclosures is that, in liberal settler states such as Canada, the 'commons' not only belong to somebody—*the First Peoples of the land*—they also deeply inform and sustain Indigenous modes of thought and behavior that harbor profound insights into the maintenance of relationships between human beings and the natural world built on principles of reciprocity, non-exploitation, and peaceful coexistence"(*Red Skin, White Masks*, 12).

8. Deplorable Alternatives

1. Wiener, *Cybernetics*, 37.
2. Wiener, 37.
3. Wiener, *Human Use*, 16. See Marx, *Capital*, 1:925. As Singh writes, "Marx's oeuvre, which frequently compares the labor of workers with that of slaves during this time, exemplifies the problem, on the one hand affirming what W. E. B. Du Bois once called the 'slavery character' of capitalism in its Anglo-American ascendancy, yet on the other contributing to a problematic relegation of African slavery to a secondary role in capitalism's development that has haunted radical politics ever since" (*Race and America's Long War*, 76).

4. Wiener, *Human Use* (1st ed.), 213; *Human Use* (2nd ed.), 185. Emphasis in original.
5. Louis Chude-Sokei, *The Sound of Culture: Diaspora and Black Technopoetics* (Middletown, Conn.: Wesleyan University Press, 2016), 83–86.
6. In a later elaboration of machinery as slave labor, Wiener disavows this relation by making it clear that he is referring to classical (rather that Atlantic) slavery. In so doing he avoids encountering the prospect that the "human cruelty" results from the same conditions that produce the "free" person. Wiener, "Some Moral and Technical Consequences of Automation," *Science* 131, no. 3410 (1960): 1357.
7. In "The Negro and Cybernation," Boggs writes: "In the work process within American society, the role of the Negro has been that of the scavenger. He got the jobs which white Americans would not do, which they considered beneath their dignity, which they had abandoned, or in dying industries. Now, however, cybernation—i.e., automation with nerve centres operated not by man but by computing machines—is eliminating the 'Negro jobs.' Thus it is also destroying the ladder, by means of which white workers moved up, leaving the dregs behind to the Negroes." James Boggs, "The Negro and Cybernation," in *The Evolving Society: The Proceedings of the First Annual Conference on the Cybercultural Revolution—Cybernetics and Automation*, edited by Alice Mary Hilton (New York: Institute for Cybercultural Research, 1966), 169.
8. Hartman, *Scenes of Subjection*, 19.
9. Hartman, 21.
10. Ian Baucom, *Specters of the Atlantic: Finance Capital, Slavery, and the Philosophy of History* (Durham: Duke University Press, 2005), 6–7, 11.
11. Norbert Wiener, "The Future of Automatic Machinery" (1953), box 30C, folder 728, Norbert Wiener Papers, Institute Archives and Special Collections, MIT Libraries, Cambridge, Massachusetts.
12. Marx, *Capital*, 1:377.
13. Wiener, *Cybernetics*, 37–38.
14. Norbert Wiener, untitled 1954 article on automatic factories, box 30C, folder 746, Norbert Wiener Papers, Institute Archives and Special Collections, MIT Libraries, Cambridge, Massachusetts.
15. James Boggs, "The Challenge of Automation," in *The American Revolution: Pages from a Negro Worker's Handbook* (New York: Monthly Review Press, 1963), 37. Also see Boggs, "The Negro and Cybernation."
16. Wynter, "Unsettling the Coloniality of Being/Power/Truth/Freedom," 324–25.
17. Jodi Melamed usefully tracks the movement between these positions, from white supremacy to "a series of successive official or state-recognized US antiracisms: racial liberalism (1940s to 1960s), liberal multiculturalism (1980s to 1990s), and neoliberal multiculturalism (2000s)," each of which functions through the "trick of racialization, a process that constitutes differential

relations of human value and valuelessness according to specific material circumstances and geopolitical conditions while appearing to be (and being) a rationally inevitable normative system that merely sorts human beings into categories of difference." Melamed, *Represent and Destroy: Rationalizing Violence in the New Racial Capitalism* (Minneapolis: University of Minnesota Press, 2011), 1–2.

18. Achille Mbembe identifies the longer history of this tendency when he writes that capitalism is fundamentally anthropophobic, continually reformatting humans through the addition of natural, mineral, organic, machinic, and digital properties. "Conversation: Achille Mbembe and David Theo Goldberg on *Critique of Black Reason*," https://www.theoryculturesociety.org/conversation-achille-mbembe-and-david-theo-goldberg-on-critique-of-black-reason/.

19. As George Lamming writes, "It must have been clear to the owner that the mournful silence of his property contained a danger which would last as long as their hands were alive. One day some change akin to mystery would reveal itself through these man-shaped ploughs. The mystery would assume the behavior of a plough which refused contact with a free hand." Lamming, *The Pleasures of Exile* (London: Michael Joseph, 1960), 121. Chude-Sokei argues that Lamming's text shows how plantation imaginaries anticipate conversations about intelligent, conscious, and/or agential machines (*The Sound of Culture*, 40–41).

20. Orit Halpern, *Beautiful Data: A History of Vision and Reason since 1945* (Durham: Duke University Press, 2014), 240. Irani shows how the distinction between upgradable and unupgradable (or high and low bandwidth users) informs the division of labor in crowdsourcing platforms such as Amazon's Mechanical Turk, producing "hierarchies of value" under which "some humans are hackers, builders, and programmers and other humans are computational power" ("The Cultural Work of Microwork," 728).

21. Wiener, *Human Use* (1st ed.), 59; *Human Use* (2nd ed.), 50.

22. Wiener, *Human Use* (1st ed.) 59; *Human Use* (2nd ed.), 50. Emphasis added.

23. Sylvia Wynter, "On How We Mistook the Map for the Territory, and Re-Imprisoned Ourselves in Our Unbearable Wrongness of Being, of *Désêtre*: Black Studies toward the Human Project," in *Not Only the Master's Tools: African-American Studies in Theory and Practice*, edited by Lewis R. Gordon and Jane Anna Gordon (London: Routledge, 2016), 142. See also Wynter, "Unsettling the Coloniality of Being," 324.

24. Wynter, "On How We Mistook the Map for the Territory," 143.

9. The Digital Atlantic

1. See Baucom, *Specters of the Atlantic*; and Brenna Bhandar, "Property, Law, and Race: Modes of Abstraction," *UC Irvine Law Review* 4, no. 1 (2014): 203–18.

2. Baucom argues that, unlike earlier Turner paintings in which the pictorial planes correspond to successive historical moments, with "past" objects and relations in the distance being looked back upon by "present" spectators in the foreground, in *Slave Ship* Turner distributed the "past" event across the planes, placing the ship in the background and the drowning slaves in the foreground. In so doing, Baucom argues, Turner positions the painting's "present" in front of the picture plane, presenting the Middle Passage as a constitutive historical event both for Turner's present—1840—and that of any future viewer. Baucom, *Specters of the Atlantic*, 291–92.
3. For example, in a rich essay on Perry's work, Soyoung Yoon observes how through "the animating close-up, Perry further abstracts the swell and dissipation of the waves, the morph, warp, mutation of the sea-as-flesh" of Turner's painting, but doesn't mention the purple waves that alternate with the *Slave Ship* sequence in *Typhoon coming on*. Soyoung Yoon, "Figure versus Ground, White versus Black (Blue), or: Sondra Perry's *Blue Room* and Technologies of Race," in Sondra Perry, *Typhoon coming on* (London: Koenig Books/Serpentine Galleries, 2018), 81.
4. Tamar Clarke-Brown, "Adrift in the Chroma Key Blues: A Chat with Sondra Perry on Black Radicality + Things That Are Yet to Happen in *Typhoon coming on*," May 1, 2018, https://www.aqnb.com/2018/05/01/adrift-in-the-chroma-key-blues-a-chat-with-sondra-perry-on-black-radicality-things-that-are-yet-to-happen-in-typhoon-coming-on/.
5. Nora N. Khan, "Acquisition, God Object; Acquisition, Source Code," in Perry, *Typhoon coming on*, 22.
6. On numerical representation as a precondition for fungibility see Manovich, *The Language of New Media*, 27–48.
7. Galloway, *Interface Effect*, 11–12.
8. Spillers theorizes these processes in her account of shipped bodies "suspended in the oceanic," separated from "indigenous land and culture" but not yet "American," and rendered "neither female nor male" but instead "taken into 'account' as quantities," as differences in mass or weight that are eventually erased by "rules of accounting" ("Mama's Baby," 72).
9. "Opacities can coexist and converge, weaving fabrics. To understand these truly one must focus on the texture of the weave and not on the nature of its components. For the time being, perhaps, give up this old obsession with discovering what lies at the bottom of natures." Édouard Glissant, *Poetics of Relation*, translated by Betsy Wing (Ann Arbor: University of Michigan Press, 1997), 190.
10. These more overt influences include the written account of the *Zong* massacre in Clarkson's *History* and Théodore Géricault's painting *Raft of the Medusa* (1818–19). Baucom, *Specters of the Atlantic*, 268.
11. Baucom, 288.

12. Baucom, 288.
13. In the same way, Baucom's rigorous accounts of the relationship between Atlantic slavery and the growth of modern finance and of Turner's projection of liberal subjectivity both leave untheorized the role of race and racialization in the production of abstract social forms. As Bhandar puts it, "While Baucom certainly does not shy away from expressing the horrific levels of violence that were prerequisite to treating African slaves as chattels and also the basis for financial speculation . . . race is nowhere to be found" in his analysis of the process through which slaves are rendered empty bearers of value ("Property, Law, and Race," 216).
14. As Chen puts it, race functions today as both "a probabilistic assignment of relative economic value" and "an index of differential vulnerability to state violence" ("Limit Point of Capitalist Equality," 210).

10. Redundant Life

1. "The colonial world is a Manichean world. It is not enough for the settler to delimit physically, that is to say with the help of the army and the police force, the place of the native. As if to show the totalitarian character of colonial exploitation the settler paints the native as a sort of quintessence of evil. Native society is not simply described as a society lacking in values. It is not enough for the colonist to affirm that those values have disappeared from, or still better never existed in, the colonial world. The native is declared insensible to ethics; he represents not only the absence of values, but also the negation of values. He is, let us dare to admit, the enemy of values, and in this sense he is the absolute evil. He is the corrosive element, destroying all that comes near him; he is the deforming element, disfiguring all that has to do with beauty or morality; he is the depository of maleficent powers, the unconscious and irretrievable instrument of blind forces." Fanon, *The Wretched of the Earth,* 41.
2. Linebaugh and Rediker, *The Many-Headed Hydra,* 3–4.
3. Linebaugh and Rediker, xi–xii.
4. Robinson, *Black Marxism,* 309.
5. Marx, *Grundrisse,* 251.
6. For an account of this relationship between abject formlessness and the imposition of form that is focused on the deep history of logistics, see Amanda Armstrong, "Looting: A Colonial Genealogy of a Contemporary Idea," *Postmodern Culture* 27, no. 1 (2016): n.p.
7. Georges Bataille, "Formless," in *Encyclopaedia Acephalica,* translated by Iain White (London: Atlas Press, 1995), 51–52.
8. Weaver, in Shannon and Weaver, *The Mathematical Theory of Communication,* 19.

9. As shown by one of Shannon's key influences, R. V. L. Hartley, a principal source of noise in the communication system is "the storage of energy in reactive elements such as inductances and capacities, and its subsequent release." Hartley, "Transmission of Information," *Bell System Technical Journal* 7, no. 3 (1928): 544. The informatic character of these operations is underscored in Foucault's observation that, in eighteenth- and nineteenth-century classification systems, monsters are introduced as "the background noise," the "obvious aberration of forms" whose nonliving counterpart is the "drama of the earth and waters." Michel Foucault, *The Order of Things: An Archaeology of the Human Sciences* (London: Tavistock, 1970), 155–56.
10. As Michel Serres puts it in his grand treatise on noise and communication, "The difference is part of the thing itself, and maybe it even produces the thing. Maybe the radical origin of things is really that difference, even though classical rationalism damned it to hell. In the beginning was the noise." Serres, *The Parasite*, translated by Lawrence R. Schehr (Baltimore: Johns Hopkins University Press, 1982), 13.
11. Charles Babbage, *Passages from the Life of a Philosopher* (London: W. Clowes and Sons, 1864), 337. For Babbage's work on labor rationalization, see *On the Economy of Machinery and Manufactures*; for his work on computing machinery, see *A Letter to Sir Humphry Davy, Bart. President of the Royal Society etc. etc., on the Application of Machinery to the Purpose of Calculating and Printing Mathematical Tables* (London: J. Booth and Baldwin, Cradock, and Joy, 1822) and *Passages*, 41–167; for his digital philosophy, see *The Ninth Bridgewater Treatise: A Fragment* (London: John Murray, 1837).
12. Babbage, 337.
13. Babbage, 345.
14. Babbage, 348.
15. Babbage, 354.
16. Babbage, 345.
17. Babbage, 342, 345, 339.
18. Marx, *Capital*, 1:852.
19. See Ferguson's critique of Marx's heteropatriarchy in the first chapter of *Aberrations in Black*. As Ferguson observes, "Marx's use of the prostitute as the apocalyptic symbol of capitalism's emergence points to his affinity with bourgeois discourses of the day," discourses which, through reports of prenuptial pregnancies, masturbation, and sexually active youth, "conflated the reality of changing gender and sexual relations with the representation of the prostitute and the working class as pathologically sexual" (9).
20. Henry Mayhew, *London Labour and the London Poor*, vol. 3 (London: Griffin, Bohn, 1861), 158–214. On "Ethiopian serenaders" see vol. 2, 152, and vol. 3, 190–204.

21. Mayhew, *London Labour*, vol. 3, 193.
22. "N***** Minstrelsy," *Saturday Review*, May 11, 1861, 447.
23. Harris, "Whiteness as Property," 1735–36. Harris writes: "Although many of the cases were decided in an era when the social and legal stratification of whites and Blacks was more absolute, as late as 1957 the principle was reaffirmed, notwithstanding significant changes in the legal and political status of Blacks. As one court noted, 'there is still to be considered the social distinction existing between the races,' and the allegation was likely to cause injury. A Black person, however, could not sue for defamation if she was called 'white.' Because the law expressed and reinforced the social hierarchy as it existed, it was presumed that no harm could flow from such a reversal."
24. Charles Babbage, *A Letter to Sir Humphry Davy*, 3–5. Babbage's letter contains an exemplary account of rationalization, deskilling, and shifting organic composition of capital on pp. 9–11. These accounts foreshadow the discourse of microwork, which, in the words of one advocate, comprises "any number of dull, brainless, low-paid tasks that keep the internet economy, for better or for worse, firing on all pistons," and "allows clients to farm out the kinds of menial clickwork that we all wish computers could do, but can't." Jeff Howe, "Mechanical Turk Targets Small Business," http://www.crowdsourcing.com/cs/2008/08/index.html, cited in Irani, "The Cultural Work of Microwork," 728.
25. In this respect, Babbage's listening practice evidences the value-informatic character of what Jennifer Lynn Stoever calls the "sonic color line" and the "listening ear." Stoever defines these concepts in the following terms: "The sonic color line describes the process of racializing sound—how and why certain bodies are expected to produce, desire, and live amongst particular sounds—and its product, the hierarchical division sounded between 'whiteness' and 'blackness.' The listening ear drives the sonic color line; it is a figure for how dominant listening practices accrue—and change—over time, as well as a descriptor for how the dominant culture exerts pressure on individual listening practices to conform to the sonic color line's norms." Stoever, *The Sonic Color Line: Race and the Cultural Politics of Listening* (New York: New York University Press, 2016), 7.
26. Neferti X. M. Tadiar, "Life-Times in Fate Playing," *South Atlantic Quarterly* 111, no. 4 (2012): 795. Relatedly, Weheliye notes that an exclusive focus on resistance and agency occludes "the manifold occurrences of freedom in zones of indistinction" because they "assume full, self-present, and coherent subjects working against something or someone." A "more layered and improvisatory understanding of extreme subjection" might become possible, Weheliye suggests, "if we do not decide in advance what forms its disfigurations should take on" (*Habeas Viscus*, 2).
27. Saidiya Hartman, "Venus in Two Acts," *Small Axe* 26 (2008): 12.
28. Hartman, "The Belly of the World," 171.

29. Hartman, "Venus in Two Acts," 12.
30. Saidiya Hartman, "The Anarchy of Colored Girls Assembled in a Riotous Manner," *South Atlantic Quarterly* 117, no. 3 (2018): 465–90. In a methodological note Hartman writes that "the New York State Archives required that the names of the prisoners be changed to maintain the privacy of the records" and that the files "are very detailed," being composed of materials from an intake process that "included personal interviews, family histories, interviews with neighbors, employers, and teachers, psychological tests, physical examinations, intelligence tests, social investigators' reports, as well reports of probation officers, school report cards, letters from former employers, and other state records (from training schools and orphanages)" and "personal correspondence, discussions of sexual history, life experiences, family background, hobbies, as well as poems and plays written by the prisoners." The case files, Hartman continues, were "intended to produce deep knowledge of the individual in a genre that combined sociological investigation with literary fiction creating a statistical portrait of the young women" (486).
31. Hartman, 470.
32. Hartman, 474–75.
33. Hartman, 467.
34. Hartman, 481–85. Hartman cites "Girls on 'Noise' Strike," *New York Times,* January 25, 1920.

11. Anatomizing "Freedom"

1. J. L. Moreno, *Who Shall Survive? A New Approach to the Problem of Human Interaction* (Washington, D.C.: Nervous and Mental Disease Publishing Co., 1934), 3. Emphasis in original. Hartman details Brown's confinement at Hudson: "Even the white teachers at the training school, who disliked her and were reluctant to give a colored girl any undue praise, conceded that she was very smart, although quick to anger because of too much pride. She insisted on being treated no differently than the white girls, so they said she was trouble. The problem was not her capacity; it was her attitude. The brutality she experienced at the Hudson Training School for Girls taught her to fight back, to strike out. The teachers told the authorities that she had enjoyed too much freedom. It had ruined her and made her into the kind of young woman who would not hesitate to smash things up" ("The Anarchy of Colored Girls," 468–69).
2. See https://www.humanyze.com/about/ and James B. Stewart, "Looking for a Lesson in Google's Perks," *New York Times,* March 15, 2013. On the sociometric badges see Benjamin N. Waber, Daniel Olguín, Taemie Kim, Akshay Mohan, Koji Ara, and Alex Pentland, "Organizational Engineering Using Sociometric Badges," http://hd.media.mit.edu/tech-reports/TR-620.pdf; and Lynn

Wu, Ben Waber, Sinan Aral, Erik Brynjolfsson, and Alex Pentland, "Mining Face-to-Face Interaction Networks Using Sociometric Badges: Predicting Productivity in an IT Configuration Task," http://vismod.media.mit.edu//tech-reports/TR-622.pdf. Also see Joshua Rothman, "Big Data Comes to the Office," *New Yorker,* June 3, 2014. On sociometry and networked logics of workplace organization, also see Tiziana Terranova, *Hypersocial: Digital Networks between Markets and Commons* (Minneapolis: University of Minnesota Press, forthcoming). Yuk Hui briefly discusses the continuity between Moreno and Jennings's sociometry and Facebook's Graph API, noting that "social networking websites like Facebook stay within the sociometric paradigm by materializing social relations in terms of digital objects and allowing new associations based on different discovery algorithms to emerge." Yuk Hui, *On the Existence of Digital Objects* (Minneapolis: University of Minnesota Press, 2016), 250–51.

3. The consistent theme of reticular interaction as a natural law is marked in the phrase Waber's mentor Alex Pentland borrowed from Auguste Comte for the title of his 2014 book on social network analysis: *Social Physics.*

4. Stewart, "Looking for a Lesson in Google's Perks."

5. Bernard Mandeville, *An Enquiry into the Causes of the Frequent Executions at Tyburn* (1725; Los Angeles: William Andrews Clark Memorial Library, 1964), 26. Also see Peter Linebaugh, "The Tyburn Riot against the Surgeons," in Douglas Hay, Peter Linebaugh, John G. Rule, E. P. Thompson, and Cal Winslow, *Albion's Fatal Tree: Crime and Society in Eighteenth-Century England* (London: Allen Lane, 1975); David McNally, *Monsters of the Market: Zombies, Vampires, and Global Capitalism* (Leiden: Brill, 2011), 18–23; and Jordy Rosenberg, "Trans/War Boy/Gender: The Primitive Accumulation of T," *Salvage,* no. 2 (November 2015): 87–96. Rosenberg emphasizes and complicates the imbrication of dissection and the instrumentalization of labor power by connecting Mandeville's desire for the corpses of the condemned to demands (such as those made by Daniel Defoe) to transport living bodies to the colonies as indentured labor.

6. Mandeville, *Enquiry,* 26.

7. As Federici puts it, the centrality of executed prisoners' bodies to the history of anatomy shows how the "course of scientific rationalization was intimately connected to the attempt by the state to impose its control over an unwilling workforce" (*Caliban and the Witch,* 145).

8. See Spillers, "Mama's Baby," 68. Snorton's more sustained historical analysis focuses on three and a half years of experiments on three chattel women— named Anarcha, Betsey, and Lucy—conducted by James Marion Syms, widely regarded as the "father" of modern gynecology. Through these experiments, Snorton writes, "White femininity is conferred in relation to an unwillingness to view white female genitalia, that is, to look upon white women as flesh. On

the other hand, the unrelenting scopic availability that defined blackness within the visual economy of racial slavery becomes the necessary context for producing a field of sex/gender knowledge." C. Riley Snorton, *Black on Both Sides: A Racial History of Trans Identity* (Minneapolis: University of Minnesota Press, 2017), 33. On the longer history of dissection and sex/gender see Katharine Park, *Secrets of Women: Gender, Generation, and the Origins of Human Dissection* (New York: Zone Books, 2010).
9. Mandeville makes clear his feelings toward those who opposed practices of criminalizing, executing, and dissecting the poor when he writes that whatever "Disgrace" might have resulted from people having "Lectures read upon their bodies . . . would seldom reach beyond the Scum of the people" (*Enquiry*, 27).
10. Moreno, *Who Shall Survive?*, 3.
11. The first is that at any given moment, every individual has a given number of acquaintances, and when aggregated the acquaintances of a given group constitute an "acquaintance matrix." The second is that every individual lives in a social atom—a group of "*special*" acquaintances—that stays with them from birth onward. Note that this more or less explicitly posits the "natural" family as a privileged form of social arrangement; social atoms are a given society's "lowest common denominators . . . the seeds from which societies grow," and although "the modern family is not a social axiom," the "nuclear part of a family, f.i., mother and child, are usually an essential *part* of a social atom." The third is that there are also "cultural atoms" that distribute universal roles, producing cultural differentiation on top of the universal social substrate. And finally, the fourth of the "sociometric universalia" is that every society is "traversed and held together by networks of communication of which sociometric networks are the elementary model." J. L. Moreno, *Who Shall Survive? Foundations of Sociometry, Group Psychotherapy, and Sociodrama* (Beacon, N.Y.: Beacon House, 1953), 617–18.
12. Moreno, *Who Shall Survive?* (1934 ed.), 5.
13. Moreno, *Who Shall Survive?* (1953 ed.), 115.
14. On reproductive respectability, see Hong's definition of neoliberalism: an "epistemological structure of disavowal" that differentially allocates "reproductive respectability, *so as to* disavow its exacerbated production of premature death." Grace Kyungwon Hong, *Death beyond Disavowal: The Impossible Politics of Difference* (Minneapolis: University of Minnesota Press, 2015), 7.
15. Moreno, *Who Shall Survive?* (1934 ed.), 19.
16. See A. Paul Hare and June Rabson Hare, *J. L. Moreno* (London: SAGE, 1996), 18. On the work at Sing Sing, see J. L. Moreno, *Application of the Group Method to Classification* (New York: National Committee on Prisons and Prison Labor, 1932).
17. Richard Firestone, "In Memoriam: Fanny French Morse: 1866–1944," *Sociometrica* 7, no. 1 (1944): 78. The Hudson experiment was so central to the

development of sociometry that Moreno dedicated the first edition of *Who Shall Survive?* to Morse, "Educator and Liberator of Youth."
18. Moreno, *Who Shall Survive?* (1934 ed.), 19.
19. Moreno, *Who Shall Survive?* (1934 ed.), 69.
20. Moreno, *Who Shall Survive?* (1934 ed.), 3.
21. Moreno, *Who Shall Survive?* (1934 ed.), 70–79, 164–67, 177. Moreno defines the sociometric test as an "instrument to measure the amount of organization shown by social groups" (11).
22. Moreno, *Who Shall Survive?* (1934 ed.), 69.
23. Moreno, *Who Shall Survive?* (1934 ed.), 202.
24. Moreno, *Who Shall Survive?* (1934 ed.), 216–17.
25. Moreno, *Who Shall Survive?* (1934 ed.), 217.
26. Moreno, *Who Shall Survive?* (1934 ed.), 257.
27. Moreno, *Who Shall Survive?* (1934 ed.), 259.
28. Moreno, *Who Shall Survive?* (1934 ed.), 260.
29. As Moreno reiterates in the 1953 edition, although there are differences in terms of inputs and outputs, "*the sociometric structures found in closed communities do not differ in their basic features from the ones found in open communities*" (555; emphasis in original).
30. Moreno, *Who Shall Survive?* (1934 ed.), 264.
31. Hartman, "The Anarchy of Colored Girls," 466.
32. Moreno, *Who Shall Survive?* (1953 ed.), 527, 531.
33. Moreno, *Who Shall Survive?* (1953 ed.), 531.
34. Moreno, *Who Shall Survive?* (1953 ed.), 551–52 (336 in the 1934 ed.).
35. Moreno, *Who Shall Survive?* (1953 ed.), 553, 557. The "crystallized social or economic structure" appears on 343 of the 1934 edition.
36. Moreno, *Who Shall Survive?* (1953 ed.), 596.
37. Moreno, *Who Shall Survive?* (1953 ed.), 598.
38. Moreno, *Who Shall Survive?* (1953 ed.), 607. Emphasis in original.
39. Galloway writes that "while the forces of ludic distraction are many, they coalesce around one clarion call: be more like us. To follow such a call and label it nature serves merely to reify what is fundamentally a historical relation. The new ludic economy is in fact a call for violent renovation of the social fabric from top to bottom using the most nefarious techniques available. That today it comes under the name of Google or Monsanto is a mere footnote" (*Interface Effect*, 29).
40. Moreno, *Who Shall Survive?* (1934 ed.), 10.
41. Moreno, *Who Shall Survive?* (1953 ed.), 596–97.
42. Moreno, *Who Shall Survive?* (1934 ed.), 98.
43. Moreno, *Who Shall Survive?* (1934 ed.), 98.
44. Moreno, *Who Shall Survive?* (1934 ed.), 112–13.
45. Moreno, *Who Shall Survive?* (1934 ed.), 219.

46. Moreno, *Who Shall Survive?* (1934 ed.), 225–27.
47. Moreno, *Who Shall Survive?* (1934 ed.), 309.
48. Hartman, "The Anarchy of Colored Girls," 467.
49. Tadiar, "City Everywhere," 71.

12. The Cybernetics of Capacity

1. Markus Krajewski, *The Server: A Media History from the Present to the Baroque*, translated by Ilinca Iurascu (New Haven: Yale University Press, 2018), 328.
2. Krajewski, 3. Krajewski derives the concept of the "absolute metaphor" from Hans Blumenberg, who defines it as a metaphor that "determines a particular attitude or conduct," gives "structure to a world, representing the nonexperienceable, nonapprehensible totality of the real," and "prove[s] resistant to terminological claims and cannot be dissolved into conceptuality." Blumenberg, *Paradigms for a Metaphorology*, translated by Robert Savage (Ithaca: Cornell University Press, 2010), 14, 5.
3. "Not unlike a paterfamilias, a lord of the mansion, the end user can indulge in the illusion that everyone and everything conforms to his command and that he reigns supreme over the entire system of heterogeneous actors. File-, print-, database-, name-, web-server-, mail demons, and transfer agents quietly go about their tasks, linked into a local and simultaneously universal network. Even the time server seems to obey and submit to the user's configurations. The complex system of digital domestics—or, rather, everything the human agent is able to perceive—is a more or less well-designed user interface." Krajewski, *The Server*, 316.
4. Krajewski, 3.
5. Krajewski, 303.
6. Krajewski, 11–13.
7. Krajewski, 317–18, 257. When slavery does appear in *The Server*, it is either in Athenian form and used to underscore the features specific to the servant, or in the question of whether the machine is the slave of its user or vice versa (22–23, 332–33).
8. These omissions and substitutions appear particularly egregious because the passage on Jefferson's Monticello residence is bracketed by discussions of slaves in ancient Greece and the ways that service work conflates human and machine. Krajewski, 256, 259.
9. Reinhold Martin, "Unfolded, Not Opened: On Bernhard Siegert's *Cultural Techniques*," *Grey Room* 62 (2016): 110–11.
10. Martin, 111.
11. Krajewski, *The Server*, 257.
12. R. S. Hunt to J. B. S. Haldane, January 30, 1951, box 9, folder 133, Norbert Wiener Papers, Institute Archives and Special Collections, MIT Libraries, Cambridge, Massachusetts.

13. Hunt to Haldane.
14. At the time of his letter to Haldane, Hunt had spent most of his working life as an engineer, first in the telephone industry and then with "all types of servo- and electronic equipment save for the major computers." "After the war," he writes, "I hoped to regularize my position by going to the Massachusetts Inst. of Technology to acquire some sort of degree of diploma. I had not foreseen currency restrictions and certain other obstacles." "I read four languages," he goes on to state, "and am prepared to mind babies and fold laundry." Hunt to Haldane.
15. G. B. Baldwin to R. S. Hunt, February 13, 1952, box 10, folder 146, Wiener Papers.
16. Hunt to Haldane. In the same letter Hunt boasts of his prodigious technical ability, stating: "I could read morse at 30 words a minute when I was 12 years old, and made a 4-valve radio when I was 14."
17. Hunt to Haldane.
18. In particular see Marx's critique of Samuel Bailey in Marx, *Theories of Surplus Value*, part 3, translated by Jack Cohen (London: Lawrence and Wishart, 1972), 124–68.
19. Although Hunt states the manuscript was completed in 1947 and that he had "not tried to revise it," the bibliography includes texts published in 1948, suggesting either that the bibliography was completed later or that Hunt recalls incorrectly the date of completion.
20. R. S. Hunt, "Two Kinds of Work," 1–2 (unpublished, ca. 1947), box 34B, folder 1000, Wiener Papers. Page numbers are given in parentheses for all subsequent references.
21. Hunt does not discuss the significance of his selection of A and G to define these types of work beyond a (perhaps redundant) note that "the prefix 'A-' confirms that a word has its ordinary physical meaning. Prefix 'G-' implies the analogous meaning in relation to G-energy. A-energy is the key-quantity of A-physics. G-energy is the key-quantity in what is termed (by analogy) G-physics" (1).
22. See Anson Rabinbach, *The Human Motor: Energy, Fatigue, and the Origins of Modernity* (New York: Basic Books, 1990).
23. Rabinbach, 4.
24. Marx, *Grundrisse*, 361. Arthur calls Marx's "form-giving fire" an "idealist" reading of concrete labor that "freezes into fixity" (*The New Dialectic*, 169). Patrick Murray suggests that it in fact captures capitalism's particular imbrication of abstract and concrete. Calling it "'idealist,' even in scare quotes," Murray writes, "is surprising. Marx is here talking about action. There is nothing 'idealist' in that unless we assume Marx's materialism excludes action and form from the world." *The Mismeasure of Wealth: Essays on Marx and Social Form* (Leiden: Brill, 2016), 453n49.

25. In another of Hunt's examples, "A mathematician spends 1 hour setting in data to an electronic computer. In 1 hour thereafter the computer does G-work which it would take the mathematician 6 years to perform unaided" (8). The G-work transmitted in the setting of the data requires "cleverness," while that which is transmitted through the machinic processing of that data requires "drive."
26. Rabinbach, *The Human Motor*, 3–4.
27. "The designation of labour as productive labour has absolutely nothing to do with the determinate content of that labour, its special utility, or the particular use-value in which it manifests itself. The same kind of labour may be productive or unproductive." Karl Marx, *Theories of Surplus Value*, part 1, translated by Emilie Burns (London: Lawrence and Wishart, 1969), 401.
28. Federici, *Caliban and the Witch*, 15.
29. Hartman, *Scenes of Subjection*, 125.
30. On the formal rendering (by capital) of enslaved people as fixed capital see Karl Marx, *Capital: A Critique of Political Economy*, vol. 2, translated by David Fernbach (London: Penguin, 1992), 554: "In the slave system, the money capital laid out on the purchase of labour-power plays the role of fixed capital in the money form, and is only gradually replaced as the active life of the slave comes to an end." Also see Nick Nesbitt, "The Slave Machine: Slavery, Capitalism, and the 'Proletariat' in *The Black Jacobins* and *Capital*," *sx archipelagos* 3 (2019), http://smallaxe.net/sxarchipelagos/issue03/nesbitt.html.
31. Marx, *Capital*, 3:945.
32. This isn't the only outcome of racialization at the interface between human and machine. For example, Day shows how Asian racialization in the United States and Canada functions through the parallel abstraction of Asian laborers as money and machines, both of which are aligned with "the destructive value dimension of capitalism" (*Alien Capital*, 191–98).
33. Tadiar, "Life-Times in Fate Playing," 789.
34. Saidiya Hartman, *Wayward Lives, Beautiful Experiments: Intimate Histories of Social Upheaval* (New York: Norton, 2019), 77–79.
35. Neferti X. M. Tadiar, "Decolonization, 'Race,' and Remaindered Life under Empire," *Qui Parle* 23, no. 2 (2015): 140, 152.
36. The "primary work" of this stratum "is to save as well as produce the valuable time of their clients/employers—that is, to serve as the means of facilitating the latter's value-productive movements." Tadiar, "City Everywhere," 71.
37. Tadiar, 73.
38. Vora, *Life Support*, 3. Emphasis added. The category of life support includes and identifies continuities between gestational surrogacy, call center work, and devalued and precarious types of information technology work.
39. Vora, 113. Emphasis added.

40. In Tadiar's words, "social practices of making viable life on the part of those who serve as the means of reproduction of others" are exemplified by acts and stories of "running away" ("Decolonization, 'Race,' and Remaindered Life," 149–51).
41. R. L. describes the imposition of this absence as desocialization. When labor power is dissolved through superfluization, "the human container that would have possessed this labor power endures as an empty shell," appearing as "a thing that is without any social utility." Blackness, R. L. continues, appears as a representation of this lack, "its positive instantiation." R. L., "Inextinguishable Fire: Ferguson and Beyond," *Mute*, November 17, 2014, http://www.metamute.org/editorial/articles/inextinguishable-fire-ferguson-and-beyond.

Coda

1. This character is named Alf in a number of articles, listings, and reviews, but he is not addressed by that name in the film. A coworker addresses him as Marcio.
2. Neta Alexander, "Rage against the Machine: Buffering, Noise, and Perpetual Anxiety in the Age of Connected Viewing," *Cinema Journal* 56, no. 2 (2017): 19.
3. On electronics manufacture and use in sites of attenuated reproduction, see Dyer-Witheford, *Cyber-Proletariat*, 102–23. Dyer-Witheford identifies five ways in which cell phones are "integrated into the lives of the poor and the dispossessed": employment ("the compelled necessity of mobiles for the poor in conditions where subsistence has become dependent on fluctuating and unpredictable wage labour"); emergency (strengthening "social networks of kin or community," securing "the means of circulating scarce resources, which today include money," and thus helping to "download the costs of socially reproducing proletarian life away from capital and onto proletarians themselves"); migration (making it "easier for transnational families to stay in touch; to get help with visas; to seek out information about new destinations; to reach relatives, friends and communities," and to find work "often, of course, in the new country's version of the precarious or informal labour sector"); money (via mobile financial systems that enable users to transfer credit, pay bills, and transfer funds); and crime (whether as "shadow capitalism," outlawed social reproduction, or the organization of rebellion through riots and looting).

INDEX

abolitionism, 2, 87, 114, 120, 123–24
abstract labor, 10, 23, 47, 70–71, 75, 101, 135, 163; as the "data" to value's "information," 49–50, 170, 214n34
Adorno, Theodor: on value and the transcendental subject, 54
Agre, Philip E.: on capture and grammars of action, 32–33, 35, 200n7; on the mirror world of informatics, 33
Alexander, Neta: on buffering, 183
analog, 11–14, 103, 181, 222n24
anatomy, 139–40, 233n7
Armstrong, Amanda: on looting, 229n6; on Marx, 205n12
Arthur, Christopher: on form-determination, 202n25; on labor as a content penetrated by value, 51; on labor as "form-giving fire," 237n24
Ashby, W. Ross: on information and variety, 24–28, 36, 74, 198n70
Atanasoski, Neda: on technoliberalism (with Kalindi Vora), 221n13
Atlantic Ocean, 1–2, 106, 120–25, 216n9
Auden, W. H.: on "unrectored chaos," 92, 219n22
automata, 13–14, 32, 44, 64, 98

automation, 35, 98–99, 112–17, 134–35, 151, 185, 204n9, 226n7

Babbage, Charles: on intellectual labor, 128, 130–31; on machinery and the unreliability of living labor, 56, 134–35, 154, 167, 231n23; on street nuisances, 128–35
Baldwin, G. B.: correspondence with R. S. Hunt, 161
Balibar, Étienne: on connection and structure, 49–50
bandwidth, 118–19, 126, 166
Barlow, John Perry, 110–11, 193n39
Barrett, Lindon: on race and value, 215n8
Bataille, Georges: on the formless, 127
Bates, John A. V.: on information, 24–28, 36, 74
Bateson, Gregory, 11; on information as a difference that makes a difference, 45–46
Baucom, Ian: on compensation, 115; on Turner's *Slave Ship*, 123–24, 228n2, 229n13; on the *Zong* massacre, 120, 229n13
Beller, Jonathan, 203n28

· 241

Bernal, J. D.: on information as the imposition of pattern, 45, 51, 81
Bernes, Jasper: on logistics, 33, 200n6, 200n10
Best, Beverley: on capitalism's perceptual economy, 19, 196n61
Bhandar, Brenna: on dispossession (with Davina Bhandar), 215n37, 215n3; on William Petty, 224n13, 224n18; on racial regimes of ownership, 109, 224n12, 224n15; on the *Zong* massacre, 120, 229n13
Bhandar, Davina: on dispossession (with Brenna Bhandar), 215n37, 215n3
Bigelow, Julian: on the digital, 11, 103; on the nature of information, 198n71
biopolitics, 66, 117–18, 127, 142, 151–53, 159, 197n65, 198n76
blackface minstrelsy, 133–34
"black poor" (in eighteenth century London), 130, 134
Blender (graphics software), 120–23
block diagram, 20–23
Blumenberg, Hans: on the absolute metaphor, 236n2
Boggs, James: on cybernation, 114, 226n7; on struggle, 117
Boltanski, Luc, and Eve Chiapello, 203n27
Bonefeld, Werner: on primitive accumulation, 60
Braden, Robert T.: on network tolerance and robustness, 210n73
Braudel, Fernand: on abstraction and material life, 218n6; on the market economy as self-regulating network, 83–84
Brenner, Robert: on capitalism as generalized market dependence, 47; on the long downturn, 194n49

broken windows policing, 130
buffering, 177, 183

capacity: of a channel, 2, 5, 17, 19, 39–41, 46; of people, value-informatic distribution of, 14, 41, 54–55, 57–58, 63–68, 72–73, 74–76, 82, 102, 105–6, 114–19, 160, 165–74, 207n49
Čapek, Karel, 112
capitalism: as self-regulating system, 35, 45; *as if* self-regulating system, 6, 10, 57–58, 59, 64, 67, 70, 85–86. *See also* informatics of value
capitalists, 4, 17, 64, 84, 126, 190n15, 200n12, 207n49, 208n53; competition among, 63, 65; as positive feedback loops, 47, 53
cathode, 26
Chakravartty, Paula: on dispossession and debt (with Denise Ferreira da Silva), 61
Chaturbate, 177–80, 183
Chen, Chris: on racialization, 73, 229n14
chess-playing machine, 25
Chiapello, Eve, and Luc Boltanski, 203n27
Chude-Sokei, Louis: on George Lamming, 227n19; on Wiener's "mechanical slaves," 113
circuit diagram, 1, 43–44
circuits: electrical, 13, 15, 43–44, 56–57, 74, 148, 164, 181, 204n9; psychological, 148; of value, 19, 28, 48, 56–57, 59, 67, 71, 82, 88, 109, 117, 128, 136, 139, 166, 168, 174, 186, 214n32
circulation, 1–2, 5, 14–15, 31–37, 40–43, 81–83, 105–9. *See also* logistics
coding: of labor as value, 50, 71; media-technological, 33, 40–41, 45, 222n24

colonialism, 22, 33, 42, 62, 73, 87, 93, 104–11, 126–27, 197n65, 216n9, 229n1. *See also* settler colonialism

coloniality, 73, 104–11

commodity, 1–7, 10, 31–35, 41–42, 47–54, 71, 74, 76, 122, 159, 162–74. *See also* enslaved people: rendered as commodities

communication: and the human, 55–56, 98–100, 105, 107, 115, 116–17, 124, 162, 169–70; information-theoretical formulation of, 26–27, 31–32, 34, 38–39, 43–44, 203n1, 205n20; networks of, 141; production and circulation modeled as, 40–41; value as, 36, 47, 49–51, 101–2, 166

component: electronic, 13, 15, 25–27, 81, 181; faulty, 25–27; gene as, 25–27; neuron as, 13; optimal, person as, 97; unreliable, person as, 16, 56–57, 64, 67–68, 74–76, 100, 102, 109, 132, 156, 160, 168–69, 175, 184–86, 213n11

computation: machine, 24, 158–59; of value from labor, 5–11, 12–13, 47–49, 52, 71, 75, 88, 100–102, 124, 161–74

computer network, 32, 126, 170, 175–86

confinement. *See* incarceration

congelation, metaphor of in Marx, 5–8, 23, 186, 190n15

constant capital. *See under* fixed capital

control, 16, 20, 22, 27, 32–33, 41, 44–45, 50, 97, 100, 169, 201n15, 202n22

convict-leasing system, 41–42

Coulthard, Glen Sean: on the commons, 225n23; on Indigenous dispossession in Canada, 212n8, 224n18

Cowen, Deborah: on logistics, 32, 199n4, 200n5, 201n15

Cubitt, Sean, 3

cybernetics, 8, 11–15, 33, 98, 100–102, 160–62, 220n6, 223n5

cybernetic sciences, 19, 34, 97, 112. *See also* information theory; operations research

Cybernetics, or Control and Communication in the Animal and the Machine (Wiener), 112–19

Dalla Costa, Mariarosa, and Selma James: on the family, 214n29

Day, Iyko: on abstract labor and differentiation, 71; on racialization and machinery, 238n32; on romantic anticapitalism, 13

debt, 61–62, 66, 127, 137, 171, 184, 211n4

Delany, Samuel R: on informatics, 85–86; *Neveryóna*, 20, 77, 78–94; on racialization, 102, 219n18; "The Tale of Dragons and Dreamers," 90; "The Tale of Old Venn," 90–92; *Tales of Nevèrÿon*, 92–94

Deleuze, Gilles, and Félix Guattari: on dispossession, 213n12, 222n25; on global capitalism, 214n32

Denning, Michael: on market dependence, 59

desire, distribution of, 9, 17–18, 22, 28, 53–54, 56, 61, 136

Deutsch, Karl: on information as the transmission of pattern, 45

differential valuation, of labor, 5, 16, 19, 28, 41–42, 53, 62, 67–68, 69–72, 85, 91, 94, 115–18, 124, 132, 137, 143, 168–72, 175, 186, 227n17, 229n14. *See also* informatics of value: and differential valuation

digital, the, 11–14, 24, 67, 103, 181, 222n24
digital computer: electronic, 11–12, 24, 39, 158–59, 168, 176–83; idealized, 118; mechanical, 128; and periodization, 164–65
digital culture, 2, 10, 20, 67, 94, 102, 175, 184, 186
digital imaginary, 13, 59, 76–77, 99, 185
digitality, as cultural logic, 2–3, 76
digital-liberal: fantasy, 116; humanism, 115; imaginary, 111, 114, 134, 183; optic, 101, 136; person, 100, 118, 122, 124, 126, 175
digital "natives," 110–11
discipline, 18, 34, 50, 60, 67, 70, 73–74, 82, 91–92, 127, 137, 145, 211n4
dispossession, 11, 22, 34, 42, 60–68, 85–94; and feminization, 73–74, 91–92; and racialization, 67–68, 69–74, 77, 85–94, 104–11, 136–37, 215n37, 215n3; relationship to the digital imaginary, 170; as social automation, 67, 102, 134–35, 150, 174, 185
disruption; as post-industrial ideal, 106, 126; of production and circulation, 33–34, 56, 154, 167, 201n14, 201n15
dissection, 139, 233n5
Dunayevskaya, Raya: on the value theory of labor, 50
Dyer-Witheford, Nick: on capitalism as a computer, 195n50; on cellphones, 239n3

economics, 10, 50, 64, 161, 164
el auge del humano (Williams), 175–86
Electronic Frontier Foundation, 111–12
Elias, Peter: satirical treatment of information theory, 203n2

Ellison, Ralph: on formlessness, 102
Elson, Diane: on racialized and feminized wage differentials and the attribution of skill (with Ruth Pearson), 53, 73–74; on value as a historical process of forming, 36, 163; on value as objectified abstract labor, 206n36; on the value theory of labor, 50, 163, 207n38
Encyclopædia Britannica, 38–43
Endnotes (collective): on form-determination, 202n25; "The Logic of Gender," 74
energy, 6–8, 13, 40, 45–46, 79, 81, 101, 153, 161–63, 230n9; R. S. Hunt's concept of G-energy, 161–74; vital, 172–74
enslaved people: death by suicide of, 108; extraction of labor from, 116; fungibility associated with (*see under* fungibility); at Thomas Jefferson's Monticello, 159–60; medical examination of, 139; regarded as machines, 7–9, 61, 112–15, 118, 171, 238n30; rendered as commodities, 107, 115, 123–24, 159, 201n19; resistance to capitalism by, 8, 127, 191n20; valuation of, 72, 115, 171. *See also* slavery
entropy, 27, 205n20, 220n2
Equiano (internet cable), 1–2, 5, 10, 11, 17, 19, 28
Equiano, Olaudah, 1–2, 4–5, 7, 8, 17, 28, 35, 48, 108
eugenics, 117, 152
evolution, 25–26
expectation: as modulated by the informatics of value, 9, 17, 19, 24, 28, 54, 56, 64, 71–72, 82, 170, 174
extraction: of knowledge, 139; of labor power, 62, 67–68; of materials, 33, 42, 67, 74, 104–5; of value, 6–7, 16, 35, 50, 64–67, 72, 110, 169

factory, 20–24, 34, 98, 112–17, 129–30, 138, 181–82, 184–85, 201n14

failure, media-technological, 175–84, 210n73

Fanon, Frantz: on the "becalmed zone" of coloniality, 108; on the construction of natives, 126, 229n1; on the zone of nonbeing, 102–3

Federici, Silvia: on anatomization, vivisection, and labor power, 57–58, 139, 233n7; on the body as abstraction, 171; on dispossession and gendered divisions of labor, 22, 91, 211n7; on microcredit, 213n16; on structural adjustment in Nigeria, 61

Ferguson, Roderick: on Marx, 230n19; on the racialization and gendering of surplus populations, 69

Ferrante, Elena, 20–24

finance capital, 104–6, 108, 118, 120–23. *See also* debt; microcredit

Finelli, Roberto: on value and the concrete, 51, 53

fixed capital, 41, 63, 106, 127, 165–66; enslaved people rendered as, 115, 171, 202n25

flexibility, 66, 94, 102, 106, 110, 126, 140, 150–54, 168, 200n12; as precarity, 73–74, 107, 156

flexibilization, 73–74, 107, 168, 184

form: commodity, 4; and computation, 100–101; differential allocation of, 9, 11, 18–20, 36–37, 62–68, 71–77, 87–89, 92–94, 101–3, 107–9, 122, 124, 149, 153–54, 160, 168–74, 183, 227n17; information and, 80–81, 85–86; labor, as transmission of, 160–74; social, 6, 9, 34–36, 42, 45, 47, 51–52, 80, 85, 101–3. *See also* formlessness

formlessness: abjected, 92–94, 102–3, 107–10, 119, 124, 126–28, 130–31, 133, 136–37, 139, 145, 152, 164; dynamic relationship to form, 93–94, 103, 107, 109–10, 119, 128, 222n25; valorized, 94, 102–3, 108, 110, 119, 126, 128, 149–50, 183

forms of disposal, 5, 18–20, 28, 37, 54, 56, 196n59, 196n62

Foucault, Michel: on monsters, 230n9

freedom, 35–36, 59, 61, 75–76, 90, 106, 110–11, 118, 134, 142, 156; abjected forms of, 131–32, 135–37; connection as, 54–55, 69, 82–84, 89, 98, 150, 185

free trade, 65–66

frontier, 104–7, 110–11, 150–51

fungibility: of the commodity, 4–5, 123; of the enslaved, 4–5, 114, 118, 123; as a property of digital media, 5, 33, 123, 200n10

Galloway, Alexander R.: on abstract compression (with Jason R. LaRivière), 223n8; on interfaces, 102; on the ludic economy, 235n39; on photography and computation, 123

Galton, Francis, 152

general communication system (Shannon), 31–32, 34, 39; and the informatics of value, 49–50

general communication system (Shannon), 31–32, 39; labor mapped onto, 49–50, 67; lumber mill analogy, 39–40

genetics, 25–27, 80, 85–86, 118, 142

gentrification, 130

Gerard, Ralph, 11–12

Gilmore, Ruth Wilson: on gender, criminalization, and racialization, 69–70

Gitelman, Lisa, and Virginia Jackson: on data, 214n34

Glenn, Evelyn Nakano: on convict-leasing, 41–42
Glissant, Édouard, 123, 228n9
Gómez-Barris, Macarena, 199n77
Google: as exemplar of the "post-industrial" workplace, 138, 157; and internet infrastructure, 1–3, 5, 10, 11, 17, 19, 28, 175, 189n11
Googleplex, 2, 157
Gramsci, Antonio, 197n65
Grey Walter, William, 8
Guattari, Félix, and Gilles Deleuze: on dispossession, 213n12, 222n25; on global capitalism, 214n32

Haldane, J. B. S.: correspondence with R. S. Hunt, 160–61
Hall, Stuart: on capitalism as if self-regulating system, 57
Halpern, Orit: on the user, 118–19
Hardt, Michael, and Antonio Negri, 223n3
Harney, Stefano: on logistics (with Fred Moten), 201n19
Harris, Cheryl: on self-possession, 17; on whiteness as reputation, 132–33, 231n23
Hartley, R. V. L.: on noise, 230n9
Hartman, Saidiya: on the abjection of black women's labor and social reproduction, 136–37, 145, 150, 156, 219n19; on "black noise," 136; on Esther Brown, 136–37, 156, 232n1; on the burdened individuality of freedom, 36, 87, 90, 171; on the differential attribution of legal personhood, 213n14; on fungibility, 4–5, 114; on the genre of inmates' records, 232n30; on liberalism, 114–15; on manual labor, 172; on self-possession, 24, 54, 197n67; on vagrancy, 136–37, 145

Hayles, N. Katherine: on immateriality, 193n39; on information, 33, 205n21; on the posthuman, 55, 209n64; on Norbert Wiener's liberalism, 98, 220n6
Heims, Steve Joshua: on Norbert Wiener's revisions to *The Human Use of Human Beings*, 98
Heinrich, Michael: on abstract labor, 49; on racialized and gendered differentials, 71–72; on rationality and social validity, 52; on value as a relational mechanism, 51–52
Hemings, Sally, 159–60
Hennessy, Rosemary: on unmet and outlawed needs, 195n55
homeostat, 7–9. *See also* social reproduction: and homeostasis/self-regulation
Hong, Grace Kyungwon: on abstract labor and whiteness, 23; on reproductive responsibility, 234n14
HSBC, 1–3, 5, 10, 11, 17, 19, 28, 175, 189n11
Hui, Yuk: on sociometry, 232n2
human, 16, 18–19, 48–49, 56, 70, 98–103, 105–11, 112–19, 138, 151, 153–54, 158–59, 166, 170–72, 191n20, 195n56, 213n14, 215n8, 221n14, 227n18, 238n32, 239n41
humanism, liberal, 98, 100, 113–15, 123–25, 142, 220n6. *See also* digital-liberal: humanism; liberalism; personhood, liberal; subject, liberal
Human Surge, The (Williams), 175–86
Human Use of Human Beings, The (Wiener), 97–102, 104–11
Humanyze (analytics company), 138
Hunt, R. S.: information theory of value, 160–74; on the measurement of "ethical quantities," 161

incarceration, 66–67, 127, 136–37, 138–57, 173–74
informatics of value: and abjection, 92–94, 134; as abstract domination, 49–54, 80–84; as the basis of liberal personhood, 54–56, 97–100, 114–15, 123–25, 151–52; and capacity (*see* capacity: of people, value-informatic distribution of); and coloniality, 106–7; and differential valuation, 66–68, 115–19, 139, 168–74; and dispossession, 59–68, 173–74; and feminization, 67, 73–74, 91–92; and formlessness (*see* formlessness); and "freedom," 54–55, 83–84, 105–6, 119, 171; optimization of, 138–40; and racialization, 66–67, 69–74, 82, 86–91, 102–3, 109–10, 115–19, 168–74; and the senses, 69, 124, 130–31, 137, 156; and skill (*see* skill, value-informatic allocation of); and social form, 46, 51, 54, 92–94, 102 (*see also* form: social); and social reproduction, 47, 54, 61, 69–72, 114, 123, 171–74; and surplus populations, 62–65, 86–89, 131–32; as the synthesis of reliable circuits from unreliable components, 56–57, 64, 67, 71, 82, 128, 139, 168–74, 175, 186, 213n11. *See also* integration, differential; prospects
information, 11, 16, 34–37; as abstract domination, 43–45, 47, 75, 84; applications of, 38–39, 204n9; as constraint, 44, 128; contested definition of, 25–28, 38–39, 41, 45–46, 80, 198n71, 205n20, 205n21; and form, 80, 84–85, 93, 102; and the human, 118; immateriality of, 33, 45, 81, 86; and literature, 201n16; and logistics, 31–37, 39–42, 200n5; and meaning, 43, 51; and noise, 127–28, 230n9; processing of, 39–40; as relation, 43–46, 52, 55, 101; and subjectivity, 75; and value, 46–50, 56, 67, 69, 92, 162–74, 201n6; as variety, 27
information age, 13, 54, 92
information economy, 21, 106
information theory, 25–28, 31–32, 37, 38–41, 43–46, 161–65, 168, 203n2
integration, differential, 36–37, 56, 63, 73, 79, 88–90, 107–8, 123, 160, 166–74, 184, 196n67
Invisible Man (Ellison), 102
Irani, Lilly: on microwork, 227n20

Jackson, Virginia, and Lisa Gitelman: on data, 214n34
James, Selma, and Mariarosa Dalla Costa: on the family, 214n29
Jameson, Fredric: on expressive causality, 194n45
Jefferson, Thomas: Monticello residence of, 159–60
Jennings, Helen H.: sociometric work at the New York Training School for Girls (with J. L. Moreno), 137, 140–50, 153–56, 172
Johnson, Walter, 15, 194n44

Khan, Nora N., 122
Kittler, Friedrich: on digitization, 33; on information and the "sociology of literature," 201n16; on Claude Shannon, 34; on "the traffic of persons and goods," 31–32, 34–36, 50
Kline, Ronald R., 204n4, 220n2
Krajewski, Markus: on the (human) servant and the (digital) server, 158–60, 172, 236n3, 236n8

labor: app- or platform-mediated, uberized, 3, 15, 17, 66, 73, 106, 153,

169, 175, 189n11, 227n20; creative, 118, 140, 151–54, 164, 184, 202n22; differential valuation of (*see* differential valuation, of labor); of enslaved people, 42, 60, 73, 79–80, 112–15, 226n6; "free," 24, 49, 59, 73, 85, 90, 113, 159; immaterial, 11, 15, 54, 94, 202n22; intellectual, 128, 130–35, 164–66, 171; manual, 82, 118, 151, 164–66, 172; service, 24, 50, 62, 66–67, 73, 137, 140, 153, 156–57, 158–60, 163, 172–73, 184–85, 189n11, 214n32; skilled and unskilled (*see* skill, value-informatic allocation of); surplus (*see* surplus labor); "unupgradable," 117–19, 123, 125, 126, 136–37, 140, 151, 153, 157, 171–73, 184, 227n20; "upgradable," 117–19, 122, 124, 126, 128, 132, 135, 150, 151, 154, 171, 184–85, 227n20. *See also* abstract labor

Lacan, Jacques: on homeostasis, reproduction, and slavery, 7–9, 61

lag, 14

Lamming, George: on the slave imagined as "man-shaped plough," 227n19

LaRivière, Jason R.: on abstract compression (with Alexander R. Galloway), 223n8

Latour, Bruno: on connection as emancipation, 55, 83–84

liberalism, 27, 88–89, 113, 119, 120–22, 130, 134, 164. *See also* humanism, liberal; personhood, liberal; subject, liberal

Licklider, J. C. R, 11

Linebaugh, Peter, and Marcus Rediker: on the many-headed hydra, 126–27; on the technologies of global capitalism, 189n11

Locke, John, 17, 109

logic, 13–15, 18, 32, 43–44, 56–57, 64, 86

logistics, 6, 11, 32–37, 65, 67, 73, 87, 199n4, 200n6, 200n7, 200n10, 200n12

long downturn, 16, 65–66, 77

Lowe, Lisa: on abstract labor, social validity, and difference, 70–71; on coloniality, 73; on indentured Chinese laborers in the Americas, 216n9

lumber, 40–44, 67

lumber mill, informatic model of, 40, 67

machines, 7–9, 25, 56, 63, 98, 112–19, 134–35, 151, 154–56, 185, 223n8, 226n7; chess-playing, 25; computing, 11, 24, 39, 100–102, 120–23, 128, 134, 158–60; cybernetic, 77, 81, 85–86, 106–7; enslaved people analogized to (*see under* enslaved people); "free" people rendered as, 22, 98, 113, 138–39, 158–60, 164–66, 171–73, 220n6, 236n8, 238n32

MacKay, Donald M., 38

MacPherson, C.B.: on the possessive individual, 55, 209n60

Macy conferences, 11–12, 38–39, 198n70, 198n71, 205n20

Mandel, Ernest: on the "cobweb" of exchange, 47

Mandeville, Bernard: on the dissection of executed "malefactors," 139, 234n9; on the ideal form of homeostatic reproduction, 53, 64–65, 208n53

Manovich, Lev, 33, 200n10, 228n6

market dependence, 19, 42, 47–48, 59–61, 63, 65–66, 77, 82–83, 90, 91–92, 94, 102, 107, 134–35, 150, 170, 175, 185–86, 211n6. *See also* dispossession

Marshall Plan, 22

Martin, Reinhold: on slavery and the architecture of Jefferson's Monticello, 159

Marx, Karl: on abjected forms of social reproduction, 70, 131–32, 137, 230n19; on capitalism as a medium of "spontaneous interconnection," 37, 46–58, 98–99, 206n30, 207n37; on capitalism as network, 46–47, 51–52, 65–66, 206n27; on capitalism as "never-ending circle," 8; on capitalists, 4; on the commodity, 41; on the differential valuation of labor, 71–72, 170; on expanded reproduction, 208n54; on the "flow" of labor into production, 65–66; on form-determination, 202n26; on freedom and "free" labor, 54–55, 70–71, 209n62; on the imbrication of abstract and concrete, 10, 12, 14, 35; on labor as "form-giving fire," 164; on the labor theory of value, 50, 161; on machinery, 98; on the organic composition of capital, 63, 213n22; on productive and unproductive labor, 238n27; on the senses, 101; on skill, 52–53; on slavery, 15, 116, 171, 194n46, 212n8, 225n3, 238n30; on so-called primitive accumulation, 59–61, 210n4; on social reproduction, 208n52; on surplus populations, 62–68, 131–32; translations of, 5–6, 190n13, 202n25; on value and form, 163–64; on wages, 62, 71–72, 207n49

"Mathematical Theory of Communication, A" (Shannon), 43–45, 127–28, 162

Mayhew, Henry, 133

Mbembe, Achille: on capitalism's anthropophobia, 227n18

McKittrick, Katherine: on the racialized production of space, 109

McCulloch, Warren, and Walter Pitts, 11, 13

media archaeology, 159–60

Melamed, Jodi: periodization of racialized sorting in the US, 226n17

mercantilism, 83–84, 107–8, 216n9

merchants, 4, 42, 78, 83–84, 87, 104–8

Merrill, Heather: on structural racism in Italy, 197n65

microcredit, 61

microwork, 73, 227n20

Middle Passage, 1–2, 5, 106–18, 122

Mirowski, Philip: on operations research (with Edward Nik-Kah), 199n4

modulation, 18, 20, 33, 40–41, 64, 66, 76–77, 102, 116, 122, 170, 214n32, 222n24

Moore, Jason: on Nature, 12–13, 193n35

Moreno, J. L.: on coloniality and spontaneity, 150–51; distinction between "creative" man and zootechnical animal, 151–53; sociometric work at the New York Training School for Girls (with Helen H. Jennings), 137, 140–50, 153–56, 172; on the "sociometric universalia," 234n11, 235n29

Morse, Fannie French, 142, 234n17

Moten, Fred: on logistics (with Stefano Harney), 201n19; on the reduction of phonic materiality, 193n32

Murray, Patrick: on labor as "form-giving fire," 237n24

Nakamura, Lisa: on racialized and feminized electronics labor, 18

needs, 22, 119, 134, 137, 149, 170, 172. *See also* unmet needs

Negri, Antonio, and Michael Hardt, 223n3
Negroponte, Nicholas, 13
nervous system, 13–14, 39, 166
network: commodity (*see* circulation); computer, 1–3, 6, 11, 15, 32, 33, 83, 118–19, 126, 175–86; electrical, 13–14; Jefferson's Monticello as, 159; neural, 39; person as, 55–56, 97, 118–19; social, 37, 97–99, 138–57. *See also* value network
neurons, 13–14
Neveryóna (Delany), 20, 77, 78–94
Ngai, Sianne: on congelation in Marx, 190n15; on value and social synthesis, 84
Nichols, Robert: on dispossession, 60, 212n10; on the paradox of self-possession, 221n19
Nik-Kah, Edward: on operations research (with Philip Mirowski), 199n4
noise, 25, 82, 131–32, 136–37, 159, 174; incapacity rendered as, 167–68, 170; information-theoretical treatments of, 26–28, 39, 67, 86, 127–28, 167, 203n2, 230n9, 230n10

Ong, Aihwa: on spirit possession in electronics factories, 34, 201n14
operations research (OR), 35, 199n4
optical character recognition (OCR), 101
optimization, 35, 39–41, 72, 81, 138–40, 145, 149, 150, 152–54, 156, 160, 165, 168–69
organic composition of capital, 114, 123, 231n24
oscilloscope, 26

packet switching, 5
Panasonic, 111

Pashukanis, E. B., 211n69
pauperization, 62–63, 70, 137, 143
Pearson, Ruth: on racialized and feminized wage differentials and the attribution of skill (with Diane Elson), 53, 73–74
Pentland, Alex, 233n3
Perry, Sondra, 20, 120–25
personhood, liberal, 2, 23–24, 54, 56, 64, 76, 107. *See also* digital-liberal: person; humanism, liberal; liberalism; subject, liberal
Petty, William: on Ireland, 109
physics, 12, 161, 165, 168; social, 223n3
piecework, 131, 157, 170
Pitts, Walter, and Warren McCulloch, 11, 13
plantation, 8, 41, 118, 127, 189n11, 216n9, 227n19
police, 128, 130, 142, 149
post-Fordism, 11, 18, 21, 28, 110, 116, 118, 138, 150, 156
possessive individual, 54–55, 66, 99, 102, 109, 145, 169, 185, 209n60, 212n8, 215n3. *See also* self-possession
posthuman, 55, 209n64
Postone, Moishe: on abstract domination, 35, 84, 219n12
primitive accumulation. *See* dispossession
processing: of data, 31; of labor, 6–7, 67–68; of materials, 40–41, 67–68
programming, 16, 20–25
prospects, 2; differential allocation of, 7–9, 19–20, 50, 76, 86, 114–18, 120, 123, 135, 229n14
Puar, Jasbir K.: on debilitation, 191n25

quantification, 12, 109, 127, 160–61, 163–64, 166, 168, 195n50

Rabinbach, Anson: on energy and labor, 163
racial capitalism, 9–11, 28, 72, 92–93, 117–18, 126, 136, 175, 186, 192n26, 221n14, 227n17
Radin, Margaret, 17
radio, 32, 39, 42, 237n16
Rankin, John, 114
rationalization, 12, 61, 63, 66, 68, 82, 86, 90–92, 128, 153, 169, 223n8, 231n24, 233n7
real abstraction. *See under* Sohn-Rethel, Alfred; value
rebellion, 89, 92–94, 127, 137, 154–57, 216n9, 224n18, 239n3. *See also* struggle
Rediker, Marcus, and Peter Linebaugh: on the many-headed hydra, 126–27; on the technologies of global capitalism, 189n11
relay (electrical component), 11, 13, 15, 43–44, 45, 56–57, 164, 204n9
rendering, 191n16
reproduction, expanded, 51, 57, 60, 63–64, 77, 102, 196n60
reproduction, media-technological, 44, 46, 78
reproduction, social. *See* social reproduction
Return to Nevèrÿon (Delany), 85
Reuten, Geert, and Michael Williams, 35
R. L.: on racialization and desocialization, 239n41
Robinson, Cedric: on the ideals of freedom and mobility, 83; on racial capitalism, 10, 192n26; on slave rebellions, 127
Rosenberg, Jordy: on dissection, 233n5; on the molecular, 196n62
Rubin, I. I.: on the determination of form, 202n25; on social labor, 52
running away, 92, 135, 141–42, 145–50, 172, 174, 185, 239n40
R.U.R (Čapek play), 112

Schuller, Kyla: on biophilanthropy, 198n76; on impressibility, 110, 217n31
self-possession, 17–18, 23, 54–56, 61, 69, 94, 97, 99, 101–2, 108, 110, 115, 135, 141, 170–71, 194n49, 197n67. *See also* possessive individual
self-regulation, 8. *See also* homeostat
Serres, Michel: on noise, 230n10
server, 158–59, 172
servomechanisms, 39, 161, 166, 204n9
settler colonialism, 60, 104–11, 150–51, 153, 196n62, 221n13, 224n15, 225n18, 225n23
sex work, 70, 131, 134, 177–80, 184–85
Shannon, Claude, 11, 25, 162; and automatic machinery, 204n9; on the content-indifference of informatic relations, 43–44, 49; on the definition of information, 38–40, 205n20; on the general communication system (*see* general communication system); on information and noise, 26; on information as a relation, 43–46; on information theory, 38–40, 203n1, 203n2; on logic and switching circuits, 43–44; on the synthesis of reliable circuits from less reliable components (with Edward Moore), 56–57, 64
ship, 4, 91–92, 93, 106–7, 115, 120–25, 189n11
Shukin, Nicole: on rendering, 191n16
Siegert, Bernhard: on the digital, 222n24; on the ship as a cybernetic machine, 106
Silva, Denise Ferreira da: on affectability and transparency, 75–77, 85,

217n31; on dispossession and debt (with Paula Chakravartty), 61
Singh, Nikhil Pal: on Marx's engagement with slavery, 225n3; on the technology of race, 215n8
skill, value-informatic allocation of, 52–53, 73–74, 117–18, 168–74
slavery, 1–2, 4–5; afterlives of, 41–42, 136–37; and capitalism, 15, 192n26, 194n43, 194n44, 225n3; and circulation, 42; and coloniality, 107; differential valuation through, 72, 91; and dispossession, 60–61; and "free" labor, 87–90, 112–15, 216n9, 225n6; and gender, 89, 139, 219n19, 233n8; and logistics, 201n19; Marx on (see Marx, Karl: on slavery); and social death, 8; and social reproduction, 7–9, 191n18. *See also* enslaved people
Slave Ship (Turner), 120–25, 228n2
Smallwood, Stephanie: on dispossession and social reproduction under slavery, 7, 61, 191n18
Smith, Adam: on the division of labor and the extent of the market, 189n11
Snorton, C. Riley: on James Marion Syms's gynecological experiments on enslaved women, 139, 233n8
socially necessary labor time, 48–49, 52, 57, 67, 72, 123, 206n36, 214n32
social reproduction, 21–24, 62, 116, 124; attenuated, 69, 134, 175, 183; compromised, 15, 17–18, 28, 70, 87, 88, 114, 126, 183–84, 196n59; and dispossession, 211n6; of enslaved people, 6–10, 61, 114; as feedback loop, 19, 53, 63, 75–76, 110, 169; gendered dynamics of, 22, 60, 91, 130–34, 171–73; and homeostasis/self-regulation, 6–10, 13, 18, 55, 64–65, 75–76, 80, 93, 114, 119, 145, 186; outlawed, 60–61, 70, 130–34, 145, 195n55 (*see also* running away); racialization of, 91, 107, 130–34, 171–73; and wages, 52–53, 64, 66, 68, 71, 74, 77, 109, 170
social science, 38, 199n4, 203n2, 138–57
sociometry, 138–57
Sohn-Rethel, Alfred: on the abstract intellect, 15–16; on exchange as the "source" of scientific knowledge, 19, 46, 92, 196n59; on second nature, 34–35; on value as a real abstraction, 194n47
Spillers, Hortense: on bodies "suspended in the oceanic," 228n8; on body and flesh, 36; on experimentation on the enslaved, 139
Spivak, Gayatri Chakravorty: on global capitalism, 9–11, 192n31; on value, 5–6
Starosielski, Nicole: on the processing of materials for electronics production, 67–68, 74, 214n35
Steineck, Raji C.: on the devaluation of labor power, 72
Stoever, Jennifer Lynn: on the sonic color line and the listening ear, 231n25
struggle, 9, 29, 117, 196n60. *See also* rebellion
subject, liberal, 54–55. *See also* digital-liberal; humanism, liberal; liberalism; personhood, liberal
superfluization, 36, 64–67, 107, 134, 151, 175, 239n41
supply chain, 33, 41
supply chain management, 11, 15, 32, 106, 201
surplus labor, 5, 9, 49
surplus populations, 62–68, 79, 87–89, 93–94, 128, 214n29; as a distribution

of redundant components, 168–74; as formless, 152; gendering and racialization of, 69, 73, 130–37; as raw material, 149

surplus value, 9, 16, 35, 50, 53, 56, 58–59, 65–67, 71, 74, 82, 90, 93, 116, 124, 169, 171, 208n54; relative, 63–64, 72, 89, 110, 184, 207n49

Sutherland, Keston: on Marx's use of *Gallerte*, 190n15

switch (electrical component), 8, 12, 43–44, 204n9

Tadiar, Neferti X.M: on capitalizable and commodifiable life, 172; on disposability, 196n60; on the global service stratum, 73, 172–73, 238n36; on life-making practices below the network of exchange, 135–36, 238n40

"Tale of Dragons and Dreamers, The" (Delany), 90

"Tale of Old Venn, The" (Delany), 90–92

Tales of Nevèrÿon (Delany), 92–94

Taylorism, 23

telegraph, 32, 39, 46, 166

telephone, 26–27, 32, 165–66, 175–81, 183, 184–85, 239n3

television, 39, 101

Teubner, Gunther: on the legal person as element in an information system, 55–56

Thom, René: on information and form, 80, 84–86

Those Who Leave and Those Who Stay (Ferrante), 20–24

time, 14, 49, 73, 135–36, 173, 185. *See also* socially necessary labor time

Toscano, Alberto, 194n47, 200n12

transmission: of data or information, 1–2, 31–32, 43–44, 78–81, 84, 128; of energy, 78–81; of value, 5, 36, 49–51, 56, 76, 82, 106, 160–74; of vital energy, 173–74

Turing, Alan, 13

Turner, J. M. W., 121–25, 228n2

Typhoon coming on (Perry), 20, 120–25

unmet needs, 18, 23, 59, 63, 65, 114, 184, 195n55

user, the, 3, 16, 118–19, 126, 158, 170, 183, 227n20, 236n3

vacuum tube. *See* valve

vagabondage, 70, 210n4, 212n11. *See also* vagrancy

vagrancy, 136–37, 145

value: as abstraction, 4; as animating the concrete, 13–15, 41, 51, 53, 190n14; as automatic subject, 10; as "congealed quantity," 5–6; as computed, 5–7, 9–13, 23, 47, 49, 75, 122–23, 163, 170; and digitality, 15–16, 18–20, 118, 120–23, 170, 183–86; R. S. Hunt's information theory of, 161–74; immateriality of, 6, 10, 12, 35; as objectification of abstract labor, 9, 49, 52, 163, 207n36; as real abstraction, 15–16, 194n47; as relation, 51–54; as "signal," 49–50, 97–98, 101–2, 160, 163, 166–68; and social synthesis, 6, 9, 13–15, 18, 34–37, 51, 84. *See also* informatics of value; value network

value network, 47–49, 53, 91, 101, 123–24, 141, 185; and coloniality, 107–8; gradated connection to, 63, 67–68, 69, 76–77, 102, 139, 183–84, 186; expansion of, 61–62, 66–67, 92; and freedom, 54, 61, 82–84; gendering and racialization within, 69–74, 109–10, 115, 136, 160, 169–74; interface of, 102–3, 119; life beyond, 135–37,

INDEX · 253

139; self-regulation of, 64–65; and social synthesis, 51–52, 56; and social validity, 52, 57–58, 76–77, 93, 101, 110, 116, 126, 136, 164; and survival, 54, 59–60, 186
valve (electrical component), 8, 11, 13, 45
Valve Software, 222n21
variety, 27
vocoder, 101
von Neumann, John: on the digital, 11–13, 103; on logic and its material substrates, 13–15, 18, 32, 44; on the synthesis of reliable organisms from unreliable components, 13–15, 56–57, 64
Vora, Kalindi: on life support labor, 73, 173; on technoliberalism (with Neda Atanasoski), 221n13

Waber, Ben, 138
wages: differential distribution of, 17–18, 62–66, 70–77, 168–74, 184; as means of connection, 47–58, 63, 68, 69–70, 74, 84; as operating system, 158; and reproduction, 7–9, 18, 47–49, 52–53, 70, 114, 135, 171, 184
Walker, Gavin: on primitive accumulation, 212n11; on the sublime perversion of capital, 210n70
Wallace, James: on the slave trade and financial risk, 108
Weaver, Warren: on information, 44–45; on noise, 127–28
Weheliye, Alexander: on racialization, 70; on resistance and agency, 26

Wiener, Norbert, 11, 25, 160–61; on automation, 98–100, 112–19; on coloniality, 104–7, 150, 221n13; communicational definition of the human, 98–103, 107, 109–10, 117, 220n6; on control, 97–98, 101; definition of information, 45, 81; on form, 100–102; on labor, 98, 110, 112–19; on "mechanical slaves," 110–15; revisions to *The Human Use of Human Beings*, 98, 100, 220n2; on settler colonialism, 221n13; on slavery, 226n6; on "upgradable" labor and that which "simply cannot be upgraded," 116–19, 136–37, 171–72; on white supremacy, 100, 118
Williams, Eduardo, 175–86
worker, the, as abstraction, 9–11, 16–17, 23–24
writing, 2, 34, 44, 91–92, 166
Wynter, Sylvia: on code, system, and regulation, 18, 196n57; on the Darwinian/Malthusian formulation of man, 118–19; on the differential valuation of labor, 72; on fifteenth-century mercantile networks, 107; on the plot and the plantation, 8, 61, 191n20; on selection and dysselection, 18, 118–19, 171–72, 195n56

Yoon, Soyoung: on Sondra Perry's *Typhoon coming on,* 228n3

Zong massacre, 115, 120–21

(continued from page ii)

49 *Program Earth: Environmental Sensing Technology and the Making of a Computational Planet*
Jennifer Gabrys

48 *On the Existence of Digital Objects*
Yuk Hui

47 *How to Talk about Videogames*
Ian Bogost

46 *A Geology of Media*
Jussi Parikka

45 *World Projects: Global Information before World War I*
Markus Krajewski

44 *Reading Writing Interfaces: From the Digital to the Bookbound*
Lori Emerson

43 *Nauman Reiterated*
Janet Kraynak

42 *Comparative Textual Media: Transforming the Humanities in the Postprint Era*
N. Katherine Hayles and Jessica Pressman, Editors

41 *Off the Network: Disrupting the Digital World*
Ulises Ali Mejias

40 *Summa Technologiae*
Stanisław Lem

39 *Digital Memory and the Archive*
Wolfgang Ernst

38 *How to Do Things with Videogames*
Ian Bogost

37 *Noise Channels: Glitch and Error in Digital Culture*
Peter Krapp

36 *Gameplay Mode: War, Simulation, and Technoculture*
Patrick Crogan

35 *Digital Art and Meaning: Reading Kinetic Poetry, Text Machines, Mapping Art, and Interactive Installations*
Roberto Simanowski

34 *Vilém Flusser: An Introduction*
Anke Finger, Rainer Guldin, and Gustavo Bernardo

33　*Does Writing Have a Future?*
　　Vilém Flusser

32　*Into the Universe of Technical Images*
　　Vilém Flusser

31　*Hypertext and the Female Imaginary*
　　Jaishree K. Odin

30　*Screens: Viewing Media Installation Art*
　　Kate Mondloch

29　*Games of Empire: Global Capitalism and Video Games*
　　Nick Dyer-Witheford and Greig de Peuter

28　*Tactical Media*
　　Rita Raley

27　*Reticulations: Jean-Luc Nancy and the Networks of the Political*
　　Philip Armstrong

26　*Digital Baroque: New Media Art and Cinematic Folds*
　　Timothy Murray

25　*Ex-foliations: Reading Machines and the Upgrade Path*
　　Terry Harpold

24　*Digitize This Book! The Politics of New Media, or Why We Need Open Access Now*
　　Gary Hall

23　*Digitizing Race: Visual Cultures of the Internet*
　　Lisa Nakamura

22　*Small Tech: The Culture of Digital Tools*
　　Byron Hawk, David M. Rieder, and Ollie Oviedo, Editors

21　*The Exploit: A Theory of Networks*
　　Alexander R. Galloway and Eugene Thacker

20　*Database Aesthetics: Art in the Age of Information Overflow*
　　Victoria Vesna, Editor

19　*Cyberspaces of Everyday Life*
　　Mark Nunes

18　*Gaming: Essays on Algorithmic Culture*
　　Alexander R. Galloway

17　*Avatars of Story*
　　Marie-Laure Ryan

16 *Wireless Writing in the Age of Marconi*
   Timothy C. Campbell

15 *Electronic Monuments*
   Gregory L. Ulmer

14 *Lara Croft: Cyber Heroine*
   Astrid Deuber-Mankowsky

13 *The Souls of Cyberfolk: Posthumanism as Vernacular Theory*
   Thomas Foster

12 *Déjà Vu: Aberrations of Cultural Memory*
   Peter Krapp

11 *Biomedia*
   Eugene Thacker

10 *Avatar Bodies: A Tantra for Posthumanism*
   Ann Weinstone

9 *Connected, or What It Means to Live in the Network Society*
   Steven Shaviro

8 *Cognitive Fictions*
   Joseph Tabbi

7 *Cybering Democracy: Public Space and the Internet*
   Diana Saco

6 *Writings*
   Vilém Flusser

5 *Bodies in Technology*
   Don Ihde

4 *Cyberculture*
   Pierre Lévy

3 *What's the Matter with the Internet?*
   Mark Poster

2 *High Technē: Art and Technology from the Machine Aesthetic to the Posthuman*
   R. L. Rutsky

1 *Digital Sensations: Space, Identity, and Embodiment in Virtual Reality*
   Ken Hillis

SEB FRANKLIN is senior lecturer in contemporary literature in the Department of English at King's College London. He is the author of *Control: Digitality as Cultural Logic.*

www.ingramcontent.com/pod-product-compliance
Lightning Source LLC
Jackson TN
JSHW070314120426
100741JS00008B/65